LAND DEVELOPMENT AND THE NATURAL ENVIRONMENT: ESTIMATING IMPACTS

Dale L. Keyes

The research for this report was made possible through a research grant from the Office of Policy Development and Research of the U.S. Department of Housing and Urban Development under the provisions of Section 701(b) of the Housing Act of 1954, as amended, to The Urban Institute. The publication of this report was supported by the Ford Foundation. The findings and conclusions presented in this report do not represent official policy of the Department of Housing and Urban Development, the Ford Foundation, or The Urban Institute.

THE URBAN INSTITUTE

Library of Congress Catalog Card Number 76-10104

U.I. 195-214-4

ISBN 87766-158-8

REFER TO URI 13500 WHEN ORDERING

Available from:

Publications Office
The Urban Institute
2100 M Street, N.W.
Washington, D.C. 20037

List Price $4.95

Printed in the United States of America

First printing, April 1976

FOREWORD

This is one of a series of reports by The Urban Institute's Land Use Center which discuss the evaluation of land developments and their economic, environmental, and social impacts. Increasingly, local governments are turning to formalized impact evaluation requirements in order to ascertain the likely effect of permitting land to be developed in various ways at specific locations. The degree to which this approach can improve land use decision making is largely dependent on the ability to accurately estimate a wide variety of potential impacts.

The first report in this series, *Measuring Impacts of Land Development: An Initial Approach,* established an overall framework for evaluation and suggested a series of measures which could be used to estimate impacts for a wide range of economic, social, and environmental concerns. Procedures for actually making impact estimates were also outlined, although in a general and preliminary fashion. The concluding report in the series, *Using an Impact Measurement System for Evaluating Land Developments,* reexamines the overall framework and describes potential problems and prospects for implementing an impact measurement system. This latter report thus provides a general perspective on this as well as the other reports in this series.

This report treats only those impacts related to the natural environment (primarily air quality, water quantity—including flooding—and water quality, wildlife and vegetation, and noise). In addition, natural disasters and scarce resources are discussed briefly. The discussion of environmental impacts focuses on data collection and analysis procedures, with special attention given to assessing the costs and data requirements and reliability of specific analytical techniques appropriate for making estimates in the various impact categories. It can be best described as a reference document for those who find themselves directly involved with the impact evaluation process. These would include planners, developers, and others actually making the estimates as well as decision makers and interested lay persons who wish to learn more about the costs, assumptions, and general considerations which underlie the estimates.

Companion reports in this series treat methodological issues in the following areas—fiscal balance (local revenues and the cost of public services), the private economy (employment and property values), public services (the quality and level of service), and social effects (aesthetic considerations and the perceptions and behavior patterns of local residents). Taken together, these reports offer detailed guidance in the structuring and operation of a comprehensive impact evaluation system appropriate for use by local governments.

Even with improved information concerning the probable effects of proposed developments, arriving at decisions regarding specific projects will remain a difficult task. Rarely are the impacts so one-sided that no one is adversely affected or that no one is benefitted. Rather, decision makers must sort out and compare impact estimates which are often incommensurable and then balance the interests of various affected parties, some of whom may be future generations. The task is an unenviable one and subject to much speculation. By using a well-documented and highly visible approach to impact analysis as is recommended here and in the companion reports, some of these difficulties may be mitigated. Land use conflicts will surely remain, but some of the obscurity and confusion which surrounds them may be reduced.

WORTH BATEMAN, *Executive Director*
Land Use Center
The Urban Instiute

CONTENTS

Tables

Figures

ACKNOWLEDGMENTS

The research supporting the impact evaluation study of which this work is a part was sponsored by the Office of Policy Development and Research of the U.S. Department of Housing and Urban Development. The encouragement of Wyndham Clarke and Allen Siegel from this office and the specific suggestions of James Hoben, the HUD project manager, at various points in the overall study are greatly appreciated.

The research was carried out under the general direction of Worth Bateman, Executive Director of The Urban Institute's Land Use Center. Philip Schaenman was the project manager. Their valuable insights, comments, and overall guidance are gratefully acknowledged.

Kathleen Christensen of The Urban Institute and Harry Feldman of the Indianapolis Department of Parks and Recreation made substantive contributions to the report. Ms. Christensen provided valuable background material and text to the noise discussion, while Dr. Feldman wrote a paper on urbanization and wildlife/vegetation, parts of which were incorporated into the discussion of the same subject.

The author is extremely appreciative of all who critiqued early drafts of this study and provided valuable suggestions: Roger Betson, Tennessee Valley Authority (Water Systems Development Branch); Eugene Darling, U.S. Department of Transportation (Transportation Systems Center); Aelred Geis, U.S. Fish and Wildlife Service; Donald Hey, Hydrocomp, Inc.; Michael McCarthy, University of Arizona (School of Renewable Natural Resources); Curt Miller, University of Michigan (Department of Landscape Architecture); J. A. Smedile, Northeast Illinois Planning Commission; Ethan Smith, U.S. Geological Survey (RALI Program); and Forest Stearns, University of Wisconsin-Milwaukee (Department of Botany). Members of the Advisory Group also assisted in reviewing early drafts.

Staff members from the Department of Community Development in Indianapolis and the Maryland National Capital Park and Planning Commission in Montgomery County, Maryland, are acknowledged for their cooperation and the insights they provided into impact evaluation procedures used by local governments.

The participation of the following individuals in a survey of air dispersion model users is also acknowledged: Steven Albersheim, NUS Corporation; W. Brian Crews, Oregon Department of Environmental Quality; Richard Hawthorne, Oregon Department of Environmental Quality; and Richard Thuillier, San Francisco Bay Area Air Pollution Control District.

ADVISORY GROUP

SUMMARY

That land development may adversely affect the natural environment or, conversely, that the natural environment may pose problems for development is no longer in question. Attention has now turned to designing methods for mitigating these conflicts. The use of impact evaluation to detect existing and potential problems is a valuable step in this process. This report discusses ways to estimate impacts associated with proposed development.

Purpose and Scope

The objective of this report is to provide information on (1) key issues and considerations in evaluating the impacts associated with proposed development, and (2) the relative merits of alternative techniques for estimating impacts, in light of the costs, skills, and data required by each technique and the validity of the results, where information on these topics has been found. (Wherever a technique was discovered to have been used by a local government or in a specific community, that fact is noted.)

The report discusses development impacts on man *associated with or operating through* the natural environment (air quality, water quality and quantity, noise, and scarce resource use preemption), impacts *on* the natural environment (wildlife and vegetation), and impacts *from* the natural environment (flooding and other natural disasters). Simple manual estimation procedures as well as complex, computerized assessment techniques are examined for each impact category (except for scarce resources and disasters other than flooding) and for three types of development—residential, commercial, and industrial.

The treatment of scarce resource use preemption and natural disasters other than flooding is considerably reduced in scope and detail in comparison with the other impact areas. This is largely due to the relatively primitive nature of impact estimation techniques in these areas and to the existence of an extensive body of literature documenting what is currently known.

Throughout the discussion, the emphasis is on quantification and estimation of *end impacts* on man, rather than intermediate effects. For example, information on the number of people exposed to new ambient concentrations of pollutants is preferred to simply knowing what the new concentrations will be. For each impact category, measures incorporating these concepts are suggested for use in assessing the impacts of proposed development. For certain impacts, however, the preferred measures are impractical, at least for routine use. Either the requisite analytical techniques are lacking, or the costs of data collection and analysis seem prohibitively high. For these cases, alternative or fallback measures are specified. These measures typically incorporate expressions of intermediate effects such as development output (e.g., emission levels) or they reflect qualitative assessments. Even where the preferred measures seem practical, alternatives are offered for those governments which may prefer a less detailed, albeit less satisfactory, approach. Table 1 lists preferred and fallback measures.

Rarely will a single development require detailed assessment in all areas. Evaluators must determine the type of impacts which are likely to be significant at the initial screening stage, perhaps employing the "target" planning approach suggested in the report and summarized below.

Intended Audience

The report is intended primarily for planners and other key local government staff members responsible for preparing impact evaluations. Elected officers and interested lay persons may also find selected sections of value, especially the introduction and summary sections for each of the five impact categories.

Findings and Recommendations

The state of the art of impact evaluation regarding the natural environment is very unevenly advanced across the various impact categories. For some types of impact, fairly accurate and inexpensive techniques appear to be available for routine use. For others, the desired tools are only at the research and development stage or are still too expensive for most local governments. For still others, analytical methods necessary for quantified estimates of end impacts on man have not yet been developed.

Table 1. SUGGESTED DIRECT MEASURES OF DEVELOPMENT IMPACT ON THE ENVIRONMENT

IMPACT CATEGORY	PREFERRED MEASURES	FALLBACK MEASURES
AIR QUALITY		
Health	Change in the ambient concentration of each pollutant, the frequency of exposure, and the number of people at risk	Change in the ambient concentration of each pollutant (relative to standards)
Nuisance	Change in the number and frequency of problems caused by smoke plumes, odors, and haze, and number of people affected	Change in the likelihood that aesthetic/ nuisance problems will occur or change in severity
WATER QUALITY AND QUANTITY		
Flooding	Change in the number of people endangered by flooding and the expected property damage (or value of the property endangered)	Change in flood frequency or severity
Water pollution	Change in the permissible or tolerable uses of the water in question and the number of people affected	Change in the ambient concentration of each pollutant (relative to standards)
Water consumption	a. Change in the total duration and/or severity of expected shortages and the number of people affected b. Change in the concentrations of those drinking water constituents important to health and the number of people affected	Change in the likelihood of a water shortage and the number of people affected
WILDLIFE AND VEGETATION	Change in the number of rare and endangered species; change in the population size and diversity of common species	Change in the extent and quality of vegetation and wildlife habitat
NOISE	Change in the level of noise, the frequency with which it occurs, and the number of people affected in the area surrounding the development	
OTHER NATURAL DISASTERS	Change in the likelihood of the disaster and the number of people and the value of the property endangered	
SCARCE RESOURCE USE PREEMPTION	The type and value of the scarce resource and the degree of preemption (such as farming, mining, and recreation)	

To some extent this unevenness reflects the importance that the federal government and, to a lesser extent, state governments have attached to the various types of impacts. Thus, flood prediction is much more advanced than the estimation of impacts on wildlife and vegetation. Recent air and water pollution legislation has spurred research in these areas, although affordable and accurate estimation techniques are available only for a limited number of situations. Noise legislation is likewise expected to improve the status of noise prediction models.

Following are this report's specific findings and recommendations:

1. Quantitative estimates of end impacts on man appear to provide the most useful information to the decision maker. At the same time it is important to use recognized standards or other reference points in interpreting the quantified and often technically specified estimates in several of the impact categories. *Local governments should consider using the measures suggested in this report (or similar ones) as part of their impact evaluation programs.*

2. Comprehensive land use planning and the review of individual projects can and should be coordinated. Where a few large developments or many small ones have communitywide effects, the impacts (ambient air and water quality, flooding) can be related to development out-

put (emissions or effluents) or even to design characteristics (impervious ground cover) and targets or budgets established. Individual reviews in many cases may be reduced to comparing the target with the output from or characteristic of the proposed development when added to the current levels. For example, the estimated emissions from a new development can be added to those from all existing developments in that part of the community for which an emission budget has been prepared. If the budget will not be exceeded even with the new development, then no further analysis of air quality impacts will probably be needed. *We recommend that communities consider incorporating targets or budget values of air emissions, water effluents, and impervious cover in their comprehensive plans.*

3. Even though questions regarding the cost and validity of many techniques remain incompletely answered, several of the techniques reviewed seem superior to some of the currently popular rough approximation methods and are unquestionably better than purely qualitative or judgmental approaches. Following is a general appraisal of existing techniques for estimating impacts (using the suggested measures) in each of the major categories.

   a. *Air Quality*—Air dispersion models applicable to a limited number of pollutants and types of development are available for *health* assessments, although the reported accuracies are quite low. Generally, the accuracy of the estimates increases as the models become more complex. For communitywide estimates of long-term average pollutant concentrations due to overall growth, relatively simple and, in some cases, manual techniques are available. Accuracy for a few of the latter is good. *Nuisance* impact evaluations do not require highly accurate estimates and thus are not difficult to make.

   b. *Water Quality and Quantity*—The estimation of impacts in this category frequently requires the use of more than one technique or model. Simple techniques for estimating *flood* frequency and volumes are available but tend to be unreliable. Complex models are presumably more accurate but also more expensive. Translating flood volumes into water levels requires a complex model of uncertain cost and accuracy. *Water pollution* impacts can be estimated fairly accurately for a very few pollutants and under limited conditions. Estimates of values for the preferred measure require the use of a complex model, and judgments (based on limited evidence) of the implications for water use. Some produce relatively accurate results; all are presumably expensive. Assessments of the supply aspects of *water consumption* are analogous to flood frequency and volume assessments for surface water. Only qualitative assessments are normally possible for underground sources. Water quality assessments are made with water pollution techniques. It should be noted that certain complex models can be used for combined assessments of flooding, water pollution, and water consumption (water quality); thus some economies of scale can be achieved.

   c. *Wildlife and Vegetation*—Although accurate baseline documentation of existing conditions is possible (although often expensive), techniques for producing quantitative estimates of impacts are not available. Instead, informal judgments of experts familiar with the local environment are usually necessary.

   d. *Noise*—At least one simple and accurate model is currently available for estimating noise levels. However, it is not reliable under all conditions. Another simple technique is also available but produces estimates of unknown accuracy.

   e. *Other Natural Disasters and Scarce Resource Use Preemption*—Although specific estimation techniques were not reviewed in detail, existing estimation procedures appear to provide only general approximations of the degree of risk from disasters or the value of certain scarce resources.

4. Data on costs, skill level requirements, and accuracy of the various techniques examined were extremely difficult to obtain in some cases and impossible in others. Few attempts at comparative testing and assessment of models have been made. Where the developers of individual techniques have undertaken validation studies the tests were often based on too few comparisons of estimated and observed values, and under conditions which were too similar, for validity to be established. In addition, different and frequently incomparable measures of accuracy were sometimes used. *We recommend that the federal government greatly*

expand its limited testing program for impact estimation techniques. In the meantime, local governments should be cautious about accepting the results of unvalidated or poorly validated models.

5. If some of the more complex computerized models are employed, the user should expect that initial start-up and calibration costs will be high, perhaps tens of thousands of dollars. Repeated applications of the model for project reviews (or for planning purposes) should be much less expensive, typically hundreds of dollars for computing plus some additional data collection costs. Users will generally find three sources for computerized models: those offered by a consultant, those offered by the federal government together with some user assistance, and those available in the literature but without assistance and often poorly documented. Regardless of the type selected, model users should seek to obtain data on costs of start-up, as well as continued use, from the model developer or others familiar with its application. Previous users are often the best sources for these data.

6. Where simpler techniques are used, costs may be reduced substantially. However, even though computerized techniques are not available for making estimates of impacts on wildlife and vegetation, estimates made by simple inferences will require relatively expensive field surveys (perhaps ten to twenty thousand dollars for a fifty-acre site) if the estimates are to be quantitative.

More detailed findings and assessments of current analytical methods appear in the report itself. Tables comparing the various analytical techniques are found in the summary sections for each impact category.

GENERAL INTRODUCTION

Impacts on, from, or operating through the natural environment have long been a primary concern in land use decision making but have attracted vastly increased attention and concern in recent years. This report, one of a series on impact evaluation techniques published by The Urban Institute's Land Use Center, focuses on ways to estimate the impacts of residential, commercial, and industrial development.

The intent is to provide urban planners and others concerned with evaluating the impacts of land development with basic information on the state of the art. However, this report should not be considered a manual or "cookbook" for evaluating impacts. In almost every case the referenced documents must be consulted for details of the data collection and analysis procedures. Likewise, a complete discussion of the relevant physical/biological processes which characterize the complex natural systems being assessed is not included. Instead, a brief, simplified overview of basic scientific principles related to each specific impact category is presented, followed by a discussion of impact measures and alternative data analysis procedures. References to original sources and additional readings are also given. The objective is to provide information which can be used in designing and implementing an impact evaluation program and in assessing the analytical products being promoted by private consulting firms for evaluating environmental impacts. More specifically, the report should be of value in deciding:

1. Which impact categories to include in a planning and/or project evaluation program,

2. Which measures to use within the constraints of time and available funds, and

3. Which techniques to employ, based on their identified strengths and weaknesses.

We have discussed in detail those impact areas for which several estimation techniques are currently available—air quality, water quality and quantity (including flood hazards), and noise. We have also described in some detail approaches to estimating impacts on wildlife and vegetation, even though specific analytical techniques for making estimates are not currently available. The relative unfamiliarity of most planners with wildlife and vegetation and the scarcity of relevant information justifies a more detailed discussion here. We have discussed to a much lesser extent the estimation of impacts on certain scarce resources such as prime farmland and from natural disasters in addition to floods. The more superficial treatment of these last two impact areas should not be interpreted to mean that they are unimportant. The existing analytical techniques in these areas are in a relatively primitive state of development and since what we do know about estimating these types of impacts is discussed quite well in the literature, the discussion here serves to highlight general approaches to making impact estimates and to identify key references.

The detailed treatment of estimation procedures includes a discussion of general procedures as well as specific techniques. Where individual techniques or models are treated explicitly, those in the public domain are emphasized. A few exceptions have been made, but only where the technique is extremely innovative or the model readily available at an attractive price. Although no attempt has been made to review every existing technique or model, the ones included are broadly representative of the field in each impact category.

In analyzing the comparative strengths and weaknesses of the available techniques, the focus is on inputs and outputs—what the techniques require (dollars, skills, and data) and what they produce (detail and accuracy of results). The question of accuracy is extremely important. All too often numbers appear in impact evaluations with no indication of the range of error.[1] This is not to say that information on the accuracy of the various techniques is readily available. An extensive literature search, combined with a limited survey of both developers and users of identified techniques, has produced a base of information, but a base which is far from complete. Extensive validation of both simple and complex techniques is urgently needed. Data on the costs of using the various techniques were similarly difficult to find.

In addition to its support of this project, the U.S. Department of Housing and Urban Development has sponsored a related and complementary study of procedures for estimating impacts—*Interim Guide For Environmental Assessment, HUD Field Office Edition,* prepared by Alan M. Voorhees Associates, Inc., et al., for the HUD Office of Policy Development and Research, Washington, D.C., June, 1975. *The Interim Guide* was prepared primarily for use by HUD personnel reviewing the impacts of HUD-assisted projects; however, much of the information is appropriate for use by local planners as well.

The Interim Guide lays out a system for the initial screening of development impacts to determine if special in-depth evaluations of specific impacts are required. Procedures are outlined for making initial judgments regarding the significance of potential effects for each of 79 "environmental components." The use of national standards and rules of thumb in the screening process are emphasized.

This report, *Land Development and the Natural Environment: Estimating Impacts,* focuses on techniques which could be utilized in the detailed level analyses. The two reports thus tend to complement each other and the reader is encouraged to use both in designing and implementing an impact evaluation program.

A. COMPREHENSIVE IMPACT EVALUATIONS—AN APPROACH

The emotionalism which has accompanied the use of the term "impact evaluation" in environmental debates has led to the notion that the words represent an innovative idea in decision making. A closer examination reveals that the term is fundamental to the very process of making decisions. Few would disagree that most, if not all, decisions are based on their likely outcomes, or *impact*. No decision to approve a subdivision, grant a variance, or amend a zoning plan is made in a vacuum. Each is based on some analysis of the impact of making and implementing that decision. What is suggested here is a more *comprehensive* impact analysis procedure applied *systematically* to land use decisions. Rather than introducing a new idea, we are suggesting the expansion of an old one.

This is not to say that the suggestion is not somewhat disturbing. The usual constraints of time, money, and knowledge, compounded by an intriguing web of vested interests, hidden agendas, and political pressures militate strongly against procedures which may increase costs, tax knowledge and abilities, or improve the visibility of public decision making. However, a more comprehensive and systematic impact evaluation procedure, painful as it may be in certain situations, holds the potential for improving the allocation of a scarce resource—land.

1. Impacts on Man

Further discussion of "the land use problem" and the rationale which underlies our suggested approach can be found in the overview volumes of this series.[2] The preliminary concept presented in those volumes is that the utility of impact evaluations would be increased if the impacts were specified in terms of *end impact on man* rather than in terms of intermediate effects. The fact that additional pollutants will appear in the air or water or that wildlife habitats will be destroyed are merely descriptions of changes, not impacts. It is only as these changes affect man physically or psychologically (e.g., an increase in emphysema, prohibition of swimming at a local beach, the presence of foul-smelling air), that impacts become interpretable.

It also seems likely that the utility of the analysis is increased if impacts can be quantified. Knowledge of changes in the number of people exposed to hazardous air or changes in the probability of flooding are preferable to knowing that conditions will "improve" or "deteriorate." Even a rough approximation of magnitude is better than none.

The suggested impact measures presented reflect

---

1. In this connection, two questions are relevant: what is the probability that the impact will occur; and if it does, how confident are we that the estimated magnitude is correct?

2. Philip S. Schaenman and Thomas Muller, *Measuring Impacts of Land Development: An Initial Approach* (Washington, D.C.: The Urban Institute, 1974); Philip S. Schaenman, *Using a Measurement System For Evaluating Land Development* (Washington, D.C., The Urban Institute: forthcoming, 1976).

this philosophy—they are designed to specify end impacts and are phrased in quantitative terms. Unfortunately, the state of the art is not yet advanced enough in each of the impact areas to justify the use of every "preferred" measure. Consequently, we have included alternative (fallback) measures as well. These, typically, are expressions of intermediate effects and/or are phrased in more qualitative terms. For example, the suggested fallback measure for air quality is "change in ambient concentration of each pollutant (relative to standards);" while that for wildlife and vegetation is "change in the amount and quality of wildlife habitat altered (quality rating by animal type)." Even where the preferred measure is technically feasible, the time or resources available for data collection and analysis may necessitate use of the fallback measure.

2. Comprehensiveness

Let us turn for a moment to the issue of comprehensiveness. The comprehensive master plan approach has long been both a conceptual tenet and a source of consternation for professional planners. Since the world is composed of a highly interconnected set of elements, the best way to measure the impact of any perturbation is to embrace a holistic, systematic view of the world. Unfortunately, as the scope of analysis increases both the depth of treatment and the accuracy of the output tend to decrease, at least when resources for data collection and analysis are limited.

In view of the difficulties inherent in a comprehensive approach, we advocate comprehensiveness only at the initial project screening level. This translates into a comprehensive checklist, the use of which would help assure that no significant type of impact would be ignored. A subset of important categories can then be investigated in greater depth. The amount of time and funds available for analysis will probably play as much a role in selecting this subset as the characteristics and setting of the development under consideration.

3. Impacted Populations ("Clientele Groups")

It is often desirable to divide the population at risk (or to benefit) into several distinct but not necessarily mutually exclusive groups if the impacts will not be shared equally by all community residents. One possible division is between residents or workers in the development to be evaluated and their counterparts in the surrounding community. We are primarily concerned with the latter group, since the greatest number and most severe impacts usually occur to the surrounding community. We believe that the factors

most relevant to new residents or workers (e.g., building design, unit layout, site landscaping) are best assessed by the private market. Of course, some impacts affect the entire community by acting through new residents, and these have been included in our discussion. For example, to the extent that a development endangers new residents' health or safety, the public-at-large may be required to provide specific types of relief. An example of such a danger is the location of a development in a flood plain. The public cost can be measured in terms of monetary and in-kind subsidies to those persons in the development, if and when a flood occurs.[3]

The "surrounding community" group can be further divided into localized (i.e., immediate vicinity) and nonlocalized (the rest of the community) subgroups. This is an important differentiation for those impacts which tend to have corresponding spatial components. The impact of a regional shopping center on access roads, for example, is typically far different from its impact on the entire highway network of a city. Alternative disaggregations of the population can be made on the basis of special interests, socio-economic characteristics, jurisdiction of residence, type of employment, and other attributes.[4] Disaggregating impacts by clientele group is often necessary to detect important impacts that may be masked if only community-wide effects are considered.

4. Impact Categorization

Impacts from land development can be grouped into several somewhat arbitrary and overlapping categories: Local Economy, Natural Environment, Aesthetics and Cultural Values, Public Services, and Social Conditions. Only the natural environment category is discussed in this report.[5] One danger in dividing and compartmentalizing, however, is the tendency to ignore interrelationships among the parts. Some analysts, for example, may see a change in fiscal balance as a consideration unrelated to impacts on water quality, transportation effects, or changes in neighborhood attractiveness. This results in a false picture of reality. Deterioration of water quality or overcrowding of public roads may necessitate additional expenditures of public funds for new treatment facilities or highways. The attractiveness of the neigh-

---

3. Consumer protection from unsafe construction is usually covered by local health building and fire codes, although these are not universal nor always adequate.

4. See Schaenman and Muller, op. cit., Chap. IV, for further discussion of clientele groups.

5. The others are dealt with in the companion reports in this series.

borhood will be reflected in property values, which in turn will affect public revenues.

In a system where everything tends, either directly or indirectly, to affect everything else, analysis can proceed only if most variables can be controlled while a few are manipulated, or if only a few variables are clearly dominant. Thus, fiscal impact analysis often assumes that a certain level of services will be maintained and, tacitly, that a certain threshold of environmental damage will not be exceeded. The impacts of land development are then measured in terms of changes in public revenues and expenditures needed to maintain those threshold levels. Of course, assumed levels may be changed and another analysis performed. But the point is that expenditures and service/quality levels are not varied simultaneously. Likewise, impact assessments in the other areas usually assume constant expenditures and measure impact by changes in levels of services, environmental quality, and, in the case of social impacts, changes in community activities and perceptions.

A second level of interrelatedness exists—that among impacts within the same category. For example, sulfur dioxide emitted into the atmosphere by a power plant may eventually become dissolved in nearby lakes and streams, producing dangerously acidic water conditions. These interrelations are discussed within the individual impact categories.

B. IMPLEMENTING IMPACT EVALUATION PROCEDURES—MAJOR ISSUES

Beyond the technical questions of measurement procedures and analytical methods to which this report is addressed lie more fundamental issues concerning the philosophy and strategy of implementation: (a) How can incremental decisions be coordinated with planning? (b) How can short-run outcomes be balanced against long-run concerns? (c) Is the only alternative to a specific proposed development no development? (d) Who should conduct the evaluations—specialists or generalists?

1. Comprehensive versus Incremental Reviews

Urban planners will argue, rather persuasively, that evaluating the impact of individual projects is no substitute for comprehensive planning. At best, individual evaluations capture the incremental effects of one or possibly a few large developments. The combined effects of many developments over a period of several years are not easily seen when the incremental approach is used. Even if every project, large and small, were evaluated, individual developments tend to be mutually reinforcing and synergistic. Thus, ad-

ditional levels of activity from older projects may be induced by new development.

Although the focus here is on incrementally applied evaluations, we recognize the complementary need for comprehensive planning. In discussing the concerns associated with each impact category, we have attempted to identify and differentiate between those aspects of the evaluation which are more appropriately addressed by the development of comprehensive land use and zoning plans and those which are better treated through a project review process. For example, problems created by those air pollutants which have slow decay rates and are thus dispersed throughout the community may be more amenable to solution by setting limits on the number and location of pollution sources through large-scale analysis and the adoption of zoning plans than by individual project review. On the other hand, smoke and odor problems are typically localized in their impact and are best assessed and solved on an individual project basis.

If generalizations can be made, perhaps the comprehensive planning/project review dichotomy can be clarified by considering the extent to which impacts have a community-wide versus a localized origin or effect. Sewage effluent which is collected community-wide but treated and discharged at one geographical point, air pollutants with slow decay rates and uniform dispersal patterns, and electricity generated at a single power plant for the entire community would affect community-wide pollution levels. These large-scale, long-term problems are usually best addressed by comprehensive planning. Impacts which are specific to the spatial locations of development are more appropriately treated on a case-by-case basis. Of course, many developments generate impacts which are neither purely site-specific nor purely community-wide. Here, the interface between comprehensive planning and project review is much less clearly defined. And even where a comprehensive plan based on environmental considerations has been implemented, a more detailed incremental evaluation of proposed developments consonant with the plan may occasionally be desirable, at least as a check on the adequacy of the plan.

2. The "Spillover" Problem

Jurisdictional boundaries typically do not coincide with other manmade or natural boundaries. This leads to "spillover" of pollution from one jurisdiction to another. Not only are air pollutants blown across boundaries, but mobile sources generated by a development in one jurisdiction may be driven considerable distances in surrounding communities as well. Thus, "spillover" refers to sources as well as to the pollutants themselves.

Where the governmental unit in which the effects of pollution are experienced does not also control pollution sources, redress of grievances may not be satisfactorily achieved. In fact, it may clearly be to one jurisdiction's advantage to "export" its pollution while reaping the benefits of its pollution-generating activities, usually measured in terms of additional jobs and tax revenues.

Control of regional "spillover" problems depends on both technical and institutional solutions. Large-scale models which simulate the movement of pollutants and chemical reactions in atmospheric or aquatic environments are needed to estimate the location and magnitude of regional-scale pollution problems. Once the problem has been identified and solutions in terms of source and/or land use controls proposed, regional bodies must be organized and empowered to act. The federal government is now either assuming this role or mandating regional cooperation.[6]

For communities where the problems are defined more in terms of individual shopping centers, planned unit developments, or industrial plants than in terms of large industrialized areas, state or federal mediation is much less likely. For these situations we urge that project evaluations include the other affected communities as "clientele groups." This certainly does not insure resolution of the conflict, but it would serve to heighten the level of the debate and may help to reduce suspicion and mistrust.

3. Proposal Alternatives

One of the most difficult tasks in preparing specific impact evaluations is to identify realistic alternatives to the project under review. Ideally, several proposals for a single tract of land would be submitted simultaneously. Decision makers would then be able to select on a comparative basis. Typically, however, the only alternative is no development. No development is not synonymous with no effect, however. Care must be exercised to gauge the effects in all impact categories of diverting the demand for the proposed activity to other sites. The difficulties in attempting this, however, are enormous. Who can

predict with any degree of confidence where, for example, ten thousand new residents will choose to reside if the project being evaluated is rejected? Still, the reality of rejection must be described, if only in the most general and qualitative way.

4. Planning Department/Line Agency Interrelationships

Comprehensive planning departments are usually charged with conducting evaluations of proposals for variances, rezonings, special zone adoptions, and other types of land use changes. Yet the technical expertise required for a competently conducted impact evaluation may well reside in line agencies. The quality of the evaluations produced is thus dependent on the extent to which this expertise can be marshaled and coordinated. The comprehensive planning staff should make a special effort to find out what tools exist (and their limitations) in the line agencies and to work with the agency staff in developing a checklist of measures and formats for expressing the results.

5. Applicable Federal, State, and Local Laws

The development of local impact evaluation programs occurs within the context of federal, state, and local laws which relate to and, at times, overlap with comprehensive evaluation requirements.

Federal legislation now exists in the areas of air, water, and noise pollution. Although the thrust of this legislation is towards *control* at the source, the air and water laws also contain explicit language regarding land use *planning* and *evaluation*. Other relevant areas for which federal legislation exists include flood hazards and transportation, the former through the flood insurance program and the latter as a product of extensive federal support of highway programs.

State activities related to land development typically include granting permits for water and sewage treatment facilities (both community-wide and on-site), for activities which affect the level or location of surface waters, and for new sources of air emissions or water effluents.

At the local level, government review activities emphasize the application of building and subdivision codes. Some communities have broadened their approach by adopting ordinances such as those requiring "adequate public facilities." This represents a major step toward comprehensive evaluation.

Before any evaluation program is developed, a thorough inventory should be made of relevant legislation and activity at all levels of government. Simply adding one more layer to the already bewildering

---

6. An insightful, although sobering, examination of one area's approach to regionalizing the analysis and solution of environmental problems caused by urbanization is documented in B. A. Ackerman et al., *The Uncertain Search for Environmental Quality* (Riverside, N.J.: The Free Press, 1974).

array of overlapping requirements which guide the developers' application process does little to advance orderly and efficient land development. Coordination is an overworked but pertinent word. In many cases the successful application for federal, state, or local development permits can substitute for the submission of additional data. Where the scope of the permits is more limited, additional data will be necessary at the time of impact evaluation.

C. NEEDED RESEARCH

The results of the methodological review reported in this volume reveal that the state of the art of impact evaluation is unevenly advanced in the various impact categories. Predictive techniques are not available for estimating impacts on wildlife and vegetation, as they are under certain conditions for air and water pollution. But even for the latter, additional validation of available techniques is sorely needed. Adequate validation should be based on carefully performed (and usually expensive) retrospective studies of individual developments (such as the power plant impact study in progress at the University of Wisconsin[7]), as well as less ambitious studies on the ability of a technique to estimate current conditions. Until such studies are made, progress toward developing improved techniques will be slow and the accuracy of many impact estimates will remain suspect. This is not to say that the use of any current impact estimation model is unjustified. Some produce results clearly superior to purely qualitative approaches or "quick and dirty" quantitative methods. But without better information on the accuracy of many of the more complex mathematical models, cost/benefit decisions on their use are most difficult to make.

---

7. D. E. Willard, *Preliminary Documentation of Environmental Change Related to the Columbia Electric Power Generating Site,* Working Paper II (Madison: Institute for Environmental Studies, University of Wisconsin, May, 1973).

PART 1
AIR QUALITY

I. INTRODUCTION AND BACKGROUND

The word "pollution" is tightly tied to the concept of impacts on humans. Only to the extent that emissions and resulting ambient concentrations of certain substances from either natural or manmade sources negatively affect the health or welfare of man are substances considered pollutants.[1] Thus, carbon dioxide (CO_2) is not considered a pollutant while sulphur dioxide (SO_2) is, even though the former is generated by natural processes and human activities and subsequently emitted to the atmosphere in much larger quantities than the latter.[2]

A. HEALTH AND WELFARE EFFECTS

The effects of air pollution on human health and welfare[3] can be categorized as follows:

1. Effects on health (morbidity and mortality).
2. Effect on other living organisms (which then impact upon man).
3. Effects on materials (e.g., soiling and corrosion).
4. Aesthetic and nuisance effects (e.g., odors and smoke plumes).

1. Human Health Effects

Data that bear on the health effects of air pollution are obtained from laboratory studies of animals, clinical observation and limited human experimentation, studies in controlled, nonlaboratory settings (e.g., industrial plants), and epidemiological studies of large populations. The highly controlled environment of a laboratory is ideal for manipulating the level of a single pollutant while holding all other pollutants and environmental conditions constant. However, animals must usually substitute for human subjects and only short-term (acute) effects can be measured. In addition, the possible exacerbation of existing disease conditions by air pollution is difficult to test in the laboratory.

Epidemiological studies (at the other extreme) focus on the "real world"—ambient pollutant concentrations and man in his normal setting. But even when correlations between health and exposure levels are found, it is often difficult to prove a causal relationship. Urban activities may produce air pollution, but they may also create stressful situations which, in turn, cause an increase in morbidity and mortality. Thus, in spite of much effort, there remains considerable uncertainty about the hazard actually presented by various suspect pollutants.

Table 1-1 briefly summarizes current knowledge of

---

1. "Ambient" refers to the surrounding atmosphere to which man, plants, and other receptors are exposed. The ambient concentration of any pollutant depends on the quantity emitted and the degree of dispersal.

2. Carbon dioxide may yet prove to be a pollutant if the long-term effect of increasing concentration on a global scale is an increase in climatic temperature. This is a subject of considerable debate among meteorologists.

3. For further discussion of this subject, see Lester Lave and Eugene Seskin, "Air Pollution and Human Health," *Science* 69 (1970): 723–33; The National Academies of Sciences and Engineering, *Air Quality and Automobile Emission Control,* vols. 2 and 4, Senate Committee on Public Works (Washington, D.C.: Government Printing Office, September, 1974); and George L. Waldbott, *Health Effects of Environmental Pollutants* (St. Louis: C. V. Mosby Co., 1973).

air pollutant health relationships, and the major development-related sources for each pollutant. These relationships are only probabilistic. It is known that exposure to high levels of SO$_2$ will cause ill health in some people. But for any individual the probability of becoming ill is influenced by present health, genetic susceptibility, duration and frequency of exposure, presence of other pollutants, and a host of other factors. Air quality standards based on cur-

rent knowledge of health/air pollution relationships are listed in Table 1-2.

The strongest case for unambiguous effects on health can probably be made for SO$_2$ and particulates, for which a statistical relationship between ambient concentration and mortality rate (aggregated on a national basis) has been ascertained.[4] Evidence for the

---

4. Lave and Seskin, op. cit.

Table 1-1. A SUMMARY OF HUMAN HEALTH-AIR POLLUTANT RELATIONSHIPS[a]

POLLUTANT	MAJOR SOURCES	HEALTH EFFECTS	SUSCEPTIBLE POPULATIONS	COMMENTS
Carbon monoxide (CO)	Transportation, industrial processes	Reacts with hemoglobin reducing mental attentiveness, physical exertion, and exacerbating cardiovascular disease symptoms	Persons with cardiovascular disease and others	Past knowledge was based on study of high exposure for short periods with healthy, young individuals. New data show possible health effects for susceptible persons at CO levels in the blood found in urban populations.
Nitrogen oxides (NO$_x$)	Transportation, space heating/cooling, power generation	Interfere with respiratory functions producing long-term (chronic) disease symptoms	Persons with respiratory or cardiac disease, the young and the elderly	Conclusions are based on limited exposure of healthy adults to low doses, extensive animal studies, and only limited data relevant to ambient conditions.
Hydrocarbons (HC)	Transportation and industrial processes	See photo-oxidants	See photo-oxidants	Indirectly polluting through the production of photochemical oxidants upon reaction with NO and NO$_2$ in the presence of sunlight.
Photo-oxidants (O$_x$)	See nitrogen oxides and hydrocarbons	Interfere with respiratory functions and cause eye irritations	Persons with chronic respiratory diseases, especially bronchial asthma	Ozone (O$_3$) is the most common type and the key indicator for photo-oxidants. Health effects are based on limited and inadequate data.
Particulates[b]	Power generation, space heating/cooling, industrial processes, soil erosion	Interference with respiratory functions, possible contribution to lung cancer	Persons with respiratory disease, the young and the elderly	The effects of particulates are difficult to separate from those of sulfur dioxide.
Sulfur oxides (SO$_x$)	Power generation, space heating/cooling, industrial processes	Little effect in the pure gas form; similar effects as particulates when combined with them	Persons with respiratory or cardiovascular disease, the young and the elderly	Sulfur dioxide is readily converted to SO$_3$ and then to sulfuric acid (a particulate). Determining which effects are due solely to SO$_2$ is difficult.
Heavy metals, radioactive agents, others[c]	Power generation, industrial processes	Specific to each pollutant	Specific to each pollutant	Pollution from these agents can be intense at the source, but tends not to be widespread.

a. Information in this table is based primarily on the following references: National Academies of Sciences and Engineering, op. cit., vol. 2: *Health Effects of Air Pollution;* Waldbott, op. cit.; J. D. Williams, et al., *Interstate Air Pollution Study, Phase II Project Report, VI. Effects of Air Pollution* (Cincinnati, Ohio: Public Health Service, U.S. Department of Health, Education, and Welfare, December, 1966).

b. Particulates, also known as aerosols, are either solids or fine liquid droplets which vary by size, shape, and composition. Sulfuric acid formed from SO$_2$ is one of the most biologically significant particulates. Some particulates such as dust can be rather innocuous considered alone, but become lethal transport agents when toxic gases are adsorbed to their surfaces.

c. For a more complete discussion of other pollutants see, for example, Waldbott, op. cit.

Land Development and the Natural Environment

Table 1-2. NATIONAL AMBIENT AIR QUALITY STANDARDS

POLLUTANT	PERIOD OF MEASUREMENT	PRIMARY STANDARD		SECONDARY STANDARD	
		μg/m^3	ppm	μg/m^3	PPM
1. Carbon monoxide (CO)	8 hours	10,000	9	Same	Same
	1 hour	40,000	35	Same	Same
2. Hydrocarbons (HC) (nonmethane)	3 hours	160	0.24	Same	Same
3. Nitrogen dioxides (NO$_2$)	Year	100	0.05	Same	Same
4. Photochemical oxidants (O$_x$)	1 hour	160	0.08	Same	Same
5. Sulfur oxides (SO$_x$)	Year	80	0.03	None	None
	24 hours	365	0.14	None	None
	3 hours	None	None	1,300	0.5
6. Total suspended particulates (TSP)	Year	75	—	60	—
	24 hours	260	—	150	—

SOURCE: *Federal Register,* Vol. 36, No. 84 (April 30, 1971).
NOTES:

Concentrations are averaged over each period of measurement. The annual TSP concentration is a geometric mean of 24-hour samples; all other concentrations are arithmetic mean values. Standards for periods of 24 hours or less may not be exceeded more than once per year.

Units of measurement are micrograms per cubic meter (μg/m^3) and parts per million (ppm).

Primary standards are designed to protect human health.

Secondary standards are designed to protect human welfare (i.e., eliminate damage to vegetation and materials and aesthetic problems).

other pollutants is highly suggestive. Extreme levels are known to cause illness and even death, but these levels are much higher than normal ambient concentrations. The effects of long-term exposure to lower concentrations are still highly speculative.

2. Vegetation and Material Effects

Table 1-3 summarizes the known or suspected impact of air pollution on vegetation, materials, and man in terms of aesthetic and nuisance concerns. Much of the data for vegetation and materials impact is based on laboratory or controlled field studies. As with health effects, sorting out causative agents and mechanisms of action is difficult. Vegetative damage can be mimicked, masked, or exacerbated by a variety of factors, such as rainfall, plant disease, and sunlight. Impact on materials is likewise a complex phenomenon. Aesthetic and nuisance effects are more easily identified, although the seriousness of effect is open to considerable question.

B. APPLICABLE STATE AND FEDERAL LAWS

The federal government has assumed major responsibility for the maintenance of air quality in the United States. Pursuant to the 1970 amendments to the Clean Air Act, the Environmental Protection Agency (EPA) has promulgated both primary and secondary ambient air standards (Table 1-2) together with an elaborate list of policies, guidelines, and requirements for their implementation.

The primary ambient air standards were established by identifying the lowest concentration for which health effects have been observed (usually in clinical situations among patients with respiratory or cardiovascular illnesses) and then reducing this level by a "safety factor." The secondary standards were established using data on damage to plants, animals, and materials.

State governments are required to designate geographic areas which fail to meet the standards (air quality control regions) and to submit implementation plans for stationary source emission and transportation management controls adequate to solve the problem by 1975–77.[5] These requirements were designed to satisfy the letter of the law, but two highly significant court decisions have greatly expanded EPA's role, thrusting the federal government fully into land use planning.

The first decision resulted from a challenge to EPA by the Sierra Club (May 30, 1972) regarding EPA's practice of allowing the deterioration of air in relatively clean areas. As a result, no significant deteri-

---

5. More specifically, the control plans may include emission limitation, relocation of sources, economic (dis)incentives, changes in operating procedures and schedules of sources, motor vehicle emission control and inspection, limitations in motor vehicle use, expansion of mass transportation, and other unspecified land use and transportation measures. In addition, EPA will establish new source emission standards for all stationary source categories deemed to endanger public health or welfare.

Table 1-3. A SUMMARY OF AIR POLLUTION EFFECTS ON VEGETATION, MATERIALS AND MAN[a]
(AESTHETIC AND NUISANCE CONCERNS)

POLLUTANT	VEGETATION	MATERIALS	AESTHETICS/NUISANCES
Carbon monoxide (CO)	None	None	None
Nitrogen oxides (NO$_x$)	Reduction in growth of plants with broad leaves (e.g., beans, tomatoes)	Accelerated deterioration of dyes and paints	Creation of a brownish coloring in urban air
Photo-oxidants (O$_x$)	Severe reduction in growth and eventual death of leafy vegetables, field and forage crops, shrubs, fruit and forest trees caused by ozone and PAN[b]	Ozone causes the cracking of rubber and the accelerated deterioration of nylon, rayon, dyes, and paints	Ozone has a distinct although not terribly offensive odor
Hydrocarbons (HC)	None	None	None
Particulates	Reduction in plant growth by physical blockage of light when deposited on leaf surface	Soiling of fabrics and buildings and corrosion of metals when combined with SO$_2$	Creation of smoke plumes, scattering of sunlight to produce haze and colorful sunsets, and formation of hydroscopic nuclei to produce fog
Sulfur oxides (SO$_x$)	Reduction in growth of plants with broad leaves	Corrosion of iron metals, accelerated deterioration of building stone, cotton, paper, leather, paints and other finishes	Scattering of sunlight to produce haze, production of unpleasant odors
Others[c]	Floride causes long-term damage to selected field crops (and animals)	Tarnishing of metals by hydrogen sulfide	Hydrogen sulfide produces extremely unpleasant odors

a. The information in this table is taken primarily from Public Health Service, *The Effects of Air Pollution* (Washington, D.C.: U.S. Department of Health, Education, and Welfare, 1967).

b. Peroxyacylnitrate, an oxidation product of hydrocarbons.

c. Other pollutants, such as hydrochloric acid and ammonia, are present in small quantities on a national basis and are not discussed.

oration in these areas will be allowed in the future.[6] At issue now is the definition of "significant deterioration." Although final regulations had not been promulgated, EPA's expressed intention was to shift the definitional burden to the states. The draft regulations would allow the states to place planning areas (presumably analogous to air quality control regions) into one of three categories, which range from "no deterioration allowed" to "deterioration allowed up to a large fraction of the national standards." Regardless of how literally "significant" is interpreted, it is clear that new development in atmospherically clean as well as degraded areas must be controlled in order to minimize air pollution. Thus, state and designated local governments will have to review land use plans as well as individual projects for their impact on air quality.

The second court decision was a product of a challenge to EPA-certified state implementation plans (January 1, 1973). The Natural Resources Defense Council, Inc., successfully asserted that the imple-

mentation plans addressed only the issue of remedial actions to be taken in areas presently violating national standards. The plans did not assure that air quality would be *maintained* once the standards were achieved. In response, the EPA is applying two new approaches, Indirect Source Review[7] and the development of Air Quality Maintenance Plans (AQMPs).[8] Under the first approach, states, or preferably local governments, must review all new developments (above certain thresholds) which threaten to cause new or exacerbate existing violations of the national standards by inducing transportation-related emissions.[9] These developments include parking facilities, shopping centers, airports, and sports arenas. Where such developments are estimated to cause the specified deterioration in air quality, they are to be prohibited.

The second approach requires states to designate areas which, due to projected growth rates, present threats to the continued maintenance of national stan-

6. The Court of Appeals for the District of Columbia reaffirmed a lower court's order and the Supreme Court could not reach a decision, thus allowing the original order to stand.

7. See *Federal Register*, vol. 39, no. 38 pp. 7269–92 (February 25, 1974).

8. See *Federal Register*, vol. 38, no. 116, pp. 15834–37 (June 18, 1973).

9. The thresholds are expressed in terms of number of cars.

Land Development and the Natural Environment

dards. These areas are to be known as Air Quality Maintenance Areas (AQMAs). Once the nature and magnitude of the problems have been ascertained, air quality maintenance plans are to be developed specifying preventative measures. These are primarily land use and transportation control measures, including emission-density zoning and a requirement for environmental impact evaluations antecedent to and serving as a basis for decisions on requests for land use changes.[10]

Aside from implementing various aspects of the Clean Air Act, states may, and in some cases have, specified standards and implementation programs more stringent than the federal ones (e.g., California). In every state and in many local communities, public agencies have been designated to implement and enforce federal and state air pollution laws. Some states, such as Florida, have also added air quality impact evaluation requirements to the review of certain large-scale developments.[11] A few of the larger cities, such as New York, have also established region-specific standards and regulations.[12]

C. EMISSIONS AND ATMOSPHERIC DISPERSION: FUNDAMENTAL PRINCIPLES

1. Emissions and Emission Sources[13]

Virtually every substance now identified as a pollutant is produced to some extent by natural processes. These background levels are the product of oil and coal field leaks, volcanic eruptions, weathering of rock, biological production and decay, sea spray, forest fires, and a variety of other occurrences. In some situations background levels may be high enough to be a cause of concern. Typically, however, manmade emissions far exceed the natural ones.

Man-related emission sources are numerous and varied. The general categories in Table 1-1 refer to the type of development-related activity which produces the emission. Concentrating on physical aspects of emission sources, most air pollution meteorologists recognize three types of sources: point,

area, and line. *Point* sources are those which are stationary, can be readily identified and located, and usually are substantial contributors to total pollutant loads in the atmosphere. Power plant smokestacks are an obvious example. *Area* sources are either sources of considerable areal extent (e.g., a burning landfill site) or combinations of small, difficult-to-identify stationary or mobile sources averaged over an area (e.g., residential structures). *Line* sources are transportation corridors through which mobile sources pass and, over time, can be represented as a continuous source in the shape of a line.

2. Atmospheric Dispersion[14]

The escape of noxious materials from point, area, and line sources is only the first stage in the development of air pollution problems. In the path from source to receptor (who or what is exposed to or "receives" the pollution), atmospheric gases and aerosols are driven by forces with disparate origins, magnitudes, and directions. The actual path that the materials take will largely determine their strength at the receptor and thus their effect on man.

The forces which control atmospheric dispersion are the product of differential heating of the earth's surface by the sun and gravitational attraction between the earth and atmospheric constituents. These forces are most conveniently categorized by the scale of effect. *Synoptic* or large-scale forces produce major weather events and affect large land and water areas, *meso* or medium-scale forces produce conditions which affect air quality for an entire community (or subarea thereof), and *micro* or small-scale forces create localized conditions in the immediate vicinity of a source. The most dramatic impacts from development will normally be localized and thus controlled to a large extent by micro factors. However, cumulative effects and extreme conditions (i.e., those producing the hazards) are caused by factors at all three scales.

a. Principal Factors Affecting Dispersion

Ambient concentration of pollution at any point in space is largely dependent on the extent to which pollutants have mixed with surrounding "clean" volumes of air. This in turn is a function of *wind speed* (the greater the speed the faster the removal from the source and the greater the dilution) and *mixing depth*. The latter is an expression of the vertical distance from the ground to the inversion layer or area of

10. For further information on the designation of AQMAs see, Environmental Protection Agency, *Guidelines for Air Quality Maintenance Planning and Analysis, vol. 1: Designation of Air Quality Maintenance Areas* (Research Triangle Park, N.C.: EPA, September, 1974).

11. The Environmental Land and Water Management Act, Chapter 380, Florida Statutes, 1972.

12. See "Air Pollution Control News," *The American City* (August, 1972).

13. For additional information, see National Academies of Sciences and Engineering, op. cit., vol. 3 and The California State Air Resources Board, *Current Methodologies for Determining the Spatial Distribution of Air Polluting Emissions* (Sacramento: CSARB, July, 1974) (NTIS No. PB-237864).

14. For more information, see Brian J. L. Berry et al., *Land Use, Urban Form, and Environmental Quality,* Research Paper No. 155 (Chicago: Department of Geography, University of Chicago, 1974).

warmer air aloft and represents the volume of air available for pollutant dispersal. When inversions are located close to the ground (i.e., the depth is small), pollutants are trapped in relatively small volumes of air and ambient concentrations are consequently increased.[15] The average mixing depth and the potential for low-level inversion formation (and thus the potential for dangerous pollutant build-ups) can be predicted from historical records. Published data are available on mixing depths on a rather gross scale nationally.[16] More disaggregated information is also available, at least for the state of California.[17]

Wind speed and direction are determined by forces at all three scales (i.e., synoptic, meso, and micro). More specifically, prevailing winds, storm systems, urban heat-island effects,[18] topographic features, and manmade structures combine to create net movements of air at any point in space. The "concrete canyons" created by rows of tall buildings produce special effects. Eddy currents concentrate internally generated pollutants, while the "canyon" walls retard flushing by crosswinds.

b. Removal and Transformation Processes

Once emitted and dispersed, the fate of atmospheric pollutants is an important but poorly understood story. Some pollutants, such as CO, SO_3, nitrogen oxides to some extent, and particulates are removed by precipitation. Some particulates are also removed by gravitational settling, depending on their size. Some, such as NO, NO_2, and hydrocarbons are either nonsoluble or participate in long-term chemical reactions, being transformed into nonsoluble gases in the process. These nonsoluble gases are presumed to

"decay" by adsorption to solid surfaces, absorption by vegetation, or dilution by increasingly larger volumes of the atmosphere.[19] The transformation processes depend on pollutant concentrations, meteorological conditions, topography, and ground cover.

Tracing the fate of these pollutants is important not only from an air pollution perspective—they also affect water and "land" pollution. For example, pollutants such as SO_3 and NO_2 produce caustic acids when dissolved in water. Heavy metals, if deposited in surface water from the atmosphere, may present health hazards for many years. Radioactive materials present serious health problems regardless of their eventual place of deposition.[20]

D. AIR QUALITY IMPACTS OF LAND DEVELOPMENT

Air quality impacts resulting from land development differ by phase (site preparation, construction, occupancy) and type (residential, commercial, industrial). In addition, air quality impacts can be distinguished on the basis of source location—on-site or off-site.

For all types of developments the most significant impacts will normally be associated with the occupancy phase. Site preparation and construction tend to be relatively transitory activities and the resulting pollution (largely in the form of particulates) rather localized.[21] Consequently, attention will be focused on air quality impacts generated once the development has been occupied.

For residential and commercial developments the emission of pollutants will be caused by on-site space heating, by off-site electrical power production, and by the generation of both on-site and off-site transportation. For industrial developments one additional source will be the manufacturing processes themselves. The combustion of fuel, as well as the handling of gaseous materials, can lead to significant emissions.

---

15. Inversions can occur when warmer air masses descend, when air near the ground cools more rapidly than that above, and, in effect, creates an inversion (as typically happens in urban areas at night), or when cooler air underflows warmer air (as typically happens in valleys at night).

16. George C. Holzworth, *Mixing Heights, Wind Speeds, and Potential for Urban Air Pollution Throughout the Contiguous United States* (Research Triangle Park, N.C.: EPA, January, 1972).

17. California State Air Resources Board, *Meterological Parameters for Estimating the Potential for Air Pollution in California* (Sacramento: CSARB, July, 1974) (NTIS No. PB-237 869).

18. Urban areas are net producers of heat. This creates a "convection cell" whereby warm air in the city rises, moves out over the cooler countryside, cools, descends and returns to the city at ground level. This may produce a "recycling" of pollutants.

19. Existing evidence indicates that vegetation plays a relatively minor role in removing gaseous pollutants, although it may be effective in removing particulates. See George Hagevik, Daniel R. Mandelker, and Richard K. Brail, *Air Quality Management and Land Use Planning* (Washington, D.C.: Praeger Publishers, 1974).

20. Waldbott, op. cit. (see fn. 3).

21. However, for development occurring over extended periods of time in already developed areas, this may not be insignificant.

II. METHODOLOGICAL APPROACHES

Central to the problem of estimating the impact of land development on air quality is the relationship between emissions and ambient concentrations. Most impact assessments, no matter how crude they may be, are based on the measurement or estimation of emissions with and without the development in question and a translation of this difference into the change in ambient concentration. Since this translation is dependent on highly variable meteorological factors, the fidelity with which the translation technique represents local meteorological conditions will largely determine the accuracy of the results.

The general steps in calculating the impact of proposed land developments on air quality are as follows.[1]

1. Measure/estimate current emissions.
2. Estimate future emissions.
3. Measure/estimate current ambient concentrations.
4. Estimate future ambient concentrations.
5. Measure/estimate exposure of man, vegetation, and materials.

These steps are necessary in order to establish baseline conditions for comparison purposes and, for some techniques, to make future estimates. After a

discussion of impact measures and related topics, the remaining portion of this chapter will discuss available techniques for each step.

A. MEASURES, STANDARDS, AND INDICES

1. Measures and Standards

Measures of air quality impacts should preferably reflect changes in (a) risk or damage to human *health* and possibly vegetation and materials, and (b) *aesthetic* and *nuisance* problems. Following is a list of alternative measures, with the preferred one listed first in each category:

Health[2]

1. Change in the ambient concentration of each pollutant, the frequency of exposure, and the number of people at risk.

OR

2. Change in the ambient concentrations of each pollutant (relative to standards).

Aesthetic/Nuisance

3. Change in the number and frequency of prob-

---

1. For retrospective analyses of existing developments, simply compare the emission levels and ambient concentrations before construction with those after it has been completed.

2. These measures could be expanded to include the exposure of vegetation (areal extent and vegetation type) and materials (amount and type) most likely to be severely affected. An alternative measure is "new emissions as a percentage of the budgeted amount" meaning that a budget has been prepared for the entire community or the area in question. See Part 1, III, Section A for a more detailed discussion.

lems caused by smoke plumes, odors, haze, and the number of people affected.

OR

4. Change in the likelihood that aesthetic/nuisance problems will occur or change in severity.

Measures 1 and 3 are most directly related to the end impact on man and thus are the preferred measures. Each is a quantitative assessment of changes in ambient pollutant concentrations, including likely new levels and their frequency of occurrence. In addition, these measures suggest that a detailed estimation be made of who (or what) will be exposed to which levels and how often. Measures even more reflective of the end impact on man could be specified. We could speak of changes in morbidity or mortality rates or changes in the monetary value of property damaged by air pollution. However, values for these measures could not be obtained for individual communities due to the present lack of knowledge regarding health and damage effects of air pollution.

Measures 2 and 4 are much less desirable expressions of impact but may be more practical in certain situations. They are more general indications of changes in area-wide pollutant levels, relying on long-term concentration averages rather than the more detailed data needed for measures 1 and 3. These should thus be considered proxy measures.

One important consideration in choosing between measures is the probable magnitude of the impact. If one or more new developments have the *potential* of significantly degrading air of currently acceptable quality (based on a cursory qualitative assessment), then a detailed and comprehensive analysis may be justified, unless the initial assessment clearly shows an unambiguous violation of a standard. Small developments, or those located in relatively noncritical areas, on the other hand, probably do not warrant the expense of an elaborate evaluation.

Data collection and analysis procedures appear to be available for all of the measures listed, although the accuracy of values generated remains an important and, in some cases, an unknown quantity. Issues related to the cost and accuracy of impact evaluations are discussed in the next section.

The four measures are intended to be objective statements of impacts on the affected population. However, citizen perceptions of annoying or unpleasant air pollutants are needed to define reference standards for interpreting the impacts, in addition to knowledge of pollutant concentration/aesthetic relationships based on controlled condition experiments. Where detailed impact evaluations are not feasible, data on current citizen satisfaction with air quality

may also be used to infer the general impact of future developments. The subject of measuring perceptions of air quality and other neighborhood attributes is discussed in another report in this series.[3]

Interpretation of values generated for the measures is usually made by reference to historical values or standards. In the case of the latter, federal standards are the most popular (and now mandated) reference point. Unfortunately, the relationships between pollutant concentration and health typically do not display threshold characteristics with a single value separating completely safe levels from hazardous ones.[4] As mentioned earlier, hazard is best measured as a probability of deleterious effect which depends on current health, inherited susceptibility, length and frequency of exposure, the presence of other pollutants, and other factors. Thus, single standards for each pollutant, convenient as they may be to apply, do not adequately represent the physical and biological processes involved. The point is not that the federal standards are invalid, but that they should be viewed as merely the best available knowledge on a complex and imperfectly understood subject. Local governments may well decide to specify more stringent standards as a protection against uncertainty.

Once a set of standards or targets has been specified, they can be used to interpret the results of the analysis. Since impact depends on both ambient concentration and the frequency of occurrence, the standards and the results could be expressed as the "total number of days (or, less adequately, the number of times) a certain concentration is reached." Impact can then be described as the "total number of days or the number of times the standard is exceeded (or closely approached)."

2. Indices

For the purpose of comparing one development or plan with another it is sometimes desirable to express "air quality" by a single number. Several air quality indices have been developed to "sum up" or integrate the changes in concentration of the various pollutants.[5] These are typically root-sum-squares or summations of ratios between observed concentra-

3. K. Christensen, *Social Impacts of Land Developments* (Washington, D.C.: The Urban Institute, forthcoming).

4. For documentation of the nature of this relationship, see National Academies of Sciences and Engineering, op. cit., vols. 2 and 4.

5. For a discussion of several indices, see James W. Curlin, *National Environmental Policy Act of 1969: Environmental Indices—Status of Development, Pursuant to Section 102(2) (B) and 204 of the Act,* Senate Committee on Interior and Insular Affairs (Washington, D.C.: December, 1973) and Berry et al., op. cit.

tions and the standards.[6] Indices can also be developed to reflect the number of times the standard is exceeded within a specified period of time.

However, indices have several inherent problems. The weighting schemes used are often arbitrary, and the numbers which result are difficult to interpret in terms of the severity of the problem. Although higher numbers for each of the various indices tend to indicate greater pollution, differences in scores between individual cities show wide variation, depending on the index used.[7] Also, those using an index may be unaware of the weighting.

Another problem is that indices tend to blur distinctions among pollutants. The same numerical score can be obtained from a vast number of different combinations of pollutants. Thus, low concentrations for several pollutants could overshadow a high concentration for one. We believe that expressing the results separately for each pollutant provides more usable information for the decision maker.

B. MEASUREMENT/ESTIMATION PROCEDURES

In order to obtain values for these measures, a number of discrete data collection and analysis operations are necessary. These operations were summarized in the introduction to this section and will now be discussed in detail.

1. Measuring/Estimating Current Emissions

All dispersion models used to estimate the air quality impact of development need values for the total level of emission—current levels plus those added by the proposed development. Consequently, accurate estimates of current emissions will improve the accuracy of the projected impact.

---

6. The following are formulas for root-mean-square and linear summation indices, respectively:

$$I = \sqrt{a \sum_{i=1}^{n} (C_i/S_i)^2}$$

$$I = \left(a \sum_{i=1}^{n} (C_i/S_i) \right)^b$$

where
 I = index value,
 C = recorded concentration,
 S = standard,
 i = 1, 2, . . .n time periods (e.g., 8 hours, 24 hours) or, alternatively, pollutant$_1$, pollutant$_2$, . . .pollutant$_n$.
 a and b = scaling factors chosen so that the numerical values of the index fall within desired ranges (e.g., I = 1 for the situation where no standards are exceeded).

These can be used to weight the concentrations of one pollutant for different averaging times or the concentrations of different pollutants for a single averaging time.

7. See Berry et al., op. cit.

The acquisition and assemblage of current data on point, area, and line source emissions are formidable and costly tasks. Even with a substantial investment of time and money, the results are often less than satisfactory, or worse yet, are inaccurate to an unknown degree. However, since an inventory of current emissions is a prerequisite for air quality impact evaluations at any scale, the expenditure of the necessary funds to make estimates of emissions is probably justified.[8] For most large metropolitan areas it is required under the Clean Air Act.

Both the EPA and, to a lesser extent, the U.S. Department of Transportation (DOT) have been active in developing guidelines, analytical procedures, and mathematical models for use in preparing emission inventories.[9] Rather than repeating what is covered in these reports and others they reference, only the general approaches will be described.

a. Point Sources

The most accurate method of ascertaining the type and quantity of emissions from a point source is to place a monitoring device in the effluent stream. However, the cost of applying this approach to every smokestack of every industrial firm and power plant in a metropolitan area is usually prohibitive. At a minimum, instrumentation can provide an accurate test for other less direct approaches.

A second, more practical approach is based on the quantity and type of fuel consumed or raw materials used. When multiplied by emission factors (pollutants per unit of activity)[10], these indicators will provide estimates of aggregate emissions. If information on the timing of emissions is desired, however, schedules of operation must be obtained.

Data on fuel and raw materials can be collected from surveys of each point source (or a sample of sources if many are similar). If this level of detail is not available, records of local fuel and raw material distributions can be probed. Failing this, statewide

---

8. The EPA estimates that approximately three man-years are required to inventory current emissions in a city the size of Washington, D.C. (personal communication with a member of the Control Programs Development Division).

9. See the EPA, *Guide for Compiling a Comprehensive Emission Inventory* (Research Triangle Park, N.C.: EPA, June, 1972); EPA, *Compilation of Air Pollution Emission Factors* (Research Triangle Park, N.C.: EPA, April, 1974); Federal Highway Administration, *Urban Transportation Planning and Air Quality,* Highway Planning Technical Report No. 33, and Federal Highway Administration, *Special Area Analysis* (Washington, D.C.: Department of Transportation, August, 1973).

10. The emission factors relate the quantity of pollutants emitted to levels of polluting activity (e.g., x pounds of SO_2 per y tons of coal) and are specific to the type of emission control device (if any) in use at individual sources.

data on fuel and raw material consumption (collected by such organizations as the U.S. Bureau of Mines or state pollution control agencies) can be allocated to a local community, based on the community's state-wide share of the polluting activity.

Likewise, community-wide data can be apportioned to subareas using the same concept. It is clear, however, that these approaches are several times removed from the physical measurement of emission levels; and with the loss in specificity comes a concomitant loss in accuracy.[11]

The measurement of smoke plumes presents a slightly different problem. The most common parameter measured is opacity, and the most frequently used measuring device is the Ringelmann Smoke Chart.[12]

b. Stationary Area Sources

Most area sources are groups of point sources which are too small to investigate individually. Secondary sources of information are then typically used. For residential area sources, local fuel distributors can be consulted to obtain information on the amount and mix of fuels used for space heating. A characteristic emission factor for each fuel is then applied to obtain total emissions.

Depending on the ultimate utilization of the inventory, spatial disaggregation may be desirable. Allocation methods similar to those mentioned for point sources are appropriate here as well. Alternatively, small point sources (e.g., individual homes) in different areas of the community can be sampled and heating bills used to obtain information on fuel consumption. Total consumption for each area is then calculated by multiplying the average unit consumption by the number of units in that area.

If changes over time (e.g., seasonal variations) are to be considered, additional analysis by type of area source is necessary. For example, the average number of degree-days[13] by season will provide an indication of daily residential fuel consumption over the year.

Estimates for large area sources, such as fuel depots (evaporative losses), landfills (trash burning),

building fires, and construction sites (dust) are obtained as detailed in the previously cited EPA reports (see page 17).

c. Mobile Area or Line Sources

A moving source of emissions is conveniently depicted as a line source. However, most emission inventories and most dispersion models treat line sources as area sources by aggregating and then uniformly distributing the line sources throughout the areal unit of analysis.

The data base for estimating emissions from line sources is usually much richer than that for point or area sources. Most medium to large size communities have transportation departments which maintain detailed data on street capacities, traffic volumes, and sometimes vehicle mixes (both by type and age). This allows calculation of vehicle miles of travel at various speeds at various times of day. Knowing in addition the average mix (light duty and heavy duty) and the age distribution of vehicles allows calculation of the level of emissions. The analytical procedures are detailed in the EPA and DOT publications previously cited (see page 17).

Again, if this level of detail is not available or appropriate, indirect data can be used. These include data on total gasoline sales for the community (obtainable from state tax departments) and on motor vehicle registrations (obtainable from state motor vehicle departments). It must be remembered that increasing aggregate data usually means decreasing accuracy when these data are disaggregated and allocated to individual communities.

d. Estimation Problems

Potential sources of error in an emission inventory are obviously numerous. If every source could be physically monitored, then only instrumentation errors would be present. Unfortunately, except for a few large point sources, this is not practical for most local governments today. Once secondary and tertiary sources of data are used, four possible error types multiply rapidly:

1. Errors in collecting and recording the secondary/tertiary data.

2. Inherent errors in using surrogate data (e.g., how accurately do gasoline sales reflect vehicular emissions?).

3. Inherent errors in using aggregate data (e.g., how accurately can statewide data on fuel consumption be allocated to local communities?).

4. Errors in ascertaining the effectiveness of pollution control equipment.

11. If data on fuel and raw material consumption are to be used on a scale larger than individual sources, then the utilization of emission control devices must also be aggregated and averaged—another possible source of error.

12. R. Kudlich, (rev. by C. R. Burdick), *Ringelmann Smoke Chart,* Information Circular 7718 (Washington, D.C.: Department of the Interior, Bureau of Mines, August, 1955).

13. "Degree-days" is an expression of heating load and is numerically equivalent to the outside temperature expressed as the average number of degrees below a threshold temperature for a given day. The threshold is that temperature which, when reached, will require some indoor heating (usually 65°F.).

Land Development and the Natural Environment

Information on the first type of error is typically nonexistent. The second type of error relates to the use of emission factors and other coefficients which relate tertiary indicators (e.g., gasoline consumption) to secondary data (e.g., vehicle miles). EPA has employed a combination of approaches in deriving its emission factors for various pollutant-generating activities, from detailed source testing to engineering appraisals.[14] Consequently, individual factors vary in accuracy as reflected by qualitative rankings attached to each factor. These rankings are undoubtedly useful for judging the relative believability of the results but cannot be used to specify confidence intervals or other quantitative measures of accuracy. How believable is "believable" remains an unanswered question. The situation for coefficients other than emission factors is even worse. Typically, average values for relationships between tertiary and secondary variables are used with no indication of how local conditions may vary from the mean.

Errors of the third type are likewise extremely difficult to gauge. In selecting a method for allocating shares of aggregated data, data availability and common sense become the yardsticks.

Determining the efficiency of pollution control equipment (the fourth type of error) is affected by many factors, including meteorological conditions, maintenance practices, age of the equipment, and the mix of pollutants in the effluent stream. Errors which result from these factors are difficult at the present time to ascertain, due to a lack of data. Presumably, as experience with pollution control equipment increases, knowledge about the relative magnitude of these effects will improve. Presently, however, we can do little more than acknowledge the existence of these potential errors.

In any one situation the aforementioned errors will obviously not be of equal importance. Some a priori knowledge about local conditions should be brought to bear when the inventory procedure is designed. Where the major problem is associated with point sources, a greater investment of resources to inventory these sources would be appropriate. Where motor vehicles are the primary agents, additional funds for obtaining transportation data would be justified. If major problems occur during rush hours, accurate data on the time distribution of traffic volumes would prove useful. In this way some of the problems associated with uncertainty in the data can be reduced.

In a similar vein the ultimate use of the data will influence the relative emphasis placed on different types of data collection. If the inventory is to be used for comparison with future emission levels, data of a fairly aggregated nature can be used. On the other hand, estimating the effects of single developments requires data on spatially differentiated emission sources.

2. Estimating Future Emissions

Much of what has already been said about current emission inventories applies equally well to estimations of future emissions.

a. Aggregate or Large Area Analysis

It is often useful to consider the effects of individual developments along with those from growth in general (much of which may not require rezoning or similar changes from the existing plan and thus could not normally be prevented). For large developments with long construction times, impacts can be estimated only by adding the emissions to those from all other relevant developments at the point of ultimate occupancy.

Techniques for estimating overall increases in emissions are detailed in at least two EPA publications and will be briefly summarized here.[15] First, emissions from existing sources are modified to reflect future mandated reductions, if appropriate.[16] Second, growth factors for the various categories of point and stationary area sources are derived from the land use plan being evaluated and/or current growth rates of suitable surrogates (i.e., population, total earnings, and manufacturing earnings). These growth factors, modified by applicable new source emission standards promulgated by EPA, are then applied to the current level of activity within each category to obtain emissions in the desired future year. Mobile area sources can be projected in a similar manner, except that the effects of EPA-mandated source controls for new vehicles must also be taken into account.[17] Power plants, due to their importance as emission sources, are projected separately, using data obtained from individual companies.

b. Small Area Analysis

Large area analysis may be adequate on a "first look" basis, but it does not allow the assessment of

---

14. EPA, *Compilation of Air Pollution Emission Factors*, 2d ed. (Research Triangle Park, N.C.: EPA, April, 1973).

15. EPA, *Guidelines for Air Quality Maintenance Planning and Analysis, vol. 1*: op. cit., and ibid., vol. 7: *Projecting County Emissions*.

16. The state implementation plans for AQCRs specify planned reductions necessary to achieve the national ambient standards by 1975–77.

17. The total effect is the combination of increasingly effective controls and the attrition of older vehicles over time. EPA-mandated controls utilized after 1968 also affect the level of current emissions.

air quality impacts caused by alternative spatial distributions of future development within the community. The projection of future emissions for each subarea can be based on (a) distribution of aggregate growth, or (b) estimation of growth for each individual subarea.

The basis for distributing growth (and also for subarea delineation) can be as simple as reference to a comprehensive plan. Aggregate growth is assumed to be channeled to those areas which by designation can receive it. This approach, together with variations on the theme, was investigated by the Argonne National Laboratory as part of a general air pollution study of Chicago.[18] Since a comprehensive plan is but a rough approximation of the future, analysts have relied on simulation modeling techniques for more reasonable approximations.[19] These are based on the theoretical behavior of firms and households, observed development patterns for the test community over a period of time or in analogous communities, or a combination of the two.[20]

c. Individual Development Analysis

Project plans for major point sources (e.g., power plants and factories) are usually sufficiently specific so that the techniques outlined for estimating current emissions can be applied. That is, emissions are estimated from the manufacturing processes to be used. In fact, new point source emissions are strictly regulated by state and local pollution control agencies as mandated by EPA.

For proposed residential and commercial development, the primary effects are power plant and transportation-induced emissions. Procedures for estimating electrical energy demands of new developments are outlined in another report in this series.[21] These new demands must be translated into additional fuel consumption and then into increased emis-

sions. However, this is a question that must be addressed at the regional level. Increased power plant capacities are planned to match regional growth rates, and the impact of expanding capacity is a product of plant location, fuel type and composition, and the degree to which new capacities are created by borrowing from neighboring electric power grids. Individual power companies should be consulted on their future plans and the impact of individual developments estimated in the context of projected regional growth.

The inducement of transportation-generated emissions by new development is usually a much more important consideration for individual projects. The effects on air quality are frequently localized and thus project-specific. The following component parts of the problem can be specified:

(1) Number of trips generated (per day).

(2) Modal split (i.e., the choice of mode for each trip).

(3) Time distribution of trips (hourly).

(4) Spatial distribution of trips.

(5) Average speed of vehicles on each link or for each zone.

(6) Vehicle emission rates.

In support of the new indirect source regulations promulgated by EPA, a series of documents has been prepared specifying approaches to estimating the impact of indirect (i.e., vehicle-generating) sources.[22] As a basis for these estimations the manuals provide information from which calculations for most of the above data can be made. However, only traffic patterns in the immediate vicinity of the facility are considered. In addition, residential developments are excluded.

The chapter on transportation in the public and private service report[23] explicitly treats the issues not covered by the EPA indirect source documents. Methods for estimating trips generated by residential developments and trip distributions for various types of land developments are outlined. The spatial distribution of trips is perhaps the most difficult aspect of

18. Allen S. Kennedy et al., *Air Pollution—Land Use Planning Project Phase I. Final Report* (Argonne, Ill.: Argonne National Laboratory, November, 1971).

19. The flexibility of community zoning plans is rather notorious. Perhaps they can be more appropriately thought of as but one constraint on the pattern of future development.

20. An overview and critique of land use models can be found in Ira Lowry, "Seven Models of Urban Development: A Structural Comparison," in *Urban Development Models*, Highway Research Board, Report No. 97, 1967; William Goldner, "The Lowry Model Heritage," *Journal of the American Institute of Planners* (March, 1972): 100–09; and California State Air Resources Board, *Air Quality, Land Use, and Transportation Models* (Sacramento: CSARB, July 1974).

21. See the "Energy Services" chapter in: Philip S. Schaenman, Dale L. Keyes, and Kathleen Christensen, *Estimating Impacts of Land Development on Public Services* (Washington, D.C.: The Urban Institute, forthcoming).

22. Scott D. Thayer, Kenneth Axetell, Jr., and Jonathan Cook, *Vehicle Behavior In and Around Complex Sources and Related Complex Source Characteristics*, vols. I–VI (Shopping Centers, Airports, Sports Stadiums, Parking Facilities, Amusement Parks, Major Highways, Recreational Areas) (Research Triangle Park, N.C.: EPA, Office of Air and Water Program, Office of Air Quality Planning and Standards, August–November, 1973). See also Kevin G. Croke, et. al., *The Relationship of Automobile Pollutants and Commercial Development*, (Argonne, Ill.: Argonne National Laboratory, 1975).

23. Schaenman, Keyes, and Christensen, op. cit.

these calculations. It requires detailed information about the future inhabitants and the origins and destinations of their trips. In addition, rather complex simulation models are required to assign these trips to links in the highway network. Fortunately, only the largest[24] developments will impact significant portions of the entire network.

Once the number of new trips has been estimated and distributed, emission levels can be projected using the EPA emission factors and knowledge of vehicle age, speeds, and volumes on specific highway links.[25]

d. Estimation Problems

Although the uncertainty in predictions may be high (and in many cases is itself unknown), considering an extension of past trends and/or other plausible futures is useful for estimating future air quality. However, if growth projections are to be used as anything more than qualitative descriptions they should be generalized spatially and cover a limited interval of time, perhaps no more than ten years.

However, the primary focus of this report is on individual developments and short-time horizons. Even here, though, considerable uncertainty exists regarding the factors which will determine ultimate impact—vehicle miles of travel induced and energy requirements—which, in turn, are related to a host of other factors, such as population density, characteristics of new residents/customers/employees, and building construction features. But even where uncertainty exists, a range of estimates can be considered—the lowest, average, and highest value at each step in the calculation procedure (if these values are known). The final estimate can then be expressed in the same terms (lowest, average, highest) even though the probability of obtaining these values cannot be specified. In other words, the sensitivity of the estimates to the assumptions can be stated.[26]

The concern about data precision, valid as it may be, must be conditioned by the ultimate use of the study results. Great accuracy is not needed to predict trends or make initial assessments, especially when initial assessments show that conditions will be far below or above preselected standards or targets. On the other hand, if future emissions will produce ambient concentrations approaching threshold levels, then more accuracy may be needed.

3. Measuring/Estimating Current Ambient Concentrations

Although data on emissions constitute a valuable and necessary base of information, ambient pollutant levels must be measured in order to assess the impact of the new emissions. The measurement of ambient concentrations remains a difficult and costly activity, despite continued federal involvement and financial support.[27]

a. Quantitative Measurement

Pollutants in the atmosphere show variations in both time and space. This has important implications for the design and operation of an air monitoring network. The number and placement of stations and the frequency of recordings must be planned to capture the concentration variations. EPA's recommendations are a compromise between scientifically based design criteria and the problems of the real world.[28] Recognizing that the costs of an ideal system are prohibitive, the EPA guidelines emphasize placement of the sampling stations where the potential for pollution problems is the highest. The "hot spot" criteria include such factors as population distribution, suspected ambient levels, location of sources, and areas of future growth. Other practical considerations are presence of power supplies and security from vandalism. Thus, the number and actual location of stations may be far from ideal.

The Clean Air Act defines ambient air as "that portion of the atmosphere external to buildings to which the general public has access." Thus, measurements of air quality should logically be made at a height of five to six feet. EPA suggests a height of three to six meters (approximately ten to twenty feet), while actual locations are often at roof level.

The literature on monitoring instrumentation is well developed and will not be reviewed here.[29] Worthy of

---

24. "Large" is a relative term. The size of the development (in terms of the number of trips generated) must be compared with the size of the surrounding community.

25. EPA, *Compilation of Air Pollution Emission Factors* (Research Triangle Park, N.C.: EPA, Office of Air and Water Programs, Office of Air Quality Planning Standard, April, 1973) (Report No. AP-42).

26. For a good discussion of the way errors propagate through multistep calculations, with illustration for air quality assessment, see Hagevik, Mandelker, and Brail, op. cit.

27. EPA estimates that approximately ten man-years of effort are required annually to maintain a monitoring network the size of the one found in Washington, D.C. (personal communication with a member of the Contract Programs Development Division).

28. R. A. McCormick, *Air Pollution Measurements* (Research Triangle Park, N.C.: EPA, National Environmental Research Center, February, 1972) (NTIS No. Com-73-10016); and EPA, *Guidelines: Air Quality Surveillance Networks* (Research Triangle Park, N.C.: EPA, Office of Air Programs, May, 1971) (Publication No. AP-98).

29. For a summary of available methods and techniques, see National Academies of Sciences and Engineering, op. cit., vol. 3.

note, however, is research on measuring ambient concentrations using airborne sensors. Advances in these techniques may significantly improve the accuracy of the measurements.[30]

b. Measurement Problems

Despite the existence of more than 7,000 federal, state, and locally operated monitoring stations throughout the country,[31] knowledge of ambient conditions remains rather primitive. Even if all the stations recorded each of the major pollutants, there are simply too few stations to reflect geographical variations adequately. With the possible exception of Chicago and New York, the number of stations for any one city is insufficient to allow satisfactory interpolation between stations and the construction of isopleths (lines of equal concentration). Thus, diffusion models will be needed in most communities to obtain isopleths of current ambient concentrations or to obtain estimates for areas within the community which are not located near monitors. (Diffusion models are discussed in the next section.)

Aside from problems of location, there remains a serious concern regarding data reliability. Variations in station operation and maintenance, combined with poor quality control procedures, especially for stations requiring manual chemical analysis, has rendered the data recorded for many cities of questionable accuracy. The inappropriate height of many stations further hampers meaningful interpretation.[32]

There is also some evidence that the EPA-recommended sampling frequency is too low for the desired degree of certainty in the results.[33] Compared with the other problems, however, this seems to be of lesser importance.

What then can be said about the concentration of pollutants in the atmosphere? Certainly the data from even a single station are useful, not as a definitive statement about air quality for a city, but at least as an indicator of a potential or general problem. Con-versely, if ambient concentrations at a single station at a "hot spot" during the worst meteorological conditions are satisfactory, then probably no part of the city faces a serious problem. These data may also be useful in answering questions regarding planning at a community-wide level. (E.g., is any additional development within city limits feasible?) But for other assessments there is no substitute for accurate data on the variable conditions found in different parts of the community, which must be obtained from properly located, well-maintained, and competently operated stations. Diffusion models can be used, but their validation depends on the existence of a good profile of current conditions. A series of simple procedures for calculating the current ambient levels in localized areas (i.e., several blocks) using simple mathematical relationships is outlined in a recent HUD-sponsored report.[34]

c. Vegetative Indicators

For many communities the quantitative monitoring of ambient air quality is simply too expensive, while for others one or a few sampling points must suffice. In order to obtain an objective, albeit *very* qualitative "sense" of community-wide or subarea air quality, strategically placed vegetative test plots may offer one alternative. Although plant damage from air pollution remains a poorly understood phenomenon, carefully controlled field studies continue to provide information by which various plant species can be rated for sensitivity.[35] Local governments interested in utilizing plants as pollution indicators should contact state air pollution agencies for additional information and assistance.

4. Estimating Future Ambient Concentrations

The next step in the analytical procedure involves the estimation of future ambient concentrations for each of the various pollutants. In a sense, this is the culmination of all preceding calculations. Data on current and future emissions and current ambient levels are combined with meteorological and surface feature inputs to produce the net change in future ambient levels. The analysis can be performed at varying levels of sophistication and complexity. Manual techniques as well as those requiring computer support are available.

The various techniques for estimating future am-

30. L. J. Duncan, E. J. Friedman, E. L. Keitz, and E. A. Ward, *An Airborne Remote Sensing System for Urban Air Quality* (Washington, D.C.: The Mitre Corporation, February, 1974).

31. EPA, *Inventory of Air Pollution Monitoring Equipment Operated by State and Local Agencies* (Research Triangle Park, N.C.: Air Pollution Technical Information Center, 1971).

32. Even New York has recently recognized the inadequacy of its network. Forty-five new CO monitoring stations placed at a height of five to eight feet above street level will be added to the sixteen presently in operation. See Richard Severo, "City to Augment Monoxide Gauges," *New York Times,* 20 April 1975, p. 42.

33. Harold E. Neustadter and Steven M. Sidik, *On Evaluating Compliance with Air Pollution Not to be Exceeded More Than Once Per Year* (Cleveland: Lewis Research Center, June, 1974) (NASA No. N74-25879).

34. T. M. Briggs, *Air Pollution Considerations in Residential Planning, vol. I: Manual* (Cincinnati: PEDCO-Environmental Specialists, Inc., July, 1974).

35. See Atle Habjorg, *Air Pollution and Vegetation II* (Research Triangle Park, N.C.: EPA, June, 1974) (NTIS No. PB-237-880-T).

Land Development and the Natural Environment

bient concentrations will be discussed both generally and specifically. The material to be presented is partly a synthesis and recombination of information and ideas contained in other overviews.[36] However, only the Darling report contains specific information on the cost and accuracy of individual dispersion models.[37] The information presented here is designed to supplement the Darling report. The emphasis is on models which have wide geographic applicability and which are used routinely by planning or pollution control agencies.

a. Types of Models

There are many ways to differentiate approaches to estimating the transport and dispersion of atmospheric pollutants. The various typologies described below highlight different yet important aspects of dispersion models.

Theoretical versus Empirical Models—"Theoretical" models are those which are grounded on basic principles of the physical sciences. They are rigorous, and only a few purely theoretical models have advanced beyond the research stage. Empirical models are derived purely from observed patterns over time or for different settings. Models which embody empirically justified modifications of theoretical relationships are in the middle.

Theoretical air dispersion models are based on the *conservation of mass law,* which, in simplified mathematical terms, is:[38]

$$C_i = T_i + D_i + R_i + Q_i$$

where: C_i = the change in concentrations of pollutant i over time in a small volume of air

T_i = the net transport of i into or out of the small volume

R_i = the amount of i created in the volume by photochemical reaction

D_i = the change due to turbulent diffusion of i out of the volume

Q_i = the amount of i emitted directly into the small volume from outside

With the improved understanding of the way turbulent diffusion varies with wind speed, temperature, humidity, sunlight, and surface roughness, and with the advent of high-speed computers, the mass conservation equation is now being used as the basis for recently developed dispersion models. The obvious advantage is that, in theory, all emission sources (including photochemical generation) and time variations can be represented, along with data on surface roughness. The disadvantage is that the theoretical models tend to be costly to operate.

The next category (semi-theoretical, semi-empirical) includes a family of models derived from the *Gaussian dispersion equation,* which is depicted schematically in Figure 1-1.[39] This equation represents the concentration at any point in space of a single puff of pollutant i which is transported by local winds and diffuses three-dimensionally in a Gaussian or normal manner in the process.[40] The extent to which the puff will continue to disperse in horizontal and vertical directions is related to the stability of the atmosphere. Turner has developed empirical relationships between stability categories and the standard

where: C_i = concentration of pollutant i

t = time

∇ = change with respect to the x, y, and z directions in space

$$\left(\frac{\partial}{\partial x} i + \frac{\partial}{\partial y} j + \frac{\partial}{\partial z} k \right)$$

V = wind velocity with components in the x, y, and z direction

K = turbulent diffusivity with components in the x, y, and z direction

R_i = rate of generation or removal of pollutant i by photochemical reaction

Q_i = rate of emission of pollutant i

36. See Eugene M. Darling, Jr., *Computer Modeling of Transportation-Generated Air Pollution* (Cambridge, Mass.: U.S. Department of Transportation, Transportation Systems Center, June, 1972) (NTIS No. PB-213013); Joe J. Mathis and William L. Grose, *A Review of Methods for Predicting Air Pollution Dispersion,* (Washington, D.C.: NASA Langley Research Center, 1973) (NTIS No. N73-20658); Harry Moses, *Mathematical Urban Air Pollution Models* (Argonne, Ill.: Argonne National Laboratory, April, 1969) (NTIS No. ANL-ES-RPY-001); R. A. Papetti and F. R. Gilmore, *Air Pollution* (Santa Monica, Calif.: The Rand Corporation, February, 1971).

37. Darling surveyed private research and consulting firms regarding the mathematical underpinnings and technical aspects of their dispersion models.

38. Or more formally:

$$\frac{\partial C_i}{\partial t} = -\nabla \cdot (VC_i) + \nabla \cdot (K \nabla C_i) + R_i + Q_i$$

39. The mathematical representation is as follows:

$$C_i = \frac{Q}{(2\pi)^{3/2} \sigma_x \sigma_y \sigma_z} \exp - \left[(x - ut)^2 + \frac{y^2}{2 \sigma_y^2} \right] \left\{ \exp - \left[\frac{(z-H)^2}{2 \sigma_z^2} \right] + \exp - \left[\frac{(z+H)^2}{2 \sigma_z^2} \right] \right\}$$

where: C_i = concentration of pollutant i at time t after emission at any point in space

Q = amount of pollutant emitted

x,y,z = distances in 3-dimensional space

u = mean wind speed

$\sigma_x, \sigma_y, \sigma_z$ = standard deviation of the distribution of concentration in the x, y, and z directions

H = height at which the pollutant is emitted

exp = e raised to the expression which follows

40. A Gaussian or normal distribution when graphed is the familiar bell-shaped curve.

FIGURE 1-1
SCHEMATIC REPRESENTATION OF THE
GAUSSIAN MODEL

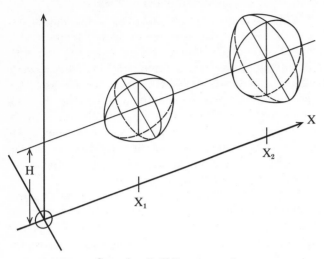

a. Gaussian Puff Representation

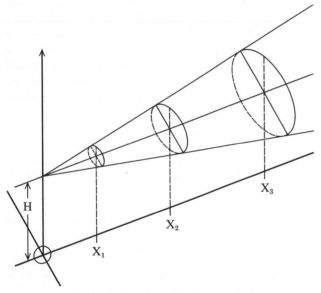

b. Gaussian Plume Representation

NOTES:
H = height at which emissions are released
X = downwind distance

SOURCE: Modified from Darling, op. cit.

deviations of dispersion.[41] However, atmospheric stability is but one factor, albeit a very important one, which influences the degree and rate of dispersion. Mechanical turbulence from surface roughness is another, but the roughness dispersion relationship has

not yet been quantified. The selection of appropriate values for a given local situation remains a serious weakness in the utilization of Gaussian dispersion models.

Similarly, the model is not easily adapted to reflect photochemically produced pollutants or pollutant removal processes. On the other hand, the puff model retains the conservation of mass model's ability to reflect changes in wind speed, wind direction, and emissions over time.

In order for the instantaneous Gaussian puff model to reflect a realistic urban setting (i.e., continuous emissions from many sources), the equation is mathematically integrated over time and summed for each source.[42] The result is an integrated puff or a Gaussian plume model.[43]

The third category of models embraces those which are empirically derived, that is, those which attempt to explain observed data in the simplest way. The most obvious example is the use of regression equations to relate changes in ambient concentrations with such variables as emission levels, meteorological conditions, and terrain.[44] In fact, attempts at reproducing the results obtained from more sophisticated models have proven quite successful.[45]

The obvious advantage of such an approach is its simplicity and built-in validation properties. By definition, unless the regression equation "explains" a considerable amount of the variance in the dependent variable, it will not be used. Thus, fairly high agreement with observed data is assured. However, since regressions only reveal associations and not causal relationships among the data, future patterns may be significantly different from present ones.

Another empirically based, simplified dispersion

42. $C_i = \int_{-\infty}^{\infty} C_i \, dt = \dfrac{Q}{2\pi \, \sigma_y \, \sigma_z \, u} \exp - \left[\dfrac{y^2}{2 \, \sigma_y{}^2} \right]$

$\left\{ \exp - \left[\dfrac{(z - H)^2}{2 \, \sigma_z{}^2} \right] + \exp - \left[\dfrac{(z + H)^2}{2 \, \sigma_z{}^2} \right] \right\}$

$C_{total} = \sum_{i=1}^{n} C_i$ $\quad$ n = the total number of sources
∞ = infinity

43. These are closely related, yet distinct models. The difference is that in the integrated puff version, the emission times over which the equation is integrated can be quite short. The resulting puffs or segmented plumes (depending on how elongated a puff can be and still retain the name) can then be tracked separately. The plume version incorporates the dispersion equation integrated over an infinite period (the resulting effluent is simply a stream of effluent). It consequently does not retain the ability to reflect changes in meteorological and emission variables with time.

44. Regression equations are simply mathematical expressions which relate one variable with one or more others, based on a number of observations of each.

45. Alan Horowitz, William S. Meisel, and David C. Collins, *The Application of Repro-modeling to the Analysis of a Photochemical Air Pollution Model,* (Washington, D.C.: EPA, December, 1973) (EPA No. EPA-650/4-4-74-001).

41. D. Bruce Turner, *Workbook of Atmospheric Dispersion Estimates* (Cincinnati: Department of Health, Education and Welfare, Rev. 1970) (NTIS No. PB 191 482). The standard deviations are the parameters which determine the rate of puff expansion.

Land Development and the Natural Environment

model is that known as a "box" model. When the mixing depth of the atmosphere is roughly equivalent to the extent of plume expansion vertically once it has begun to disperse, the warm layer of air aloft acts as a lid on a box, causing the pollutants to be uniformly dispersed within. Under these conditions (usually referred to as an inversion aloft), the concentration can be estimated by a very simple equation:

$$C_i = \frac{Q_i}{u\ d}$$

where: C_i = ambient concentration of pollutant i
$\quad\quad Q_i$ = amount of pollutant i emitted per unit of time
$\quad\quad u$ = average wind speed
$\quad\quad d$ = mixing depth

Simple versus Complex Models—The theoretical-empirical classification scheme includes most but not all models. Pressed by legislative and judicial edicts, EPA has begun to use simple linear approximations to predict future air quality. These can be classified neither as theoretical nor empirical. They have no theoretical justification except in the most fundamental sense (i.e., increases in emissions cause a proportional increase in ambient concentrations) and no empirical verification. These models will be discussed in more detail subsequently, since they are widely used and thought to be satisfactory for rough approximation.

Source versus Receptor Models—Some models are designed to estimate the concentration levels at various points due to pollutants emitted from a *single source*. Conversely, some models focus on air quality at *single points* due to the contributions from many sources. The former (source-oriented) are useful when a new development will be a major source (e.g., a new industrial plant), while the latter (receptor-oriented) are more appropriate for developments which may expose additional people or other receptors to existing concentrations and for evaluating air quality of comprehensive plans.

Models Based on Type of Source—The nature of the source is another important consideration in model design, especially for the Gaussian dispersion models.

The Gaussian puff and plume models described previously assume a *point* emission source. *Area* sources can be depicted by the use of an imaginary virtual point source located upwind of the area over which individual area sources are to be aggregated. The plume from the virtual point source is allowed to disperse so that by the time it reaches the area in question the concentration approximates that from the area sources combined. Alternatively, the Gaus-

sian point source model can be integrated in both the x and y direction. The emission rate (Q) for area sources is expressed in terms of emission level per unit time per unit area (e.g., grams/second-meter squared).

Line sources are simulated by mathematically integrating the point source Gaussian plume equation over the length of the line in the y direction (assuming that the line is perpendicular to the wind direction).[46] Furthermore, if the source is on the ground and effectively of infinite length (as is the case for most mobile sources), and if the wind is blowing at an angle with respect to the source, then the equation is greatly simplified.[47]

Since the conservation of mass model is used with an emission source grid, all sources are in effect area sources. This means that point, area, and line sources must be aggregated on a unit cell basis. The cells can be as small as several acres or as large as several square miles.

Models Based on Type of Pollutant—Most of the models developed to date treat the relatively inert pollutants—particulates, SO_2, and CO. The ambient concentration of these is independent of chemical reactions, which may occur subsequent to emission.[48] Some modelers have also attempted to treat NO_x as inert gases, but their success has been limited.

Photochemical models are now being developed and validated for specific cities. They are largely based on smog chamber and other closed vessel experiments. This is an inherent weakness, since the atmospheric reactions are not confined by the walls of a container. The extent to which open and closed system reactions differ is still largely unknown.

Models Based on Scale of Application—A scale of application has two components: (a) the magnitude of the emissions to which the model is sensitive, and (b) the degree of spatial disaggregation of the calculated ambient concentrations. Most models are sensitive to any major point source and cumulative

---

46. $C = \dfrac{2Q}{\sqrt{2\pi}\ \sigma_z u}\ \exp\ -\left[1/2\left(\dfrac{H}{\sigma_z}\right)^2\right]\displaystyle\int_{y_2/\sigma_y}^{y_1/\sigma_y}\dfrac{1}{\sqrt{2\pi}}$

$$\exp\ -\left(\dfrac{y_i/\sigma_y}{2}\right)^2\ d\left(\dfrac{y_i}{\sigma_y}\right)$$

where: Q = emission level per unit time, per unit length of the line source (e.g., grams/second-meter)

47. $C = \dfrac{2Q}{\sin\Theta\ \sqrt{2\pi}\ \sigma_z u}$

where: Θ = the angle between the source and the wind direction

48. Strictly speaking, this is not true for SO_2 which is oxidized and hydrolyzed to sulfuric acid. Also, CO may play a role in photooxidant production. However, for both, the rates of reaction seem to be small.

changes in small point sources (i.e., significant changes in area sources). However, the models vary considerably in the spatial disaggregation of the output. Some reflect changes in ambient concentrations at a single point in the community, while others estimate changes for smaller subareas.

A few models are sensitive to individual area, line, and less-than-major point sources. Typically, these will also specify the change in ambient concentrations at a large number of points within the community or as a continuous function of downwind distance from the source.

Translating this into types of development to which the models apply is not a straightforward task. Much depends on the size of the development in terms of source strength. Residential and commercial developments are important primarily as vehicle-trip generators and thus as line sources. Whether an individual development will produce significant changes in air quality will depend on the number and distribution of new trips and whether localized or large area effects are considered. At least two models, to be reviewed here, will estimate roadside concentrations for single roads (although the accuracies may be quite low) while others estimate community-wide impacts from changes over the entire road network.

b. Description of Individual Models

Those readers who would like an initial overview of the models to be discussed here are advised to turn first to the Summary and Comparison section of this chapter. The most salient features of each model are summarized and compared with those of the other models utilizing a tabular format.

The preceding background material will now be used to describe specific dispersion models in a concise manner. Each model will be characterized according to the previously discussed typologies. This will be followed by a description of the type and scale of application and an assessment of costs of operation and accuracy of results where this information is known. Some data on the latter points have been collected by means of a questionnaire mailed to selected model users.

Several simplified reviews of air quality models with an orientation toward land use/air quality analysis and planning have recently been prepared.[49] In most cases these supplement and expand the material presented here. The EPA document is especially useful for comparing the most readily available public domain models.

The word "model" as it is used here has a very general definition. It refers to simple numerical formulas, the utilization of which requires nothing more than pencil and paper, as well as to highly developed packages of complex mathematical expressions requiring the assistance of a digital computer. In other words, "model" refers equally well to general techniques or specific computer programs. Of the models reviewed here, the first four (rollforward, Miller/Holzworth, Hanna/Gifford, and California Highway) do not require the use of a computer. The others do.

Rollforward Models—The rollforward models are identical to the rollback models (also known as linear models) advocated by EPA, with one exception. Rather than being used to estimate the reduction (rollback) in emission required to meet the national ambient standards, they are used to estimate future ambient levels (rollforward) from various levels of future emissions.

EPA has published an excellent description of the basic rollback model and modifications thereof.[50] Other publications report on specific applications in Los Angeles and San Diego.[51]

The rollforward models currently in use can be characterized as extremely to moderately simple, receptor-oriented, and applicable to all types of sources but only to inert pollutants (CO, SO_x, particulates). The models are normally used on a community-wide scale, but with some modification can be used for subarea analysis as well.

The basic equation from which all rollforward models are derived is as follows:[52]

$$\frac{C_{pi}}{C_{fi}} = K \frac{E_{pi}}{E_{fi}}$$

---

49. California State Air Resources Board, *Introduction to Manual Methods for Estimating Air Quality* (July, 1974) (NTIS No. PB-237-871) and *Air Quality, Land Use, and Transporation Models, Evaluation and Utilization in the Planning Process* (July, 1974) (NTIS No. PB-237-867); and EPA, *Guidelines for Air Quality Maintenance Planning and Analysis*, vol. 12, *Applying Atmospheric Simulation Models to Air Quality Maintenance Areas* (Research Triangle Park, N.C.: EPA, September, 1974) (NTIS No. PB-237-750).

50. Noel H. DeNevers and J. Roger Morris, "Rollback Modeling—Basic and Modified" (Paper presented at the sixty-sixth Annual Meeting of the Air Pollution Control Association, Chicago, June 24–28, 1973).

51. William T. Mikolowsky et al., *The Regional Impacts of Near-Term Transportation Alternatives: A Case Study of Los Angeles* (Santa Monica, Calif.: The Rand Corporation, June, 1974); and Mikolowsky, *San Diego Clean Air Project, Appendix 2* (Santa Monica, Calif.: The Rand Corporation, December, 1973).

52. More formally,

$$\frac{(C_{ai} - b_i)_{future\ year}}{(C_{ai} - b_i)_{base\ year}} = \frac{\sum\limits_{j=1}^{n} [K_{aij} e_{ij}]_{future\ year}}{\sum\limits_{j=1}^{n} [K_{aij} e_{ij}]_{base\ year}}$$

where: C_{ai} = concentration of pollutant i at point a

b_i = background concentration of pollutant i (i.e., that

where: C_{pi} = present ambient concentration of pollutant i

C_{fi} = future ambient concentration of i

E_{pi} = present emission level of i

E_{fi} = future emission level of i

K = a constant

This is a simple proportional relationship which assumes that the ratio of future year to base year ambient concentration is the same as the ratio of future to base year emissions, with emissions broken into categories so that the importance and growth of each category can be weighted separately. The *simple version* of this general relationship does not differentiate among emission categories and further assumes that one geographical point can be selected to represent the whole community.[53]

Several modifications to the simple version have been proposed in order to render it more theoretically accurate. The *semi-diffusion version* incorporates the relationship between height of emission release and dispersion as estimated by the Gaussian dispersion equation. The K values are made to reflect the relative contributions of the various emission categories by specifying average height of release for each category.[54]

The *location version* further modifies the K values by incorporating the general location of emission categories into the mathematical expression. The community is first subdivided into concentric zones centered about point A. Emissions for each category are then disaggregated by zone and are assumed to be uniformly distributed throughout each zone. The relative contribution to the concentration at point A are then made inversely proportional to distance from A.

The *wind direction version* represents yet another step in rendering the simple version more realistic. Here the effect of differences in wind direction are factored in by further subdividing the community into wind sectors and further disaggregating the emission

sources by sector. The K values are then modified to reflect the frequency with which the wind blows from various directions. Thus, those portions of the concentric zones which normally lie upwind from point A are weighted more heavily.

The rollforward models thus far discussed are applicable only to nonreactive pollutants where the ambient concentration is linearly related to the emission level. For pollutants which undergo photochemical reactions this assumption of linearity does not hold. Smog chamber experiments reveal that a complex relationship exists between ambient concentrations of oxidants and the emission level of their precursors (nitrogen oxides and reactive hydrocarbons). However, at least one attempt to apply the rollforward model to reactive pollutants has been reported.[55] In other words, proportionality was made slightly nonlinear for these pollutants.

The advantages and disadvantages of the various rollforward models are as follows:

Advantages

1. These models are the least complicated and least expensive to use of all dispersion models.

2. Current emissions and meteorological data required are available from local or state pollution control agencies and Weather Bureau stations located at all major airports.

Disadvantages

1. The models are unvalidated.

2. The point chosen as being representative of the community must be the location of an existing monitoring station and, therefore, may not be truly representative.

3. The lack of spatial disaggregation means that all present emissions are assumed to increase in a proportional manner and maintain their present spatial distribution in the future. (This is somewhat less of a problem for the location version.)

4. Meteorological and surface roughness factors are either ignored or treated simplistically. (Complete atmospheric mixing is assumed.)

5. The models are not applicable to short-lived pollutants (such as CO) unless their half-life is comparable to their travel time across the community at the predominant wind velocity.[56]

6. Reactive pollutants have not yet been routinely

---

transported in from other regions and that due to natural sources)

e_{ij} = emissions of pollutant i from category j (categories can be by industrial activity groupings or by type of source)

n = total number of categories

K_{aij} = contribution of a unit emission of pollutant i from category j to the ambient concentration at point a

53. Thus:

$$\frac{(C_i - b)_{future}}{(C_i - b)_{base\ year}} = \frac{(K_i e_i)_{future}}{(K_i e_i)_{base\ year}}$$

Here C_i is the average community-wide ambient concentration for some time period (usually one year), e_i is the aggregate emissions from all sources, and K_i is a constant which reflects meteorological conditions, surface features, and other factors related to dispersion.

54. "Release height" is a function of both stack height and plume rise, the latter due to the buoyant effect of a hot gas.

---

55. Mikolowsky, et al., op. cit. As with all applications of the roll-forward model to date, the accuracy of the results is unknown.

56. "Half-life" is the amount of time required for half of the pollutant to be removed from the atmosphere by deposition, interactions with vegetation, or other processes.

FIGURE 1-2
SUMMARY OF THE MILLER/HOLZWORTH MODEL

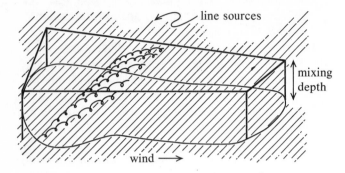

NOTES:

The community is visualized as being composed of an infinite number of infinitely long line sources of uniform strength.

Pollutants from each line source are presumed to disperse in a Gaussian manner until the plume reaches the top of the mixing layer. Thereafter, the contribution from that source is uniformly mixed in the box.

These line sources are integrated in the direction of the wind to obtain an aggregate concentration value for the downwind edge.

Average, community-wide values are obtained by a process similar to averaging the concentrations of the upwind and downwind edges.

treated by rollforward models, although some initial attempts have been made.

In general, the rollforward models are attractive and widely used because of their relative simplicity. Generalized emission data inputs and desk calculators are used for computations. However, a reduction in accuracy is the cost of simplicity. It is worth repeating that these models are completely unverified.

Although the rollforward model is typically identified with the assumption of linearity, it should be noted that many of the simpler models to follow also assume linearity between emissions and ambient concentrations. Thus, rollforward models should be considered as one type of linear model, the distinguishing characteristic of which is its application to community-wide and long-term estimation problems.

Miller/Holzworth Model—This model is relatively simple (it does not require the use of a computer), theoretical (although based on empirically validated relationships), receptor-oriented, and designed to be used with area sources and most pollutants.[57] It also treats line and point sources by assuming they behave as uniformly dispersed area sources.

A summary and schematic depiction of the model appears in Figure 1-2. The model is based on the

Gaussian dispersion equation for an infinite cross-wind line source emitting at ground level.[58] This is then integrated across the length of the entire community in the direction of the prevailing wind to obtain the highest ambient concentration (which will occur along the down-wind edge of the community). However, it does not assume that the vertical dispersion of the plume is relatively constant with distance traveled. Instead, when integrating the basic equation, two terms are produced, one which represents up-wind sources close to the receptor, the plumes from which have not had time to disperse throughout the mixing layer, and one which represents more distant sources, the plumes from which are uniformly mixed within the "box."[59] In order to obtain average values for the community as a whole (not just at one point), the values at all points are averaged by additional integration.

In order to facilitate calculations using their model, Miller and Holzworth have prepared graphs and tables which relate the normalized concentration (C/Q)[60] to wind speed[61] (the greater the speed, the lower the C/Q value), mixing depth d (the greater the depth, the lower the C/Q value), and community size (the smaller the community and thus the fewer the sources, the lower the C/Q value). Once these values are specified, the actual C value is then obtained by substituting the appropriate Q value (the estimated average emission density previously computed) for the community in question. Actual calculations are

---

58.
$$C = \frac{2Q}{\sqrt{2\pi}\ \sigma_z\ u}$$

where: C = the downwind ambient concentration
   Q = emissions per unit time and per unit *length* of the source
   σ_z = standard deviation of vertical dispersion
   ū = average wind speed

59.
$$C = \int_{t_0} \frac{2Q\ dt}{\sqrt{2\pi}\ \sigma_z} + \int_t \frac{Q}{d}\ dt$$

where: t_0 = time to travel from the nearest source
   t_d = time necessary for uniform dispersal (at average wind speed)
   t_s = time to travel the length of the community (at average wind speed
   d = mixing depth
   Q = emissions per unit time and per unit *area* of the source
   σ_z = standard deviation of vertical dispersion

The time t_d is obviously dependent on the mixing depth (i.e., the higher the lid on the box, the longer it takes for the plume to disperse upward to it). The travel times for various values of d are obtained from Turner's data as shown in the Miller/Holzworth article.

60. This expression relates the average ambient community-wide concentration (C) to a unit emission rate (Q).

61. This is the average wind speed throughout the mixing layer obtained by averaging wind speed at the surface and aloft.

---

57. Marvin E. Miller and George C. Holzworth, "An Atmospheric Diffusion Model for Metropolitan Areas," *Air Pollution Control Association Journal* 17 (January, 1967): 46–50.

thus minimized; most of the work involves finding values in tables once the input data are assembled.

The limited number of test applications have produced encouraging results. Tests in Los Angeles, Nashville, and Washington for SO_2 and NO_x produced correlations between measured and predicted values above 0.8 once the model was calibrated.[62] These results are especially surprising for NO_x, which undergo photochemical reactions. It must also be remembered that only community-wide averages were estimated.

In summary, the Miller/Holzworth model is a simple, inexpensive technique which has produced fairly accurate results. However, the limitations are quite severe.

Advantages

1. The model is extremely easy and inexpensive to use once the emission rates have been determined.

2. The results appear to be quite accurate for SO_2 and NO_x (except for situations listed below).

Disadvantages

1. Emissions from point sources with tall stacks are not estimated well since the emission height is assumed to be zero everywhere.

2. Cities of asymmetrical shape or with nonuniformly distributed sources present difficult problems and may lead to highly inaccurate results.

3. Uniform and symmetrical growth of a community is necessary in order for the model to accurately predict *future* concentrations.

4. The smallest spatial unit of analysis is an entire community.

5. Although test results for NO_x have been fairly good to date, the model is not designed to treat reactive pollutants.

Hanna/Gifford Model—Frank Gifford and Steven Hanna of the National Oceanic and Atmospheric Administration have developed a rather simple but sur-

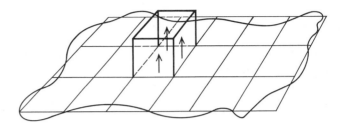

FIGURE 1-3
SUMMARY OF THE HANNA/GIFFORD MODEL

NOTES:

The community is divided into equal sized two-dimensional cells by superimposition of a gird pattern.

Area source strengths are calculated for each cell.

The ambient concentration in the cube above any one cell depends only on the emissions in that cell, the average wind speed, and the category (stable, neutral, unstable) of atmospheric stability.

Average, community-wide values are obtained either by averaging the values for all cubes, or expanding the size of the cells until one cell covers the entire community.

prisingly accurate atmospheric dispersion model.[63] The model is largely empirical, receptor-oriented, and applicable to both inert and reactive pollutants emitted from area sources.

A summary and schematic representation of the Hanna/Gifford model appears in Figure 1-3. Although it is derived from theoretical considerations (largely of the Gaussian dispersion type), the model is a result of empirical observations. Gifford and Hanna argue that for a community which is superimposed by a grid of uniform cells, the average ambient concentration for any one cell is a function of the area source emissions for that cell plus emissions from surrounding cells, attenuated by their distance from the cell in question. (The cells are usually on the order of one to several hundred square miles—the entire community.) What they discovered, however, was that the overwhelming determinant of ambient concentration is the local (i.e., source cell) emission level. This led to the following formulation:[64]

$$C_j = AQ_j/u$$

where: C_j = average ambient concentration of a

62. Correlations measure the agreement between predicted and measured data. Values of 0 signify no agreement, while values of 1.0 indicate perfect data agreement. For dispersion modeling, values about 0.7 reflect "good" agreement. Correlation coefficients as applied to data on ambient concentrations must be interpreted with caution. The specific coefficient values are a function of the adequacy of the monitoring program (e.g., network design and sampling frequency) as well as the accuracy of the model. In addition, other measures of validity can, and for some models have, been used. These measures will be discussed in the Summary. (Correlation coefficients cited in this report are the statistic "r" unless otherwise noted.)

63. E. A. Gifford, *The Simple ATDL Urban Air Pollution Model* (Oak Ridge, Tenn.: National Oceanic and Atmospheric Administration, Atmospheric Turbulence and Dispersion Laboratory, May, 1973) (File No. 78 rev.); Steven R. Hanna, "A Simple Method of Calculating Dispersion from Urban Area Sources," *Journal of the Air Pollution Control Association,* 21 (December, 1971): 774–77; Steven R. Hanna, "A Simple Dispersion Model for the Analysis of Chemically Reactive Pollutants," *Atmospheric Environment,* 7 (1973): 803–17.

64. The reader will note the striking similarity to what was previously called a box model.

chemically inert pollutant in cell j
A = constant
Q_j = emissions from cell j per unit time per unit area
u = average wind speed

Furthermore, it was shown that A is a function of the rate of vertical plume expansion, and thus of atmospheric stability.[65] The following values were obtained by fitting the equation to empirical observations:

unstable conditions A = 50
neutral conditions   A = 200
stable conditions   A = 600

For calculating long-term averages (i.e., annual or seasonal), 225 and 50 are the suggested values for A[66] for particulates and SO_2, respectively.[67] (Further analysis by the EPA has shown that particulates can be better estimated by this relationship: C = 52 + 91.7 Q/u).

The form of the model which treats reactive as well as nonreactive pollutants is more complicated, although considerably simplified over other photochemical models. It is based on a modified form of conservation of mass law and includes terms for mass movement out of the area, emission within the area, and photochemical reactions.[68] By a suitable mathematical transformation, the equation is expressed in terms of the original Hanna/Gifford model (C = AQ/u). The model is then specified by values for u, d (the mixing depth), the areal extent of the community, and the Q's for the various reacting substances.

The results of Hanna/Gifford model applications have been consistently good for the "inert model" and mixed for the "reactive model." The correlations between predicted and observed values for SO_2, particulates, and CO have been near or above 0.7 for tests in Chicago, Los Angeles, Nashville, San Francisco, and several other cities.[69] For NO_2 and reactive hydrocarbons the tests have been limited to one city (Los Angeles) and the results have been less satisfac-

tory, at least when using correlation coefficients as the yardstick. For both inert and reactive pollutants the results are usually as good, and in some cases are better, than those obtained from more complex models.

As mentioned previously, the application of the Hanna/Gifford model is restricted to area sources. However, certain types of point sources (i.e., those with short stacks) and line sources can be considered as area sources.[70] The model is also designed for large area, aggregate level application. However, the use of a grid with cells as small as one square mile has been reported.[71] It was also reported that the model has been modified to more realistically reflect urban meteorology by weighing the relative contribution of the sources as a function of wind direction.[72] However, an example of such a modification was not given.

Following is an assessment of the Hanna/Gifford model:

Advantages

1. The Hanna/Gifford Model is simple and inexpensive to use. The manual calculations for a Chicago test application of the nonreactive version are reported to have consumed approximately ½ manhour.[72] (This does not include time needed for data collection.)
2. The results have been verified in various settings and appear to be quite accurate (at least for seasonal and annual averages).

Disadvantages

1. The accuracy of the results may not be adequate when:
   a. Neighboring area sources differ in strength by more than a factor of two.
   b. The wind blows predominately in one direction.
2. Short-term concentration values are not estimated well.
3. The model has not yet been tested for a spatial resolution smaller than approximately one square mile.
4. Only point sources with short smokestacks (plus area sources and line sources treated as area sources—mobile area sources) can be modeled.

---

65. More specifically, A is a function of σ_z, the vertical standard deviation of Gaussian dispersion.

66. Thus, A reflects the average extent to which a plume, released at ground level, has been able to disperse vertically before impacting the "average" receptor.

67. EPA, *Guidelines for Air Quality Maintenance Planning and Analysis,* vol. 12, op. cit.

68. The turbulent diffusion term in the conservation of mass equation is not included since the atmosphere above the community is assumed to be a large box within which the pollutants are uniformly mixed. The photochemical reaction term is based on a simplified set of smog reactions proposed by Friedlander and Seinfeld, "A Dynamic Model of Photochemical Smog," *Environmental Science & Technology,* 3 (1969): 1175–81.

69. For specific results, see Gifford, op. cit.

---

70. For specific guidelines see, Gifford, "Applications of a Simple Urban Pollution Model "(Proceedings reprints, American Meteorological Society Conference on Urban Environment and Second Conference on Biometeorology, Philadelphia, October 31–November 2, 1972).

71. Hanna, op. cit. (1972).

72. Ibid.

5. Without additional testing, the reactive version of the model cannot yet be considered operational.

On the whole, the model combines the simplicity of the rollforward model with the empirical validity of some of the more complex models.

California Highway Model—The California Highway Model is the last of the manual techniques to be reviewed.[73] This source-oriented "model" is really a series of modified Gaussian equations for estimating the dispersion of carbon monoxide from line sources over short distances. The equations are modified to incorporate emission, meteorological, and highway design variables.

The model depicts a highway as a continuously emitting line source which produces its own mechanical mixing from the turbulence created by moving vehicles. The partially mixed CO is then dispersed away from the highway by winds, and the resulting downwind concentration is a result of wind speed and atmospheric stability.[74] The effect of highway elevation is also included.

A series of charts has been prepared relating all of these variables to normalized concentration which, in turn, is expressed as a function of distance from the highway (up to 1000 feet). Once values for the various inputs have been obtained, ambient concentrations can be determined from the charts. (Concentrations are expressed as hourly averages.) Figure 1-4 summarizes the above operations.

Unfortunately, the model has not been validated with field measurements. It thus remains unproven, despite the fact that it is widely used by transportation planning organizations. The authors of the user manual do suggest, however, a series of guidelines to be used in selecting applications. (These are incorporated in the assessment below.)

Advantages

1. The California model is simple and inexpensive to operate. (The manual contains a number of examples for purposes of self-instruction.)

2. It uses meteorological and transportation data which are usually available at local Weather Bureaus and transportation planning agencies,

respectively. (The base meteorological data are manipulated by a specially developed computer program.)

Disadvantages

1. The model is unvalidated.

2. Low wind speeds (less than two miles per hour) produce large overestimates of concentration, based on the mathematical representations alone.

3. The authors of the model recommend that it not be used near interchanges, large aerodynamic obstructions, or in the vicinity of valley winds, since the meteorological records at the Weather Bureau may not be sensitive to microscale effects near these features.

4. The model only treats CO.

ERT/MARTIK Model (Modified AQDM)—The ERT/MARTIK model is a modification of EPA's Air Quality Display Model (AQDM).[75] It is complex, semi-empirical, receptor-oriented, spatially disaggregated, and applicable to SO_2, CO, NO_x, hydrocarbons, and particulates emitted from any type of source. Annual and seasonal ambient concentration averages are estimated.

Due to the model's rather complex mathematical formulation a detailed description is beyond the scope of this review. Instead, a brief description of various model components will be given.

The model is based on the Gaussian plume equation, with the following major elaborations and modifications:

1. The equation is integrated in both the x and y directions for area sources, rather than using the virtual point source approach of the AQDM model.

2. Line sources are approximated by a series of virtual point sources.

3. A box model is used when a major part of the plume has reached the upper boundary of the mixing layer.

4. The changing vertical plume dispersion values with distance traveled are based on an alterna-

73. California State Division of Highways, *Air Quality Manual,* vol. 4: Mathematical Approach to Estimating Highway Impact on Air Quality and vol 5: Appendix (Washington, D.C.: Federal Highway Administration, April, 1972).

74. The meteorologic data is input as joint frequency distributions. That is, the probability of each stability, wind direction and wind speed category occurring simultaneously is calculated, based on historical records. This part has been computerized to facilitate preparation of the input data.

75. Byron H. Willis, *The Hackensack Meadowlands Air Pollution Study, Summary Report* (Lexington, Mass.: Environmental Research and Technology, Inc., July, 1973); James R. Mahoney, Bruce A. Egon, and Edward C. Reigenstein, III, *The Hackensack Meadowlands Air Pollution Study, Task 2 Report: Development and Validation of a Modeling Technique for Predicting Air Quality Levels,* (Lexington, Mass.: Environmental Research and Technology, Inc., July, 1973). For a description of the original AQDM see, National Air Pollution Control Administration, *Air Quality Display Model* (Washington, D.C., 1969).

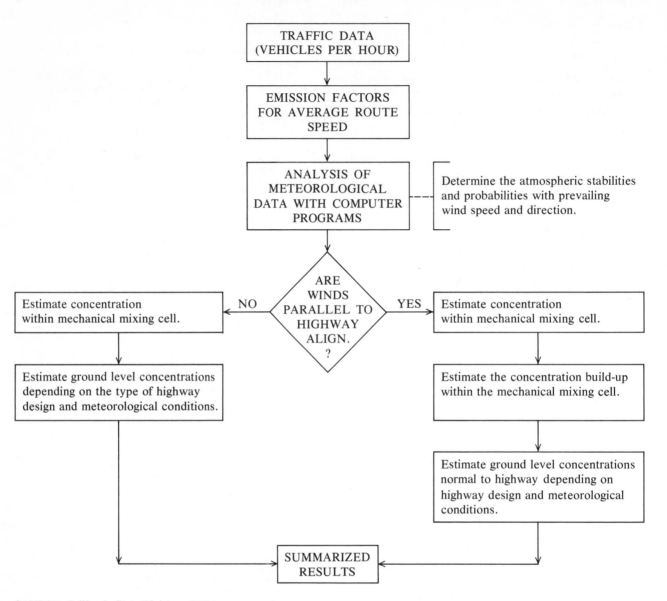

SOURCE: California State Division of Highways, op. cit.

tive empirical relationship rather than on the Turner curves.

5. Slight modifications have been introduced to partially account for the urban heat-island and topographical effects.

6. The AQDM's equations for plume rise are used (to give an effective emission release height) and special considerations are made for very tall stacks.

7. Wind speed, wind direction, and atmospheric stability joint frequency distributions are used to estimate time-averaged concentrations.

8. Ambient concentrations at receptor points are obtained by summing the contributions from all relevant sources (i.e., those that lie upwind based on the wind direction probability distributions). Isopleth maps can thus be generated from concentrations at selected receptors.

The model has been applied in only one geographical area (the Hackensack Meadows in New Jersey). Since it was carefully calibrated for this area, the generalizability of the model remains largely unknown. The results obtained for the Hackensack Meadows application are reported to be "fairly good." How-

Land Development and the Natural Environment

ever, the difference between predicted and observed values expressed as a percentage of the observed values averaged 45 percent and ranged from 0 to 180 percent. Although correlation coefficients between observed and predicted concentrations (seasonal and annual averages) were not reported (too few pairs of values were used), the results are quite discouraging.[76] On this basis alone CO and hydrocarbons were underpredicted while SO_2 and NO_x were overpredicted for all averaging times. Particulates were underpredicted for summer and annual and overpredicted for winter. However, since the number of values compared was extremely low, additional validation studies are needed.

The specific costs of calibrating and operating the model have not been reported. However, judging from the complexity of the model and the amount of data preparation and computation, the costs could be considerable (i.e., probably in the tens of thousands of dollars). Although a more detailed listing of advantages and disadvantages is shown below, the primary considerations are cost and spatial resolution.

Advantages

1. The model incorporates numerous modifications of the Gaussian plume equation, which render it much more theoretically satisfying.
2. The spatial resolution is approximately one square kilometer (approximately .39 square mile).
3. Point, line, and area sources are all modeled.
4. The model is readily coupled to "planning data" (e.g., future land use projections).
5. Isopleth maps can be produced by the program to aid in comprehension of the results.

Disadvantages

1. Operating and calibration costs could be quite high.
2. Reported accuracy from limited testing has not been very good.
3. The model, as currently constructed, is designed only to estimate long-term averages.
4. Attempts to simulate reactive pollutants with any "nonreactive" model are always suspect.

TASSIM—The Transportation and Air Shed Simulation Model (TASSIM) is a combination transportation, vehicle emission, and air diffusion model.[77] It is simple, more empirical than theoretical, spatially disaggregated, and applicable to SO_2, CO, NO_x, hydrocarbons, and particulates emitted from point and area sources. (Line sources are treated as mobile area sources.)

The diffusion submodel is a combination of the Hanna/Gifford area source model and the AQDM for point sources.[78] The previously presented descriptive material relating to these models applies equally well to TASSIM and will not be repeated again. It should be noted, however, that a more complex version of the Hanna/Gifford model is used, rather than the simple approximation employed by Hanna and Gifford.

The transportation and emission submodels are designed for high compatibility with the Department of Transportation's (DOT's) urban transportation planning model[79] and with emission data typically found in urban areas. TASSIM is consequently well suited for estimating air quality changes deriving from future patterns of development.

The spatial resolution of TASSIM is presumably that of the Hanna/Gifford model (i.e., approximately one square mile). For the Boston application the city was divided into 122 zones, most if not all of which were considerably larger than one square mile. Of course, point sources can be located much more precisely.

The model has been applied in Boston and Los Angeles. In Boston the results are very encouraging, but limited. SO_2 and particulates were estimated with correlation coefficients of over 0.9, while NO_x recorded a value of approximately 0.7. Coefficients for CO and hydrocarbons could not be obtained, however, due to insufficient monitored data. The correlation coefficients obtained in the Los Angeles application were 0.9, 0.8 and 0.7 for CO, hydrocarbons, and NO_x, respectively. The reported cost data relate only to the operation of the model ($80 per run, or $30 if only the mobile sources are modeled). Data collection and coding and model calibration could presumably push the costs into the tens of thousands of dollars for one application. Subsequent applications in the

---

76. It is often difficult to relate one measure of accuracy, (e.g., percent error) with another (e.g., correlation coefficients), and neither is a completely satisfactory measure of accuracy alone. (See the Summary section for a further discussion of these issues.) However, percent errors as large as the ones reported here are generally interpreted as being unsatisfactory.

77. Gregory K. Ingram and Gary Fauth, *TASSIM: A Transportation and Air Shed Simulation Model,* vol. 1: *Case Study of the Boston Region* and vol. 2: *Program User's Guide* (Washington, D.C.: Department of Transportation, May, 1974).

78. As noted previously, the AQDM (also known as the Martin-Tikvart model) is applicable to both point and area sources. TASSIM, however, only uses the AQDM formulation for point sources.

79. See the transportation chapter in Schaenman, Keyes, and Christensen, op. cit.

same community would be less expensive, as much of the same data could be used again and recalibration would be unnecessary.

In summary, TASSIM would appear to be a promising model. However, additional test applications are needed in order to substantiate the reported levels of accuracy.

Advantages

1. TASSIM appears to be one of the conceptually less complex computerized dispersion models currently available.
2. The accuracy appears to be excellent for CO, SO_2, and particulates, and good for the other pollutants (based on one test).
3. The model would appear to be easily adaptable to other communities. (The user manual treats the particularization problem explicitly.)
4. Operating costs are reasonable, although calibration and start-up costs may be high.

Disadvantages

1. The spatial resolution is limited to about one square mile.
2. The model is designed only to estimate long-term average concentrations.

Climatological Dispersion Model (CDM)—EPA's National Environmental Research Center has been actively involved in dispersion model development and testing for several years. One of the computerized models which the center is now making available through the National Technical Information Service (NTIS) as part of the UNAMAP program is the Climatological Dispersion Model.[80] Essentially, this is a modification of the previously discussed AQDM. As such, the model is fairly complex, semi-empirical, receptor-oriented, spatially disaggregated, and simultaneously applicable to any two nonreactive pollutants from area and point sources. Long-term (annual or seasonal) averages are estimated for any number of receptors desired.

The characteristics of the model are as follows:

1. Gaussian plume equations are used for both point and area sources.
2. The contributions from area sources are calculated by integrating all area sources surrounding a receptor (up to 2500 sources) and weighting the emissions by wind direction, wind speed, and atmospheric stability joint frequency distributions.
3. The contributions from point sources (up to 200) are calculated separately and again are weighted by the joint frequency distributions of wind speed and direction, and atmospheric stability.
4. A theoretically superior plume rise representation is used, as compared to the AQDM. In addition, winds at the emission height are extrapolated from surface wind.
5. Pollutant removal processes are simulated by simple exponential decay functions.

The joint frequency distributions of the meterological data can be obtained from the National Climatic Center (NCC) in Asheville, North Carolina. The NCC has developed a program called STAR to collect the appropriate data from each Weather Bureau station (every major urban area has at least one), calculate the joint frequencies, and appropriately format the results. The emissions data collected per EPA guidelines are also suitable as input. (All line source emissions must be expressed as mobile area sources.)

The results of attempts to estimate ambient concentrations of SO_2 and particulates in St. Louis and New York have been very good. Correlation coefficients of approximately 0.8 were reported. Again, however, the reader is referred to the Summary and Comparison section for a discussion of other measures of accuracy.

Following is a summary assessment of the CDM. In general, the model offers improved accuracy and better spatial disaggregation than most of the manual techniques, for an increase in cost.

Advantages

1. The spatial resolution is as good as that of the emission inventory.
2. Estimates can be made for an unlimited number of receptors.
3. The model appears to be quite accurate.
4. The computing time is approximately three-fourths that of the AQDM.

Disadvantages

1. The cost of calibration and operation, although unknown, is assumed to be quite high, since a computer the size of the IBM 360 series is required for storage and computation. (The computer program can be purchased from NTIS for $175.)

---

80. Adrian D. Busse and John R. Zimmerman, *User's Guide for Climatological Dispersion Model* (Research Triangle Park, N.C.: EPA, December, 1973). For information on other models in the UNAMAP series, contact EPA, National Environmental Research Center, Meterology Lab, Research Triangle Park, N.C. 27711.

2. Only long-term averages are estimated.

3. The incremental contributions of individual sources cannot be easily ascertained.

APRAC Model—Another member of EPA's UNAMAP series of models is APRAC, a transportation model originally developed by Stanford Research Institute.[81] It is fairly complex, semi-empirical, receptor-oriented, spatially disaggregated, and applicable to CO emitted from mobile area sources. Both long-term (annual) and short-term (hourly) estimates can be made. Concentrations can also be estimated for up to 625 receptors. Characteristics of the model are described as follows:

1. CO transported from surrounding areas (up to approximately 160 miles away) is simulated by a simple box model and generalized emission data.

2. For intra-community estimates, CO emissions from line sources are averaged over segments of sectors which radiate out from each receptor in the direction of the transport wind.

3. The contribution from each sector is calculated by using the Gaussian plume equation.

4. For long-term estimates contributions from the various radial sectors are made proportional to the frequency with which the wind blows in that direction and the average speed with which it blows.

5. A street canyon submodel simulates ground-level concentrations in streets bordered by high-rise buildings from data on crosswind speeds at the roof level, the height of the buildings, vehicle usage in the canyon street, and CO transported from other areas of the city.

The model is compatible with meterological and transportation data normally available in urban areas. The raw transportation data for each street are allocated to the appropriate radial sector, and emission levels are generated internally using empirically derived emission factors. Data on wind speed, wind direction, atmospheric stability, and mixing depth are acquired from the local Weather Bureau. For future projections the model readily accepts forecasts made by means of the Federal Highway Administration's suggested procedures.[82]

The model output can be expressed as either long-term or short-term concentrations for a few selected locations, usually those representing the worst conditions. Alternatively, concentrations for one time interval can be obtained at up to 625 locations and isopleths derived therefrom.

Based on correlation coefficients alone, the results of test applications in St. Louis and San Jose are somewhat disappointing. Correlation coefficients between 0.4 and 0.7 have been reported. Even more disturbing, an application by Argonne National Laboratory in Chicago yielded correlations of approximately 0.25.[83] However, most other dispersion models (especially those which only estimate long-term averages) do not attempt to estimate *ground-level* concentrations. Although these locations are more meaningful in terms of human exposure, the concentrations are more variable and more difficult to estimate.

In general, the user of APRAC will be purchasing spatial disaggregation and flexibility of application for a moderate price.

Advantages

1. The model can be extremely disaggregated spatially. Estimates for up to 625 points can be made, even for small communities.

2. With the canyon submodel, APRAC is a much more realistic representation of actual micro-atmospheric dispersion than other CO models.

3. The model can be obtained from EPA (UN-AMAP) for $175,[84] and the operating cost is quite modest ($50 per run). However, the start-up and calibration costs run into the tens of thousands of dollars.[85]

4. Both short- and long-term estimates can be made.

5. The model produces isopleth maps derived from the 625 receptors to aid in comprehension of the results.

81. Walter F. Dabberdt, F. L. Ludwig, and Warren B. Johnson, Jr., "Validation and Applications of an Urban Diffusion Model for Vehicular Pollutants," *Atmospheric Environment*, 7 (1973): 603–18; R. L. Moncuso and F. L. Ludwig, *User's Manual for the APRAC-IA Urban Diffusion Model Computer Program* (Menlo Park, Calif.: Stanford Research Institute, September, 1972); and W. B. Johnson, F. L. Ludwig, W. F. Dabberdt, and R. J. Allen, "An Urban Diffusion Simulation Model for Carbon Monoxide," *Air Pollution Control Association Journal*, 23 (June 6, 1973): 490–98.

82. See transportation chapter in Schaenman, Keyes, and Christensen, op. cit.

83. See L. J. Habegger et al., *Dispersion Simulation Techniques for Assessing the Air Pollution Impacts of Ground Transportation Systems* (Chicago: Illinois Institute for Environmental Quality, May, 1974). The authors suggest that the low correlations could also be influenced by inaccuracies in the measured ambient concentrations and windspeeds.

84. Contact EPA's National Environmental Research Center, Meteorology Lab, Research Triangle Park, N.C. 27711.

85. Based on costs experienced by the Department of Environmental Quality, Portland, Oreg.

Disadvantages

1. Only CO is simulated.
2. The accuracy is still questionable.

Other Models—Space does not permit a complete review of all relevant dispersion models. The reader will note that models based on a complete solution of the conservation of mass equation have yet to be discussed. The reasons are two-fold: (1) these models are inherently more complex and considerably more expensive to operate, and (2) the photochemical kinetics of open system reactions are still poorly understood, so that model accuracies tend to be low.

Two "reactive" models, DIFKIN[86] and the SAI model,[87] have been developed and validated with data from the Los Angeles area. Both models track projections of air parcels over extended distances. Within these presumed homogeneously mixed air parcels the complex chains of photochemical interaction are simulated. The models differ in the representation of these interactions. Both have shown promising results, although they continue to suffer from limiting assumptions regarding initial conditions and arrangements of sources. They are expensive to use[88] and require extensive testing before routine utilization.

Some organizations are developing in-house models for application in specific communities. The Bay Area Air Pollution Control District and the New York State Department of Transportation are two examples.[89] The models tend to be modifications of basic Gaussian plume and box model formulations.

Another promising but still experimental approach is that of "repro-modeling"—the attempt to use simple equations to relate the input and output data of a complex model. One effort to apply repro-modeling to the SAI model has proven quite successful, although a series of assumptions limits the generalizability of the results.[90] The concept is certainly attractive—to vastly reduce the complexity and cost of more complex models without a loss in accuracy. However, a purely empirical approach such as this suffers from the old association/causalty enigma. We may be able to predict the value of one variable simply by knowing the value of another today. But with no understanding of causality, changing values of other related variables may make future predictions impossible.

c. Summary and Comparison of Models

In order to make a cost-effective decision when choosing a model, reliable information on total cost and predictive accuracy must be at hand. The analysis in this section has shown that data on cost and accuracy are not always precise or comparable. A summary of the various models appears in Table 1-4, to aid in comparative assessment.

Correlation coefficients have been given earlier which show how well the model reproduces observed values. Although this is a widely accepted and commonly used indicator, it is but one statistic which measures the tendency of one value to agree with another. Largest positive or negative errors, error ranges, relative errors, mean absolute errors, 95 percent confidence intervals, and root mean square errors are others. Correlations alone can be misleading, since they are often reported for partially calibrated models (models to which correction factors have been applied to compensate for systematic errors), thereby inflating the correlation coefficients. In addition, the user may be interested in the error at either extremely high or extremely low values. (For air pollution measures concern is usually with high values.) A recent EPA publication reports the results of a comparative analysis of accuracy for three models and variations thereof.[91] The models are as follows:[92]

1. AQDM.
2. CDM.
3. CDM (Single Stability). (The CDM values are further averaged by using a single average wind

86. A. Q. Eschenroeder and J. R. Martines, *Concepts and Applications of Photochemical Smog Models* (Santa Barbara, Calif.: General Research Corp., June, 1971).

87. Steven Reynolds, Philip Roth, and John Seinfeld, "Mathematical Modeling of Photochemical Air Pollution—I, Formulation of the Model," *Atmospheric Environment*, 7 (1973): 1033–61; and Steven Reynolds et al., "Mathematical Modeling of Photochemical Air Pollution–III, Evaluation of the Model," *Atmospheric Environment*, 8 (1974): 563–96.

88. W. Brian Crews, Department of Environmental Quality, Portland, Oreg., reports that the start-up and calibration costs of DIFKIN are over $50,000.

89. For further information, contact San Francisco Bay Area Air Pollution Control District, 939 Ellis Street, San Francisco, Calif. 94109, and New York State Department of Transportation, Planning and Research Bureau, State Campus, Albany, N.Y. 12226.

90. Horowitz, Meisel, and Collins, op. cit.

91. D. Bruce Turner, John R. Zimmerman, and Adrian D. Busse, "An Evaluation of Some Climatological Dispersion Models (Paper presented at the Third Meeting of the NATO/Committee on the Challenges of Modern Society, Panel on Modeling, 1972) and included in the CDM users' manual.

92. Model 3 is simply the result of using averaged input data as compared to Model 2. Models 5 and 6 involve structural modifications to the Hanna/Gifford model and, as such, have not been discussed previously. They are included here only to show the effect of the most constraining assumption of the Hanna/Gifford model—that ambient concentrations for any subarea are solely due to emissions in that subarea. The reader should consult the Hanna and Gifford reference for further information on the more complex formulation of their model.

Table 1-4. COMPARISON OF ATMOSPHERIC DISPERSION MODELS

NAME	Pollutants Modeled						Sources Modeled					Inputs	Outputs	Computing Requirements	Cost	Accuracy
	CO	SO$_x$	NO$_x$	HC	O$_x$	Part.	Point	Stationary area	Mobile area	Line	Averaged[a]					
Rollforward Model	X	X	X[b]	X[b]	X[b]	X					X	Current average ambient concentrations, total emissions (for entire community or subareas) and future emissions. For more complex versions, wind speed, wind direction, and average stack heights	(1) Average ambient concentration for one or a few representative points in the community (2) Any averaging time period	Manual	Low	Unvalidated
Miller/ Holzworth Model	X	X	X			X					X	Average community-wide emission rate, average wind speed throughout the mixing layer, mixing depth, community size (along wind length of the urbanized area)	(1) Average ambient concentration for the community as a whole (2) Hourly or annual averages	Manual (essentially referencing of tables)	Low	Good (r > 0.8 for SO$_2$ and NO$_x$ for the test application)
Hanna/ Gifford Model	X	X	X[c]	X[c]		X	X	X				Emission rates for area and certain point sources and wind speed (and direction for short-term averages)	(1) Average ambient concentrations for areas as small as 1 square mile (if the areas are numerous enough, isopleths can be drawn for the community) (2) Any averaging time period	Manual	Low (approximately 1/2 hour of calculations for 150 subareas in Chicago plus the cost of emissions data collection)	Good for *nonreactive version* (r ≅ 0.7), less satisfactory for reactive version based on one application (r = 0.05–0.97)
California Highway Model	X									X		Vehicle speeds, volumes, and mixes; average wind speed, wind direction, and atmospheric stability (joint frequencies), highway elevation	(1) Average ambient concentrations as a function of distance from the highway (up to 1000 feet away) (2) Annual averages	Manual (helpful to computerize some meteorological data)	Low	Unvalidated
ERT/MARTIK Model	X	X	X	X		X	X		X	X		Average wind speed, wind direction, atmospheric stability (joint frequencies); emission rates for all sources, background emissions	(1) Average ambient concentrations for areas as small as 1/2 square mile; isopleths can be drawn (2) Seasonal or annual averages	Digital computer	Presumably high (probably tens of thousands of dollars)	Initial validation results were mediocre
TASSIM	X	X	X	X		X	X	X	X			See ERT/MARTIK and Hanna/Gifford for point sources and Hanna/Gifford for area sources. Distribution of trips and speeds by zone for line sources.	(1) Average ambient concentrations for areas as small as 1/2 square mile; isopleths can be drawn (2) Averages by hour, day, year	Digital computer with 156,000 bytes of storage	Presumably High	Good (r = 0.7–0.9) for the various pollutants
CDM		X				X	X	X	X			Emission rates for point and area sources; joint wind speed, wind direction and atmospheric stability frequencies; average mixing depth	(1) Average ambient concentrations at an unlimited number of locations (2) Annual averages	Digital computer	Presumably High	Good (r ≅ 0.8)
APRAC	X					X				X		Vehicle speed and volume per link, average hourly cloud cover, temperature, atmospheric stability and mixing depth	(1) Average ambient concentrations at up to 625 locations from which isopleths can be drawn (2) Hourly or annual averages	Digital computer, 45,000 words of storage (program modification needed for computers except CDC 6400 and IBM 360/50)	Presumably High	Mediocre (r ≅ 0.25–0.7)

a. Emissions from all types of sources are averaged together. b. The application of the model to these pollutants has been very limited. c. These pollutants are modeled by the more complex "reactive" version.

speed category and selected atmospheric stability category.)

4. Gifford '72. (This is the Hanna/Gifford model discussed previously.)

5. Modified Hanna. (This is the Hanna/Gifford model modified to include contributions to the average ambient concentrations within a given area by emissions from surrounding areas as well as by emissions in the area itself.)

6. Modified Hanna including source height. (This is the same as the preceding, with one additional modification: the average emission height for all area sources is used rather than a value of zero.)

The results of an evaluation of these models using SO_2 and particulate data from New York City are shown in Tables 1-5 and 1-6, respectively. The conclusion is that no one model is clearly superior on all measures. Furthermore, the simpler models performed better than might be expected theoretically.

The results of this test bear directly on the question of selecting among the models presented in this report. Certainly for long-term planning purposes or for evaluating the cumulative effects of development the simpler models (rollforward, Hanna/Gifford, and Miller-Holzworth) would appear to be more cost-effective. Choosing among these would have to be based on the type of pollutant being considered, the availability of required input data, and the level of spatial disaggregation (degree of resolution) needed. For example, *only the California Highway Model and the canyon submodel of APRAC* would appear to be capable of reproducing microscale effects in the *immediate vicinity of a development.* APRAC appears best suited for evaluations of *individual residential and commercial projects,* especially if the project will change traffic levels throughout the entire highway network or a large section of it, or if changes in traffic will occur within street canyons. However, APRAC is not as comprehensive nor as accurate as some of the others. The California Highway Model is appropriate for those situations where *individual developments* will cause increases in traffic on only one or a few highways. ERT/MARTIK, TASSIM, and CDM (the latter for point and stationary areas sources only) would appear to be appropriate for either *very large projects* or for *area-wide development* in general. ERT/MARTIK and TASSIM have the further advantage of being designed specifically for planning applications.

The potential user of any model requiring computer support should remember that the start-up and "tuning" activities can be expensive, time-consuming, and frustrating. Even for APRAC and CDM, two models designed for "off the shelf" application, users have reported the need to recode input data (and in the case of CDM, even to undertake some reprogramming) before operation.[93] This is not intended to dampen enthusiasm for computerized models. Certainly they are more widely applicable and, in most cases, more accurate than the simple ones. But their calibration and use can be a costly process.

A brief statement regarding general limitations and deficiencies is also in order. One need is for the development of regional models which would simulate the movement of pollutants over distances of several hundred miles and thus help to explain the high background levels found in many areas. Synoptic scale meteorology is poorly modeled as well. On the other extreme is the lack of a model which reflects urban meteorology and special microclimatic effects. But probably the greatest and certainly the most pervasive deficiency is the lack of field data to be used for model validation. Without better designed monitoring networks and a dramatic increase in the number of stations, model validation will lag far behind the development of model theory.

5. Measuring/Estimating Odor and Smoke Problems

Since the assessment of nuisance problems requires a slightly different approach, the subject will be given special, albeit brief, attention.

a. Odor Problems

Odors can be localized or widespread, of short-term duration or long-lived, constant or intermittent. In addition, the extent to which they present a problem depends on intensity, distinguishing quality, and acceptability.[94] As a result, the objective detection (to say nothing of the prediction) of odor problems is a difficult task.

As a guide, evaluators might obtain from developers a component breakdown of future emissions or, failing that, a description of the industrial process and raw materials to be used. (Paper mills, sewage plants, meatpacking plants, and chemical firms are of special concern.) A rough estimation of potential problems

93. Richard Hawthorne, Department of Environmental Quality, Portland, Oreg., and Steven Albersheim, NUS Corporation, Rockville, Md.—respondents to the Urban Institute questionnaire.

94. The Third Karolinska Institute Symposium on Environmental Health, "Measuring and Evaluating Odorous Air Pollutants at the Source and in the Ambient Air" (Report of an International Symposium in Stockholm, June 1–5, 1970). (Available from the Department of Environmental Hygiene, Karolinska Institute, s. -10401, Stockholm, Sweden.)

Table 1-5. RESULTS OF MODEL EVALUATION USING SO₂ DATA

	AVERAGE* ESTIMATED CONCEN-TRATION**	NUMBER OF COMPARI-SONS	ROOT MEAN SQUARE ERROR**	MEAN ABSOLUTE ERROR**	LARGEST NEGATIVE ERROR**	LARGEST POSITIVE ERROR**	ERROR RANGE**	LINEAR CORRELATION WITH MEASURED VALUES (r)	ERROR AT POINT OF MAXIMUM MEASURED VALUE**	MAXIMUM*** ESTIMATED CONCENTRATION **
1. Air Quality Display Model (AQDM)	211	75	121	92	−87	310	397	0.89	112	566
2. Climatological Dispersion Model (CDM)	138	75	52	37	−118	166	284	0.84	−101	368
3. CDM (Single Stability)	206	75	124	89	−112	332	444	0.84	13	577
3B. CDM (C Stability)	94	75	56	46	−128	96	224	0.82	−119	307
3C. CDM (C/D Stability)	139	75	64	45	−115	188	303	0.84	−56	423
4. Gifford '72	54	75	82	72	−175	29	204	0.81	−175	180
4B. With CDM Point Estimates	79	75	59	50	−137	49	186	0.85	−137	219
5. Modified Hanna	279	75	330	178	−145	1232	1377	0.77	1153	1503
5B. With CDM Point Estimates	305	75	348	193	−120	1270	1390	0.78	1191	1541
6. Modified Hanna Including Source Height	102	75	58	45	−151	190	341	0.84	49	399
6B. With CDM Point Estimates	127	75	56	38	−126	225	351	0.86	87	437

SOURCE: Turner et al. (1972).

* The average and standard deviation for the measured values are 135 and 72 micrograms/cubic meter, respectively.

** In micrograms/cubic meter.

*** The maximum measured concentration was 350 micrograms/cubic meter.

Table 1-6. RESULTS OF MODEL EVALUATION USING PARTICULATE DATA

	AVERAGE* ESTIMATED CONCEN-TRATION**	NUMBER OF COMPARI-SONS	ROOT MEAN SQUARE ERROR**	MEAN ABSOLUTE ERROR**	LARGEST NEGATIVE ERROR**	LARGEST POSITIVE ERROR**	ERROR RANGE**	LINEAR CORRELATION WITH MEASURED VALUES (r)	ERROR AT POINT OF MAXIMUM MEASURED VALUE**	MAXIMUM*** ESTIMATED CONCENTRATION **
1. Air Quality Display Model (AQDM)	102	113	36	28	−51	115	166	0.62	5	199
2. Climatological Dispersion Model (CDM)	74	113	22	16	−63	68	131	0.61	−48	135
3. CDM (Single Stability)	88	113	28	21	−60	98	158	0.64	−6	165
3B. CDM (C Stability)	58	113	31	26	−78	59	137	0.57	−71	126
3C. CDM (C/D Stability)	69	113	25	19	−73	75	148	0.61	−43	142
4. Gifford '72	40	113	53	47	−117	46	163	0.63	−56	151
4B. With CDM Point Estimates	51	113	47	40	−111	59	170	0.63	−44	164
5. Modified Hanna	80	113	41	30	−77	177	254	0.64	61	281
5B. With CDM Point Estimates	92	113	45	32	−71	190	261	0.64	73	294
6. Modified Hanna Including Source Height	56	113	31	26	−80	25	105	0.66	−58	129
6B. With CDM Point Estimates	67	113	25	19	−71	37	108	0.62	−53	141

SOURCE: Turner et al. (1972).

* The average and standard deviation for the measured values are 82 and 23 micrograms/cubic meter, respectively.

** In micrograms/cubic meter.

*** The maximum measured concentration was 169 micrograms/cubic meter.

can then be made based on the known odorant properties of the material to be emitted. A fairly recent article on threshold concentrations of fifty-three odorant chemicals would be a starting point, although the thresholds reported were developed under controlled laboratory conditions.[95] In order to determine the dispersion of the odorant material, dispersion models can be used as demonstrated by Hogstrom[96] and Sullivan.[97]

For measuring the magnitude of existing odor problems a variety of techniques exists.[98] The techniques range from subjective evaluations by panels of experts[99] to objective assessment made by analytical devices, such as the scentometer.[100] The subjective approach is attractive because it integrates the various odor characteristics (intensity, distinguishing quality, and acceptability). The hardware approach, on the other hand, is more objective and quantitative.[101]

b. Smoke Problems

Smoke problems are typically associated with the opacity and size of smoke plumes. Reference has already been made to the standard opacity measurement device—the Ringelmann chart—which can be used to estimate problems caused by existing developments. Future estimations are becoming less of a concern since new EPA source regulations are designed to eliminate smoke problems. All new point sources will be required to install appropriate control equipment. Thus, the assessment of smoke generation generally need not be a part of the evaluation of proposed developments, although new developments

may displace or provide an alternative to the continued use of existing nuisance sources.

6. Measuring/Estimating Exposure of People to Pollution

Once the spatial distribution of pollutants in the ambient air has been estimated, the next step is attempting to relate these concentrations to the population (or other receptors) at risk. There are at least three dimensions to the problem:

1. Specifying the *intensity* of exposure.
2. Specifying the *duration* (or frequency) of exposure.
3. Specifying the *number of people* exposed.

Since these dimensions apply to each of the several potential pollutants, and since various combinations of intensity, duration, and numbers of people exposed may occur for each pollutant in different areas, the potential amount of data generated by an air quality analysis is indeed large.

a. Intensity and Duration

One way to reduce this volume of information is through the use of intensity-duration indices (or single number scores). As was discussed earlier, index scores are typically derived from a comparison of estimated ambient concentrations to appropriate federal or other standards.

In this case, however, it is suggested that indices be used to combine concentrations of one pollutant for various averaging time periods rather than combining concentrations of several pollutants for a single time period. This mitigates much of the criticism of indices discussed in a previous section.[102] In order to calculate an exposure index, ambient concentrations for various averaging times are needed, since federal standards are specified for averaging times of one, three, eight, and twenty-four hours, and twelve months. However, most of the simple dispersion models only provide estimates of long-term average concentrations. To estimate average concentrations for any short-time averaging period (i.e., one, eight, or twenty-four hours), monitored data for several years are needed. Larsen has shown that pollutant concentrations vary in a log normal fashion with time (i.e., frequency of occurrence plotted against the logarithm of concentration produces a normal or bell-shaped curve), which means that average concentra-

95. G. Leonardos, D. A. Keudoll, and N. J. Barnard, "Odor Threshold Determinations of 53 Odorant Chemicals," *Air Pollution Control Association Journal* 19 (1969): 91.

96. U. Hogstrom, *Atmospheric Environment* 6 (1972): 102.

97. F. Sullivan and G. Leonardos, "Determination of Odor Sources for Control" (Presented at Conference on Odors: Evaluation, Utilization, and Control, New York Academy of Sciences, October, 1973).

98. G. Leonardos, "A Critical Review of Regulations for the Control of Odors," *Journal of the Air Pollution Control Association* 24 (1974): 456–68.

99. J. DeChioia and L. Koppelman, *Planning Design Criteria* (Van Nostrand Reinhold Co., 1969): and A. Dravnieks, "Measuring Industrial Odors," *Chemical Engineering* 8 (October 21, 1974): 91–95.

100. J. L. Milles, et al., "Quantiative Odor Measurement," *Journal of the Air Pollution Control Association* 13 (1963): 467.

101. In those cases where a new development will remove a source of current odor problems, the techniques mentioned above or a survey can be used to establish the severity or perceived severity of the current problem. A case in point is the replacement of a rendering plant by an office building in the Georgetown area of Washington, D.C., which produced greatly improved conditions for thousands of residents, workers, commuters, and visitors.

102. Indices are discussed in Section A on "Measures, Standards, Indices" in Chapter II, Part 1.

tions for any averaging time period can be calculated.[103] This involves calculating (a) certain standard statistics for the observed frequency distribution, and (b) using the dispersion model estimates of future concentrations and Larsen's relationships, the same statistics for the time-averaging period in question.[104] In addition to annual average values, estimates of the maximum yearly concentrations for any averaging time can be obtained from the same frequency distribution.

Some of the more complex dispersion models, such as APRAC, can be used to obtain annual averages and maximum values for short averaging times directly. As yet, no one has made a cost/accuracy comparison of simple models and Larsen's relationships on the one hand, and a complex model on the other. Where adequate historical air pollution data are available, and where estimates at only a few geographical points are desired, the first approach would certainly seem to be less expensive.

Another type of exposure index can be calculated once the frequency distribution of concentration with time has been estimated. Since total exposure is a function of both pollution intensity and duration, multiplying one by the other can give a one-number value for exposure. That is, each concentration level is multiplied by the amount of time that level is reached, and the resulting values are summed for all concentrations. (See Figure 1-5.) If a comparison with standards is desired, the index can be computed for those concentration values exceeding the standards. A format for presenting the results is also illustrated in the notes to Figure 1-5.

Both types of indices have their drawbacks. The first type (i.e., direct comparison with standards) relies almost exclusively on somewhat questionable standards as the sole measure of damage, while the second assumes a linear relationship between exposure and damages (i.e., damage from five days at ten parts per million is assumed equivalent to ten days at five parts per million. Nevertheless, these expres-

sions are a way of "summing up" the change in exposure level.

b. Number of People Exposed

Once the exposure level has been determined there remains the task of identifying the population affected. At least two of the dispersion models previously described (ERT/MARTIK and APRAC) and possibly Hanna/Gifford and TASSIM (depending on the size of the grid cells used) allow the construction of isopleth maps from the output data. At a minimum, pollution contours can be overlaid on maps of residential population distributions derived from census data. A more meaningful analysis would compare pollutant distribution and population distribution by time of day or day of the week (e.g., the number of commuters exposed to rush hour traffic or the number of workers exposed to downtown, daytime pollution levels). Although a search failed to uncover any studies of this nature, the voluminous amounts of transportation data collected by most cities should shed some light on the daily activity patterns of at least certain groups of individuals.

In judging the number of people at risk it could be argued that the extent to which people are exposed to interior ambient air should also be considered. Many persons spend a considerable portion of the day inside buildings, a large percentage of which are air-conditioned and ventilated. However, recent studies indicate that interior and exterior concentration levels tend to fluctuate together, with the indoor peak being slightly lower, although much depends on construction, air-conditioning, and ventilation characteristics.[105] For automobile interior spaces the situation may be even worse, with pollutant levels exceeding those outside.[106] Thus, estimates of exterior concentrations can be used as representative (and in some cases conservative) indicators of interior concentrations as well.

In addition to a comparison of pollutant concentrations with population density, it may be informative to identify impacts on especially susceptible population groups. Areas with large elderly or adolescent populations, or where athletic facilities are located, may be more severely affected by the same pollution levels than other areas. Some communities may also wish to single out already disadvantaged groups and

103. Ralph I. Larsen, "A New Mathematical Model of Air Pollutant Concentration Averaging Time and Frequency," *Journal of the Air Pollution Control Association* 19 (January 1969): 24–30: and Ralph I. Larsen, *A Mathematical Model for Relating Air Quality Measurements to Air Quality Standards* (Research Triangle Park, N.C.: EPA, Office of Air Programs, November, 1971) (Report No. AP-89).

104. More specifically, the geometric mean and standard geometric deviation for one averaging time are calculated from the monitored data. The future arithmetic mean for the long-term averaging time is obtained from a dispersion model or simpler analytical technique and used to calculate the geometric mean for this averaging time. The long-term standard deviation is obtained from that for the monitored data. These parameters are then used to estimate average future concentrations for all other averaging times.

105. T. M. Briggs, et al., *Air Pollution Considerations in Residential Planning, Volume II: Backup Report* (Cincinnati: PEDCO—Environmental Specialists, Inc., July, 1974).

106. New York Department of Air Resources, *Air Pollution Variations and Roadway Configurations* (New York: September, 1971).

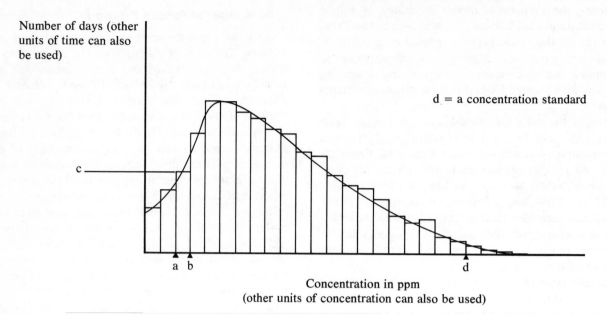

FIGURE 1-5
THE USE OF FREQUENCY DISTRIBUTIONS TO
ESTIMATE EXPOSURE INTENSITY AND DURATION

NOTES:

The curve is constructed from a histogram of concentration intervals within which short-term (usually one or eight hours) averages are observed. In the example, hourly average concentrations between the values "a" and "b" are observed to occur for a *total* of c days out of the year. (The distribution is skewed to the right because the *logarithm* of concentration is related to frequency of occurrence in a normal fashion.)

Exposure index calculations:

(a) Total exposure = total area under the curve (this is obtained by mathematical integration or approximated by calculating the area of the histogram).

(b) Exposure above a standard = area under the curve to the right of standard "d."

The units of the exposure index would be ppm-days.

The results could be displayed as follows:

	CLIENTELE GROUP*		
	A	B	C
Total population	15,000	75,000	65,000
Change in exposure level	+50 ppm-days	+150 ppm-days	+100 ppm-days
Change in exposure level above the 1-hour standard	+10 ppm-days	+8 ppm-days	+5 ppm-days

* For example, adolescent, elderly, and others.

the areas where they live or work as worthy of special consideration from an equity point of view.

7. Measuring/Estimating Damage in Monetary Units

Assuming that future concentrations of individual pollutants have been ascertained and the populations at risk identified, it may be useful to translate this data into dollar estimates of damage. A rich literature has been developed on the subject over the last few years.[107] Most studies which attempt to estimate the

107. See, for example, National Academy of Sciences, op. cit.; Thomas Waddell, *The Economic Damage of Air Pollution* (Washington, D.C.: EPA, May, 1974); Allen Kneese and Blair Bower, eds. *Environmental Quality Analysis* (Baltimore: John Hopkins Press, 1972).

costs of pollution (or the benefits of abatement) fall into one of three categories—those based on health data, those concerned with property values, and those based on vegetation and materials damages. The first type attempts to impute monetary values to loss of life and limb or ill health based on foregone earnings or data taken from court decisions. The property value studies attempt to isolate and measure the effect of air pollution by determining changes in value of property in otherwise "comparable" neighborhoods in several communities, each with different air quality. Studies in the third group attempt to attribute a percentage of crop loss and the consumption of pollutant-damageable goods and related services to the presence of airborne pollutants. All of these studies suffer both theoretically and empirically. It is safe to say that all estimates are highly approximate. No procedures were found that can be recommended for the salient concern here, evaluating community-specific development and individual projects.[108] However, current research efforts may soon make estimates feasible for small areas.

---

108. Several studies have attempted to allocate national damage estimates to smaller geographical areas. The results are highly speculative, however. See, for example, Leonard P. Gianessi, Henry M. Peskin, and Edward Wolff, "The Distributional Implications of National Air Pollution Damage Estimates" (Paper prepared for the Conference on Research in Income and Wealth, University of Michigan, May 15–17, 1974).

III. CONCLUSIONS AND RECOMMENDATIONS

A. PLANNING VERSUS PROJECT REVIEW

At various points in the discussion we have attempted to relate the evaluation of individual proposed projects to air quality planning for groups of projects or for future development in general. We stressed the need to place each project in the context of community-wide or area-wide growth, especially for large projects whose construction would extend over long periods. Since we view the relationship of large area planning to individual project review as one of the more important issues in the implementation of an impact evaluation program at the local level, we will now elaborate on these and related points.

The extent to which a planning, as opposed to a project review, approach should be utilized is primarily dependent upon two factors: (a) the scale of impact, and (b) the sensitivity of pollutant generation to design features of the development. Developments which will produce negative community-wide effects (either singly or cumulatively), such as high emission rates or the generation of pollutants with slow decay rates, are probably best controlled through planning. As noted before, however, both planning and project review may be desirable; proposed projects which are consonant with area plans (as revealed by a quick impact evaluation) may still need more detailed individual evaluations as a check on the assumptions used to make the plan.

On the other hand, developments which produce only localized effects or which generate pollutants that can be reduced by such design features as buffer areas are probably best regulated on an individual

basis at the point of project proposal. Table 1-7 is a listing of factors to be considered for each of the major pollutants, differentiated by the level of analysis. As shown, both planning and project review are appropriate for most pollutants and thus most types of developments.

At the planning level, one approach is to work backward from desired ambient concentrations to allowable emissions for various areas within the community. The allowable emissions (perhaps phrased in terms of emission densities) can then be considered targets to strive for in achieving acceptable air quality.[1] Then, as these areas develop at some point in the future, the cumulative effects of individual developments can be measured against the target by simply keeping a running sum of emissions from all developments to date. Presumably, once the target was reached, development would stop, emission levels for some developments would have to decrease, or the community would accept growth knowing that air quality would be less than desired. Emission densities (e.g., parts per million per acre) could be further translated into traffic volumes or size and types of

---

1. For a more detailed discussion of emission density zoning, see, A. S. Kennedy, et al., *Air Pollution–Land Use Planning Project,* vol. III (Argonne, Ill.: Argonne National Laboratory, May, 1973) (NTIS No. PB-239138); Richard K. Brail and George Hagevik, "Air Quality Management as a Constraint on the Comprehensive Planning Process: Emission Allocation and Emission Density Zoning Strategies" (Paper presented at 1974 AIP Conference in Denver); and J. J. Roberts, E. J. Croke, and S. Booras, "A Critical Review of the Effect of Air Pollution Control Regulation and Land Use Planning," *Journal of the Air Pollution Control Association* 25 (May, 1975): 500–20.

Table 1-7. PLANNING AND PROJECT REVIEW CONSIDERATIONS FOR EACH OF THE MAJOR AIR POLLUTANTS

POLLUTANT	PLANNING CONSIDERATIONS	PROJECT REVIEW CONSIDERATIONS
Particulates	Industrial sources (singly and collectively) plus generalized wind erosion exacerbated by construction activities can produce community-wide problems.	Smoke from individual point sources can produce localized problems. Specific construction practices may reduce wind erosion. Trees and vegetation tend to increase rates of deposition.
SO_x	Large point sources and numerous area sources can create large-scale problems.	No special problems or ameliorating factors at this level.
CO	Due to the dispersed nature of the source (i.e., the road network), CO is a community-wide problem.	CO decays rapidly with distance from the source and thus can produce local concentrations much higher than the community average. Street canyons present special problems. Project design features may affect auto vs. transit use.
NO_x, hydrocarbons, and photo-oxidants	Since all three participate in long-term photochemical reactions and since the sources are highly dispersed, the effects are experienced community-wide.	No specialized, localized problems. Project design features may affect auto vs. transit use.
Odiferous materials	Some highly pungent compounds may be detectable over considerable distances.	Most odoriferous materials are primarily localized in effect due to rapid rates of dilution.

new developments, although the latter assumes fairly invariant relationships between development characteristics and emissions, an assumption which is rarely valid.

Different air quality targets for different parts of the community may be desirable, based on population distributions or socioeconomic and demographic characteristics of population subgroups (e.g., stricter controls in areas characterized by an elderly population).

If the targets are phrased in terms of emission levels, then impact analyses of individual proposed developments need only to estimate development-produced or -related emissions. This insures the flexibility needed to accommodate changes in federal, state, and local requirements and in pollution control technology, as well as to capture the idiosyncracies of individual developments.

To determine the appropriate target emission levels from maximum desired ambient pollutant concentrations, dispersion models can be operated essentially in reverse. For this purpose the most appropriate are the Hanna/Gifford model, the Miller/Holzworth model, the ERT/MARTIK model, TASSIM, and CDM.

Another planning level approach is to compare the air quality implications of alternative land use plans developed to achieve other objectives. Emission levels determined by using gross emission factors (by land use category) are combined with long-term average meteorological conditions and with a simple dispersion model to produce the expected impact on air quality. The results can be quite good if relative

rather than absolute values are desired. Again, if the relationship between the characteristics of future developments and emission levels is tenuous, estimates of ambient concentrations are questionable.

In addition to assessing emissions from future developments for comparison with planning targets, a project level analysis could be used to assess localized effects and those sensitive to particular project design features, or, as noted before, to assess large individual developments as a check on the adequacy of the plan. Local accumulation of CO generated by development-associated traffic, for example, can best be ascertained by scrutinizing the project site plan and characteristics of the immediate environment, such as type, amount, and location of vegetation; terrain; and type and location of other manmade structures. The most appropriate dispersion models for these small area analyses are those which are sensitive to microscale effects. Of those reviewed, only the California Highway Model, the APRAC canyon submodel, and perhaps the individual source-oriented models which are part of the EPA's UNAMAP system qualify.[2]

B. SPECIFIC RECOMMENDATIONS AND CONCLUSIONS

Following is a list of recommendations and conclusions based on our investigation of issues and

---

2. EPA has two relevant point source models (PTMAX and PTDIS) which have not been reviewed here due to a lack of documentation. Readers should contact the Meteorology Lab, EPA Environmental Research Center, Research Triangle Park, N.C., in order to obtain descriptive materials as they become available.

methods of analysis relevant to the assessment of air quality impacts from proposed land developments:

1. Local governments should consider specifying emission "targets" in their land use or zoning plans, based on a dispersion analysis of those pollutants which are community-wide in scale. At a minimum, evaluations of individual developments would estimate the future on-site and off-site emissions associated with each development, add them to the development-generated emissions to date, and compare them with the target.

2. Where developments would cause emission targets to be exceeded or where the pollutants to be emitted are localized in scale (or simply as a check on the assumptions used to determine the plan), detailed evaluations of individual developments should be undertaken.

3. The detailed evaluations should focus on both health and aesthetic/nuisance problems, emphasizing end impacts on man where possible, and perhaps using the recommended measures. In choosing between preferred and fallback measures, the potential magnitude of impact and the time and funding available for evaluation will probably be the most important considerations.

4. Relatively simple yet reasonably accurate techniques appear to be available for making estimates of long-term (e.g., annual) average pollutant concentrations from community-wide development. These can also be used to establish emission targets in land use plans or to assess very large developments.

5. Some existing air dispersion models estimate short-term (e.g., one-hour, eight-hour) maximum concentrations due to emissions from single developments or groups of developments but appear to be of questionable accuracy and/or are costly.

6. Only two models reviewed have the capacity of estimating ambient pollutant concentrations in the immediate vicinity (i.e., within a few hundred feet) of a proposed development.

7. Every model reviewed needs additional validation. Models are typically validated with sparse, and in some cases questionable, field data and under too few differing conditions to allow for much confidence in the reported accuracies. Even where detailed validation studies have been performed, the accuracy of the results is difficult to measure. Statistical measures are numerous, and no one measure can reflect accuracy in a totally satisfactory way. When different measures are used for different models, comparison is difficult if not impossible.

PART 2
WATER QUALITY
AND QUANTITY

I. INTRODUCTION AND BACKGROUND

With the increase in population and advancement in the level of industrialization have come an increase in water use and a simultaneous decrease in the availability of clean water for drinking, recreation, and other uses. Man-produced changes in terrain and land cover have also affected the likelihood of flooding. Clearly, land use planning and control should consider potential impacts on the quantity and quality of water for various users and changes in flooding hazards. This part of the report discusses these water-related impacts and methods for estimating those caused by land development.

A. HEALTH, SAFETY, AND WELFARE EFFECTS

Since the legal justification for the local application of land use controls (and thus, by extension, for the existence of impact evaluation requirements) usually rests on protecting human health, safety, and welfare, it is useful to maintain this categorization in discussing water-related impacts.

1. Flooding

Flooding relates most obviously to man's safety, but floods are also frequently associated with outbreaks of communicable diseases. Although floods occur naturally as a consequence of an uneven distribution of precipitation and runoff over time, the location and design of land developments can substantially affect the extent of flood damage. One solution is to eliminate manmade structures from flood-prone areas and use these areas for parks or wildlife preserves. Not only would damage to any development in question be eliminated, but increased flooding downstream caused by the diversion of flood waters around structures could possibly be reduced.

2. Water Pollution

As used in this report, "water pollution" refers to the quality of bodies of water, such as wetlands, streams, rivers, lakes, and oceans used for purposes other than for the supply of drinking water. The quality of water used for drinking purposes, on the other hand, is mentioned in the water pollution discussion but receives primary consideration under "water consumption."

The quality of a body of water is determined by the composition of the earth material over which it lies (or in which it is located) and the composition of the inflow water (precipitation, surface and underground flow, and wastewater flow.) Urban sources of wastewater include sewage treatment facilities, septic tanks, and industrial plants. Stormwater runoff and air pollution can also lead to the contamination of surface and ground waters.

The extent to which water can be called polluted is really dependent on the use to which it will be put. The criteria for human consumption will obviously be the most restrictive, while some deterioration may be acceptable for certain agricultural, recreational, industrial, and wildlife uses.

The EPA has proposed a series of water quality criteria (for bodies of water) pursuant to the Federal Water Pollution Control Act Amendments of 1972.[1] The recommended criteria consist of maximum ambient concentrations for fifty-seven polluting substances and maximum levels for eight indicators of water quality. These are based on field and laboratory studies which measure the effects of various pollutants or their surrogates on crops, domestic livestock, aquatic life, wildlife, and man. The specified levels or concentrations applicable to plants and animals reflect a margin of safety below the demonstrated response threshold, or below the concentration which causes death within ninety-six hours to 50 percent of a test group of certain important and sensitive animals or plant species.[2] Standards for human consumption are based primarily on dose-response relationships in test animals, modified by a "safety factor.[3]

Table 2-1 shows the pollutants covered in the EPA documents and provides a brief description of some of the more common pollutants, their sources, and their effects. Also included is a description of selected water quality indicators.

The criteria or standards which appear in the EPA document have varying confidence levels. Many pollutants found in pretreatment water supplies have known health effects.[4] Numerous others, however, have only suspected deleterious effects when present in concentrations observed in drinking water. The asbestos-like fibers discharged into Lake Superior and the possibly carcinogenic chlorinated hydrocarbons recently found in New Orleans and Cincinnati are cases in point. Likewise for aquatic life, the toxic effects of environmentally significant pollutants are usually known only for laboratory conditions. Even more difficult is the determination of standards for recreational uses. Although water contact and fishing activity standards can be based on aquatic life, and, to some extent, on human health criteria, gen-

eral aesthetic considerations are difficult to quantify, although attempts have been made to do so.[5]

3. Water Consumption

Land development may affect water consumption by changing the quality and/or quantity of available water. That is, water supplies can be affected through the introduction of undesirable substances and by the increased consumption demands of the new development (or decreased demand as previous users are removed by development.) The qualitative problem includes both health impacts (from pathogenic and toxic substances) and aesthetic impacts (taste, odor, and clarity). The quantitative impact is a problem of major proportions in rapidly growing areas with only limited access to fresh water, such as parts of the arid Southwest, the Florida coast, and Washington, D.C.

B. APPLICABLE FEDERAL AND STATE LAWS

Current federal and state legislation bears directly on the question of which types of impacts can and, in some cases, must be evaluated in granting land use changes and/or in developing land use plans. These laws are extremely pertinent to any local government considering an impact evaluation program.

1. Flooding

The National Flood Insurance Act of 1968 and its successor, the Flood Disaster Protection Act of 1973, bear directly on the relationship between land development and flood hazards.[6] Both attempt to encourage the adoption of flood plain zoning and building codes by local communities, using subsidized flood insurance for existing flood plain developments as the lever. The 1973 act (which has now replaced the 1968 act) goes one step further by stipulating that no federally insured mortgage lender (i.e., almost all

1. EPA, *Proposed Criteria for Water Quality* (Washington, D.C.: Government Printing Office, October, 1973). See also, EPA, *Comparison of NTAC, NAS, and Proposed EPA Numerical Criteria for Water Quality* (Washington, D.C.: Government Printing Office, May, 1974) (NTIS No. PB-237586); and David L. Jordening, *Estimating Water Quality Benefits* (Washington, D.C.: EPA, August, 1974) (EPA-600/5-74-014).

2. The EPA recognizes that the importance of plant and animal species varies by geographical area. Local communities should thus select and apply the criteria appropriate to their area.

3. See also HEW, *Public Health Drinking Water Standards, Revised* (Washington, D.C.: Government Printing Office, 1962) and the discussion of water consumption in Part 2, II, Sec. C.

4. For a summary of the known and suspected health effects of pollutants identified by the Public Health Service see, Public Health Service, *Public Health Service Drinking Water Standards 1962* (Washington, D.C.: HEW, 1962).

5. For primarily non-aesthetic criteria see, for example, R. E. Coughlin, *Perception and Use of Streams in Suburban Areas: Effects of Water Quality and of Distance from Residence to Stream* (Philadelphia: Regional Science Research Institute, March, 1972); and Doyle W. Bishop and Robert Aukermann, *Water Quality Criteria for Selected Recreational Uses* (Urbana-Champaign: University of Illinois, September, 1970) (NTIS No. PB195164); and B. J. Mechalas, *An Investigation into Recreational Water Quality, Water Quality Criteria Data Book*. vol. 4 (Washington, D.C.: EPA, April, 1972). For an example of aesthetic criteria, see L. B. Leopold, *Quantitative Comparison of Some Aesthetic Factors Among Rivers,* Geological Survey Circular 620 (Washington, D.C.: Department of the Interior, 1969).

6. For a more detailed description of these laws see: Peter M. Williams, "Legislation Signals New Approach to Nation's Critical Flood Problem," *Mortgage Banker* 34 (March 1974): 18–28; and The League of Women Voters, "Flood Plain Management and the National Flood Insurance Program," *Environmental Update on Water,* No. 534 (January, 1975).

Table 2-1. PRINCIPAL WATER POLLUTANTS AND WATER QUALITY INDICATORS

a. Water Pollutants

POLLUTANT	SOURCE	EFFECT
Phosphorus (P)	Fertilizer, treated[a] and untreated sewage, detergents	Occurs predominantly as phosphate (PO_4) and serves as a plant nutrient which can lead to eutrophication (a process of overfertilization and overproduction of water plants) which, in turn, can produce algal blooms and other nuisance conditions.
Nitrogen (N)	Fertilizer, treated[a] and untreated sewage, the atmosphere	As dissolved nitrogen (N_2)—and like many dissolved gases at high concentrations—it is toxic to fish. As ammonia (NH_3), it interferes with drinking water chlorination. As nitrite (NO_2) and nitrate (NO_3), it is a plant nutrient and thus can lead to eutrophication. As NO_3 it can be toxic to humans, especially infants, causing methemoglobinemia.
Suspended solids (SS)	Soil, street debris, sewage	Can reduce sunlight penetration and clog animal and plant surfaces thus reducing biological activity; high levels will also cause water bodies to have a brown or muddy appearance.
Heat[b]	Nuclear generators, industrial plants	Can be toxic to fish at high levels while at lower levels, it can increase their susceptibility to disease and stress. Decreases dissolved oxygen (see Table 2-1-b).
Bacteria	Sewage, effluents with high BOD content can induce bacterial multiplication (see below)	Some forms are disease-causing in man; many cause reduction in dissolved oxygen levels through biological degradation of waste (see Table 2-1-b).
Other (e.g., metals, chlorinated compounds, exotic materials)	Industrial effluent, sewage additives from treatment plants, stormwater runoff from agricultural lands, etc.	Some are cancer-causing or otherwise toxic to man. Polychlorinated biphenyls are generally toxic to animals, especially fish and waterfoul.

b. Water Quality Indicators (in addition to pollutant levels)

INDICATOR	DESCRIPTION/COMMENTS
Biological oxygen demand (BOD)	BOD is a descriptor of effluent content. It is the amount of oxygen required to completely oxidize a quantity of organic matter by biological processes.[c] If the organic matter is being discharged into a body of water, then this is the amount of dissolved oxygen which will be depleted from the stream.
Dissolved oxygen (DO)	Water bodies with high DO levels will have abundant plant and animal life (assuming that other necessary conditions exist). Low DO levels are often the result of the discharge of effluents with high BOD levels.[d]
Turbidity	This is a measure of suspended solids (SS) concentration. High levels indicate high concentrations of SS and, thus, low light penetration.
pH	This is a measure of acidity. High quality water can display a range of values depending on natural conditions. However, very acidic or very alkaline water will not support much life.

a. Treated at the primary or secondary level.

b. This is obviously a physical state of water rather than a pollutant. However, heat can be considered a pollutant in terms of its production and effects.

c. BOD is usually expressed as BOD_5 or the amount of oxygen consumed by the decomposition of the organic matter during a five-day period. However, laboratory methods are now available to measure total oxygen demand (TOD) or ultimate BOD without having to wait long periods of time for bacterial decomposition to take place.

d. Sewage treatment plants using ozone (O_3) as a disinfective sometimes supersaturate the receiving water with DO; this can lead to fish kills.

Water Quality and Quantity: Introduction and Background

lenders) can provide financing for developments in flood hazard areas unless the local government adopts land use controls which zone these areas for nondevelopment uses or enacts special building codes for the few structures allowed.[7] Although there is no requirement that local governments prohibit all flood plain development once controls are adopted (e.g., variances could be granted), any new development in a hazardous area will not be covered by subsidized flood insurance. This in itself should be a strong deterrent to any new flood plain development.

As a consequence of federal action it now appears that a major element of the flood problem will be greatly reduced—the damage which accrues to new developments in a flood plain. However, the exacerbation of existing flood conditions by increased stormwater runoff from new development located outside flood plain boundaries is a problem which remains to be addressed.

2. Water Pollution

The federal government has an extensive history of involvement in the area of water pollution. The most recent legislation, the Water Pollution Control Act amendments of 1972 (WPCA), provides funds for wastewater facility construction and establishes both effluent and water quality standards.[8] The effluent standards apply to all existing and new point sources (primarily municipal sewage plants and industries) which discharge into navigable surface waters. The water quality standards apply to all navigable waters.[9] Either one set of standards or the other will be the limiting factor in determining the allowable effluent content from any source. In order to implement these standards an extensive permit system is being established to control the effluent content from every known point source. Under Section 208 of the act, area-wide wastewater planning programs will control nonpoint sources (e.g., urban and agricultural land) through land use and other control measures. However, the act excludes groundwater resources and

nonnavigable streams from the planning and control provisions.

Many states have also assumed an active role in reducing water pollution by means of legislation. Where state standards are stricter than federal ones the states' prevail. Even where the federal standards are used, EPA encourages and to some extent requires the states (and local/regional governments) to become actively involved in the program.

3. Water Consumption

Federal and state laws pertinent to water consumption are only tangentially related to land development. Most laws simply regulate water purification procedures. A new federal law (the Safe Drinking Water Act) extends federal authority slightly by regulating underground injection of wastes.

Section 304 of the WPCA does refer to the problem of salt water intrusion as the result of groundwater related activities, one of which could be the extraction of water for drinking purposes. However, specific land use control requirements which would follow from this section are unclear at this time.

C. FUNDAMENTAL HYDROLOGIC PRINCIPLES

The study of water resources can be approached from two quite distinct perspectives. One looks at the mechanical processes of water movement, storage, and changes in phase (solid, liquid, gas); the other places water in the larger context of aquatic ecosystems.

1. Physical Hydrology[10]

The hydrologic cycle, represented schematically in Figure 2-1, is a highly variable process requiring vast amounts of solar energy for its operation. In essence, the process involves the condensation and precipitation of water, the collection, transport, and storage of water on and beneath the earth's surface, and the evaporation of water back into the atmosphere. Surface and subsurface hydrology is seen to be a complex and interrelated series of processes including rapid surface runoff, surface percolation, subsurface interflow, and extremely slow groundwater movement (base flow). Evaporation is accomplished abiotically (i.e., direct evaporation from surfaces) and biotically (transpiration[11] by plants).

---

7. A "flood hazard area" is any area covered with water (i.e., the flood plain) according to a 100-year flood record; that is to say, a place where a flood has at least a one-hundredth chance of occurring in any one year.

8. For additional information, see Council on Environmental Quality, *Environmental Quality,* Fifth Annual Report (Washington, D.C., December, 1974); EPA, *Draft Guidelines for Areawide Waste Treatment Management* (Washington, D.C.: Government Printing Office, May, 1974); and EPA *Water Quality Strategy Paper,* 2nd ed., (Washington, D.C.: Government Printing Office, March 15, 1974).

9. The effluent standards reflect secondary treatment of sewage for all municipal plants and the best *practicable* technology for other point sources by July 1, 1977. By July 1, 1983, the standards should reflect the best *available* technology for all point sources.

10. For more information see a standard hydrology text, such as, R. K. Linsley, M. A. Kohler, and J. L. H. Paulhus, *Hydrology for Engineers* (New York: McGraw-Hill, 1975).

11. Transpiration is a physiological process whereby water is taken up by plant roots and released as water vapor at the leaf surface.

Land Development and the Natural Environment

FIGURE 2-1
THE HYDROLOGIC CYCLE

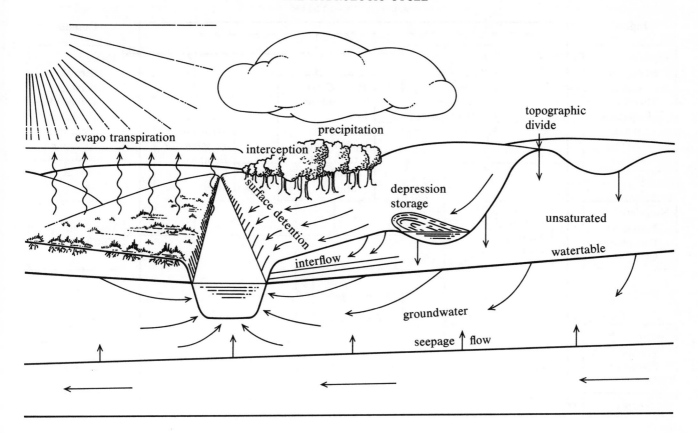

SOURCE: Clark, op. cit.

2. Biological Hydrology[12]

From the ecologist's point of view water provides the environmental support for aquatic life forms. Not only is it the medium in which life exists, but also it provides transport for life-sustaining nutrients.

Figure 2-2 is a flow diagram depicting the dynamics of an aquatic ecosystem. The living members are primary producers, plant eaters, meat eaters, and decomposers. These form a food web, the initial and final sections of which are "pools" of nutrients. The system is fueled by several forms of energy and by nutrients imported from surrounding land and water areas. The outputs of the system are energy in altered forms, nutrients, and sediments. Oxygen is produced and consumed internal to the system, and water is the medium.

These highly simplified principles of physical and biological hydrology comprise the conceptual frame-

work for understanding the hydrologic impacts of land development.

D. WATER-RELATED IMPACTS OF LAND DEVELOPMENT

As a watershed becomes increasingly urbanized, specific and frequently dramatic impacts on flooding, water pollution, and water consumption can be observed. These impacts result from (a) physical changes to the land itself, (b) wastes generated by the new inhabitants, and (c) demands for water to support various economic activities associated with urbanization.

1. Flooding

Development may affect the likelihood of flooding in several ways. First, the ability of the ground to absorb water may change due to soil compaction and changes in the amount of impervious ground cover (e.g., asphalt and concrete). This leads directly to changes in surface runoff.

Secondly, the vegetative cover may be altered. For

---

12. For additional information, see, for example, John Clark, *Coastal Ecosystems* (Washington, D.C.: The Conservation Foundation, 1974). Aquatic biology is also touched upon in "Wildlife and Vegetation," Part 3 of this report.

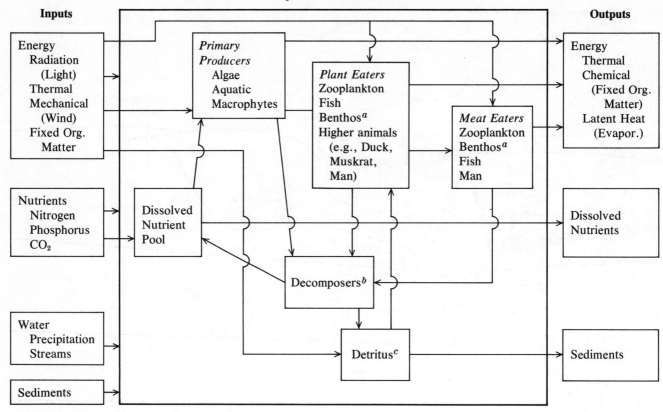

FIGURE 2-2
MATERIAL AND ENERGY FLOWS IN AN
AQUATIC ECOSYSTEM

a. Organisms living at or on the bottom of bodies of water.
b. Fungi and bacteria.
c. Small particles of organic matter.

SOURCE: D. C. Watts and O. L. Loucks, *Models for Describing Exchange Within Ecosystems* (Madison: Institute for Environmental Studies, University of Wisconsin, 1969).

example, deeply rooted plants, such as trees or native grasses, are typically replaced by lawn grass with shallow roots. Less frequently, old fields may be replaced by ornamental trees and shrubs. The result is a change in the amount of water stored in the soil and subsequently transpired by plants, leading in most cases to increased amounts of surface runoff.

Thirdly, development is frequently accompanied by topographical changes and often by a reduction in average slope. These often increase the rate of water percolation through soil and decrease the rate of surface runoff, although the removal of topsoil may negate or reverse the effect.

Urban storm drainage systems may replace natural drainage channels with culverts and storm sewers. The net effect is a decrease in the time it takes surface runoff to reach local streams and lakes.

Finally, as a large area or region becomes urbanized, slight changes in climate may be noticed. Although changes in temperature, wind velocity,

humidity, and solar radiation may be observed, the most relevant effect is on precipitation. Some cities with large point sources of air pollution have been associated with increased precipitation.[13]

The net effect of these changes will depend on the local hydrology, physiography, and soil conditions, on the extent of urbanization (both absolute and relative to the watershed), on land uses, and on the specific location of the development. It will also depend on the severity of the storm. (Since surface runoff will increase with severity, most precipitation becomes runoff once the soil is saturated, relatively reducing the effect of development.) However, most studies of urbanization have shown that the percentage of precipitation which appears as surface runoff increases, and the time lag between onset of precipitation and

13. Presumably, particulates emitted from these sources act as condensation nuclei for atmospheric moisture. See William P. Lowry, "Project METROMEX: A Review of Results," *Bulletin of the American Meterological Society* 55 (February, 1974): 86–121.

Land Development and the Natural Environment

occurrence of peak stream discharge decreases. Consequently, floods increase in both frequency and severity.

2. Water Pollution

Water pollution refers to the quality of water bodies which are affected by wastes generated by or associated with development. Residential and commercial developments will produce additional quantities of sewage and related wastes, while industrial plants often discharge a wide array of harmful wastes associated with various industrial processes.

In addition to pollutants discharged from point sources (i.e., sewage treatment plants or industrial plants), water pollution can result from nonpoint source discharges—general stormwater runoff. This type of pollution is due to natural processes as well as human activities. In natural areas the death and subsequent decay of plants and animals, natural erosion processes, leaching of soil minerals, and generation of animal wastes account for most pollutants. In agricultural areas the use (or overuse) of fertilizers, the husbandry of large numbers of animals, and the exposure of soil stripped of natural cover can contribute to a substantial increase in pollutant loadings above the natural condition. In urban areas the pollutants found in runoff derive from such sources as leaf litter, animal feces, lawn fertilizer, automobile residue, and air pollution.

On a national basis, the order of land uses (or land cover) from most polluting to least polluting based on total solids, nitrates, and phosphates is as follows: cropland, urban land (considering only residential land use), grassland, and forest. Urban stormwater runoff is the major contributor of a variety of pollutants during storms, and even on an annual basis it rivals sewage plant effluent in total loadings.[14] For example, urban stormwater runoff contributes from 40 to 80 percent of the total national BOD (biological oxygen demand) discharged to surface water.[15]

Thus, urbanization not only increases the amount of polluting material deposited in developed areas and ultimately washed off, it also eliminates natural areas where these materials could be "recycled" before reaching bodies of water. Forests and grasslands are very successful in accomplishing this recycling.

3. Water Consumption

A new development (or urbanization in general) will place additional demands on a community's or neighboring households' water supply. Residential and commercial developments will need water for domestic and other uses (e.g., lawn sprinkling), while industries may need large quantities for cooling and related purposes. Since our primary concern is for water used for drinking purposes, our interest in other uses will extend only insofar as they compete with personal consumption for the same supply.

Development may also interfere with the replenishment or inflow of water to underground sources. Placing impervious materials on land which previously allowed aquifers to be recharged is an example. Large developments which use underground sources may also remove water at too great a rate, causing water levels in surrounding wells to drop and total available volumes to decrease.

Finally, land development may decrease the pretreatment quality of water due to additional quantities of pollutants discharged from point sources, from stormwater runoff, or from septic tank leach fields. This may either increase the cost of purification or decrease the quality of the water after treatment. The withdrawal of fresh water from underground sources in coastal areas may also lead to salt water intrusion by reducing the hydraulic pressure that formerly acted as a barrier.

---

14. James D. Sartor, Gail Boyd, and Franklin J. Agardy, "Water Pollution Aspects of Street Surface Contaminants," *Journal of Water Pollution Control* 46 (1) (March 1974): 458–67; and James D. Sartor and Gail Boyd, *Water Pollution Aspects of Street Surface Contaminants* (Washington, D.C.: EPA, November, 1972) (EPA-R2-72-081).

15. Anne M. Vitale and Pierre M. Sprey, *Total Urban Water Pollution Loads: The Impact of Storm Water* (Rockville, Md.: Enviro Control, Inc., 1974) (NTIS No. PB-231 730).

II. METHODOLOGICAL APPROACHES

The conceptual framework and the individual analytical techniques for estimating water quality and quantity impacts are specific to the various impact areas. Thus, flooding, water pollution, and water consumption will be discussed separately.

The sections on flooding and water pollution emphasize the use of generalizable mathematical formulas which relate the areal extent and type of development (among other factors) to stormwater runoff. A broad range of approaches, from simple linear approximations to complex computerized models, will be discussed. The water pollution section also discusses sewage generation. Finally, the analytical treatment of water consumption impacts will focus on methods of estimating total supplies and the use of coefficients which reflect usage rates for different types of development.

A. IMPACTS ON FLOODING

With the full implementation of the Flood Disaster Protection Act discussed previously the exposure of new structures to flood hazards will be vastly reduced, although the few future proposals for flood plain development will still require careful review. However, a flood-related problem will remain—the effect of changes in stormwater runoff patterns caused by new development to existing structures within flood hazard areas. This effect can be described in terms of increased damage to structures already at risk and increased risk to structures currently safe, meaning those located just beyond present flood plain boundaries.

1. Impact Measures

Two alternative measures of flood problems are suggested:[1]

1. Change in the number of people endangered by flooding plus the change in the expected property damage (or the value of property endangered).

OR

2. Change in flood frequency or severity.

Measure 1 best expresses the end impact on man and is thus preferred. It is also the most difficult and expensive to obtain values for. Measure 2 is the fallback measure. Values for Measure 2 are used to compute values for Measure 1, but they can also be used to reflect changes in the probability of flooding alone. In this connection one speaks of a flood which can be expected to occur on the average of once in two, five, ten, fifty, 100 or 500 years. (This corresponds to a probability of occurrence of fifty, twenty, ten, two, one and 0.2 percent for any one year.) Obviously, as the frequency decreases the magnitude increases.

Since a number of dimensions are suggested by Measure 1, a tabular display of the results may be suitable. An example is shown in Table 2-2. The results are expressed as the *additional* number of peo-

---

1. A third alternative would be "the amount of impervious ground cover relative to the budgeted amount" where budgets have been prepared for the watershed in question. See section A-3 of this chapter and section A of part 2, III, for a more detailed discussion.

Table 2-2. AN ILLUSTRATIVE FORMAT FOR PRESENTING THE EFFECT OF A DEVELOPMENT ON RISKS FROM FLOODING

| FLOOD FREQUENCY OR MAGNITUDE | ADDITIONAL PEOPLE JEOPARDIZED | | ADDITIONAL PROPERTY VALUE JEOPARDIZED[a] | |
	Within Development	Outside Development	Within Development	Outside Development
			(millions of dollars)	
Floods				
Worst in 10 years	1,000	0	$10	0
Worst in 50 years	3,000	100	$40	$.5
Worst in 100 years	3,000	100	$40	$.5

a. Alternatively, the expected property damage could be used (this would be less than the total in jeopardy, as in a case where a property worth $100,000 is put in jeopardy, but where the likely damage to it may be $25,000).

ple at risk and the expected damage caused by floods of various frequencies. It may also be desirable to display the maps delineating flood plains for the ten, fifty, 100 and 500-year floods. This is extremely effective in communicating the impact on individual properties.

2. General Analytical Approaches

In order to measure the hydrologic changes that have occurred as a result of urbanization in a given watershed (i.e., retrospective analysis), one can either trace and relate the hydrologic and developmental changes over time (controlling for all other variables), or compare the changes with those observed in an "identical" watershed which has not experienced land development. The first approach is limited by the difficulty in accounting for all nondevelopment-related factors which could affect the watershed's hydrology. This is especially true for climatic factors, which can display extreme variability from year to year. In some cases simple models have been used to estimate the fraction of observed hydrologic changes due to climatic factors alone, the residual then being attributed to land use changes.

The second approach is limited by a similar problem. No two watersheds are identical. Thus, differences must be carefully measured and accounted for. These differences include physiography, soil structure, vegetation, land use, and watershed size, as well as climate.

In assessing the impact of future developments predictive techniques calibrated to local conditions are frequently employed. Alternatively, analogies to similar watersheds can be drawn. If the latter approach is used, one must again be careful to account for differences between the test and the reference situations, as in retrospective analysis.

Flood analyses which involve the use of predictive techniques or models are typically comprised of two parts, a hydrologic analysis and a hydraulic analysis.

The first estimates rainfall/runoff/stream flow relationships; the second routes the runoff into existing channels and estimates flood levels for bodies of surface water in the watershed. A few of the more complex models accomplish both types of analyses.

The sections to follow present descriptions of alternative techniques and, where possible, evaluations of them.[2] The last few years have witnessed a dramatic proliferation of the more complex hydrologic models. Selection of the techniques reviewed here was based primarily on their current popularity or representativeness of alternative approaches. Unfortunately, the dearth of information on input requirements and accuracy of the various techniques reduces our ability to appraise the various approaches. Where possible we have attempted to survey both the developers and users of particular techniques, in order to gain at least qualitative insights.

3. Estimating Impacts on Stream Flow

The extent to which a proposed land development will cause significant changes in the flow of local streams is dependent on numerous characteristics of both the development and the watershed in which it is to be located. In determining whether a particular development is large enough to justify an individual assessment, the most meaningful and widely used factor is "percent imperviousness." That is, the amount of land to be covered with impervious material, such as concrete or asphalt, is expressed as a percentage of the land on the site and as a percentage of the entire watershed. However, in order to determine

---

2. For more inclusive treatment see, for example, J. W. Brown et al., *Models & Methods Applicable to the Corps of Engineers Urban Studies* (Vicksburg, Miss.: Army Corps of Engineers, June, 1974); and Ray K. Linsley, *A Critical Review of Currently Available Hydrologic Models for Analysis of Urban Stormwater Runoff* (Palo Alto, Calif. Hydrocomp International, August, 1971). The first is particularly relevant to the subject here as individual models are described and to some degree evaluated systematically.

how large these percentages must be to justify an assessment, the sensitivity to imperviousness of individual watersheds within the community must be ascertained. This can be done through retrospective analyses (as discussed above) or by applying analytical techniques to the watersheds and observing the effect that hypothetical degrees of imperviousness have on estimated stream flow.[3]

a. Analytical Techniques

The following techniques differ in base data required, complexity of computation, type of results generated, and applicability to different types of watersheds. The simpler techniques will be presented first. Each technique is used to estimate water flow in streams and/or lakes.

Rational Method—One of the most widely but, in many cases, inappropriately used techniques is the Rational Method.[4] It is a straightforward and simple computational procedure applicable to streams and based on the following relationship:

$$Q = CiA$$

where: Q = peak (short-term) runoff rate (or stream flow) in cubic feet per second
C = a constant dependent on basin characteristics
i = average precipitation intensity in inches/hour (different values are used for storms of different degrees of severity)
A = drainage area in acres

The coefficient C is dependent on many watershed variables, such as shape, slope, soil moisture content and capacity, ground cover, and terrain, as well as on the severity of the storm.[5] (As noted previously, development can affect many of these variables.) Success in assigning appropriate values to C which reflect all of these factors has not been obtained. Typically, the total effect of urbanization is represented by "percent imperviousness," although the extent of storm sewerization is implicitly included as well.

Rantz provides rules of thumb and some empirical data (from the San Francisco area) which can be used to relate various types of development to "percent imperviousness" and thus to determine C.[6] A proposed development will change the "percent impervious" and thus values for estimated stream flow through changes in C.

As mentioned previously, the Rational Method is one of the most popular techniques for estimating stream flow, especially for watersheds undergoing urbanization. It is simple and provides estimates of peak stream flow—a quantity directly pertinent to flooding. However, it is limited in application to small watersheds of no more than a few square miles and preferably less, a fact not recognized by all users.[7] In addition, there have been few attempts to compare computed with observed values. In at least two validation studies, errors were as large as 60 percent.[8] Another test showed that only 35 percent of the estimates were within 25 percent of the observed values. It is thus of dubious utility for anything more than gross estimates.

Flood Frequency Analysis—As the name implies, this technique estimates stream flow during flood incidents from actual flood data.[9] These data are then related by empirical analysis of watersheds in the region under study to climatologic, topographical, and if possible, land use characteristics. The impact of a new development is then estimated, using these empirical relationships.

More specifically, data on peak stream flow are compiled for all streams within the region on which gauging stations are located.[10] These data are then

3. This is further discussed in Part 2, III, under the heading, "Planning versus Project Review."

4. For additional information, see American Society of Civil Engineers, "Design and Construction of Sanitary and Storm Sewers," *Manuals and Reports on Engineering Practices,* No. 37 (Washington, D.C., 1969); S. E. Rantz, *Suggested Criteria for Hydrologic Design of Storm-Drainage Facilities in the San Francisco Bay Region, California* (Menlo Park, Calif.: U.S. Geological Survey, November 24, 1971); and James K. Searcy, *Design of Roadside Drainage Channels,* Hydraulic Design Series #4, Bureau of Public Roads (Washington, D.C.: Government Printing Office, May, 1965).

5. Runoff as a percent of precipitation increases as the soil becomes saturated and the surface depressions are filled.

6. The relationship between land use categories and "percent imperviousness" for other geographical areas can be found in: Water Resources Engineers and the Hydrologic Engineering Center, Corps of Engineers, *Management of Urban Storm Runoff,* (New York: American Society of Civil Engineers, May, 1974); George Dempster, Jr. *Effects of Floods in Dallas, Texas Metropolitan Area* (Austin, Texas: Geological Survey, January, 1975); and Joachin Tourbier and Richard Westmacott, *Water Resources Protection Measures in Land Development—A Handbook* (Newark: Water Resources Center, University of Delaware, April, 1974).

7. Some have suggested the the upper limit be 200 acres (approximately ⅓ square mile). See Wright-McLaughlin Engineers, *Urban Storm Drainage Criteria Manual* (Denver: Denver Regional Council of Governments, 1969).

8. Error values are observed-estimated differences as a percentage of the observed. These occurrences were for watersheds of less than fifty acres. See D. Earl Jones, Jr., "Urban Hydrology—A Redirection," *Civil Engineering* (August, 1967): 58–62; and J. C. Schaake, J. C. Geyes, and J. W. Knopp, "Experimental Examination of the Rational Method," *Journal of the Hydraulics Division Proceedings of the American Society of Civil Engineers* (November, 1967): 353–70.

9. For additional information, see Rantz, op. cit.

10. Gauging stations are manmade structures designed to measure stream flow.

organized into frequency distributions for each stream according to standard statistical procedures.[11] Values for stream flow for floods of various recurrence intervals (typically, two, five, ten, fifty and 100 years) are then mathematically related to the basin characteristics of the test watersheds.[12] If the set of test watersheds shows wide variation in these characteristics (e.g., the gauged basins include large as well as small ones, urbanized as well as natural ones, ones with high levels of precipitation as well as dry ones), these factors can be analyzed for their effect on stream flow. If not, relationships developed for other regions can *possibly* be substituted if interregional differences are not too great. The natural basin characteristics and forecasted land use changes (either general growth or single large developments) are then used to estimate flow levels for the stream in question. Measures of development are typically very gross, such as "percent urbanization" as measured by areal extent of structures, lawns, pavements, etc. Thus, this technique is best applied only where the new development represents a large increase in a watershed's degree of urbanization. Again, more detailed guidelines can be found in the Rantz report.[13]

Table 2-3 shows the results of a Flood Frequency Analysis of forty watersheds in the San Francisco region. Storms of various recurrence intervals are related to several basin variables (only precipitation and basin size proved significant) and correlation coefficients reported.[14] As shown, the technique is highly successful in reproducing *past* events, although *future* events can only be estimated accurately to the extent that future hydrologic relationships are similar to past ones.

---

11. The data are fitted to a Pearson Type III distribution. See Water Resources Council, Hydrology Committee, *A Uniform Technique for Determining Flood Flow Frequencies*, Bulletin No. 15 (Washington, D.C.; December, 1967).

12. These relationships are determined by regression analysis, typically using an equation of the form:

$$Q = ax^b y^c \ldots$$

where: Q = flow
$x, y \ldots$ = are variables such as watershed area and precipitation
$a, b, c \ldots$ = are constants, the values for which are determined by analyzing the data for Q, x, y, etc., collected for various watersheds

13. Rantz, op. cit.

14. Correlations measure the agreement between data. Values of 0 signify no agreement while values of 1.0 indicate perfect agreement. Values about 0.7 reflect "good" agreement. Correlation coefficients as applied to stream flow data must be interpreted with caution. The specific coefficient values are a function of the adequacy of the stream gauging program, as well as the accuracy of the technique. In addition, other measures of validity can be, and for some techniques have been used. (Correlation coefficients cited in this report are the statistic "r" unless otherwise noted.)

Table 2-3. RESULTS OF A FLOOD FREQUENCY ANALYSIS
(For Illustration Purposes Only)

RECURRENCE INTERVAL (YEARS)	MULTIPLE REGRESSION EQUATION	COEFFICIENT OF MULTIPLE CORRELATION
2	$Q_2 = 0.069A^{0.913}P^{1.965}$	0.964
5	$Q_5 = 2.00A^{0.925}P^{1.206}$	0.976
10	$Q_{10} = 7.38A^{0.922}P^{0.928}$	0.977
25	$Q_{25} = 16.5A^{0.912}P^{0.797}$	0.950
50	$Q_{50} = 69.6A^{0.847}P^{0.511}$	0.902

SOURCE: Rantz, op. cit.
NOTES:

Q = stream flow, in cubic feet per second
A = drainage area, in square miles
P = mean annual basinwide precipitation, in inches

These results are specific to the unusual hydrological and climatological features of various watersheds in the San Francisco Bay area.

Other Simple Techniques—Most other techniques which do not involve the use of computerized hydrologic models are refinements of the methods already presented.[15] For example, the Unit Hydrograph Technique expands the Flood Frequency Analysis by estimating the time distribution of runoff from a storm rather than just peak discharge.[16] (A hydrograph for a hypothetical basin is shown in Figure 2-3.) This information is useful if certain flood control devices are employed in a watershed. Total, rather than just peak flows, are needed to estimate the effectiveness of storage facilities, such as levees and dams. Hydrographs are also useful for showing the impact of urbanization on the timing of peak discharge. In addition, Rantz has reported a slight improvement in accuracy for estimates of peak discharge values as compared to the Flood Frequency Analysis, although the computation procedures are considerably more involved. A recent study sponsored by EPA further documents the utility of this method.[17]

Each of the techniques discussed thus far which estimate short-term fluctuations in flow (i.e., peak flow) use a single measure to reflect the hydrologic effects of urbanization. Even though this measure is frequently called the "percent of imperviousness" it often encompasses the other major hydrologic-related

---

15. For a discussion of other simple techniques which may be used to estimate runoff, see EPA, *Water Quality Management for Urban Runoff* (Washington, D.C.: EPA, December, 1974) (NTIS PB241689/AS).

16. For much information see Rantz, op. cit., or any standard hydrologic text such as Linsley, Kohler, and Paulhus, op. cit.

17. E. F. Brater and J. D. Sherill, *Rainfall-Runoff Relations on Urban and Rural Areas* (Cincinnati: EPA, Office of Research and Development, May, 1975).

Land Development and the Natural Environment

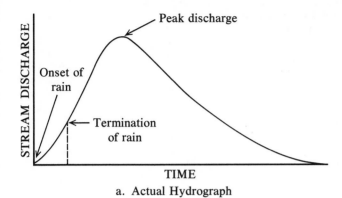

FIGURE 2-3
AN EXAMPLE OF HYDROGRAPH FOR A
HYPOTHETICAL WATERSHED

a. Actual Hydrograph

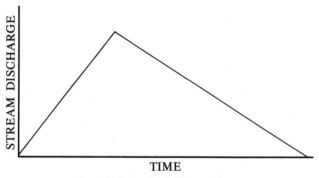

b. Mathematical Abstraction

factor as well—the extent to which natural drainage channels have been modified or replaced by storm sewers. It would, of course, be useful to know the relative effect of each so that the proposed development could be characterized by each separately.

Luna Leopold has compiled and presented in tabular and graph form the results of flood frequency studies of the effects of both factors on stream flows.[18] Since the individual studies were undertaken in different geographic regions the combined results are national averages and may or may not be applicable to specific areas. However, they could possibly be used to suggest when the other techniques may give low or high estimates when applied to specific developments. If the new development will be sewered to an unusually high or low extent when compared with the developments used to calibrate or particularize the technique, the estimates could be adjusted up or down, perhaps by a factor equal to those in the Leopold reference. The resulting estimate would still be approximate but to a lesser degree.

Another factor not accommodated well by these techniques is the influence of site design. Since the options for diverting or detaining runoff through landscaping and the construction of special facilities are numerous, it is unlikely that the impact of future development on flood potential can ever be estimated with a high degree of certainty using these methods. However, rough approximations of the mitigating effect of runoff detention devices can be made, using design specifications found in relevant engineering reports.[19]

Complex Hydrologic Models—The relatively simple techniques discussed so far are simple because they abstract only the more important features of the hydrologic cycle while ignoring the rest. The Rational Method, for example, does not treat evapotranspiration, soil moisture replenishment, or subsurface water flow explicitly (see Figure 2-1). Rather, it relies on empirical measurements of rainfall intensity and the coefficient C, which presumably encompasses the locally important variables. Likewise, the Flood Frequency Analysis attempts to associate presumed causes (e.g., basin configuration, precipitation, and land use) with effects (floods of various severity) but with no direct analysis of hydrologic processes.

Complex hydrologic models, on the other hand, attempt to simulate more elements in the hydrologic cycle. "Event models" are used to estimate stream flow during single events or storms. They are considerably more complex than the simple techniques, but stop short of simulating the complete hydrologic cycle. "Continuous models" are based on a detailed accounting procedure which traces the fate of precipitation within a given watershed on a daily, hourly, or even subhourly basis. Figure 2-4 is a flow chart for one representative continuous model. In order to compute stream flow according to this procedure, short-term data on temperature, precipitation, hours of sunlight, topography, vegetation, soil type, and land cover are necessary.

Many of the complex models also employ stream routing routines which assign surface and subsurface runoff to natural and artificial channels in various portions of the watershed. The technique used to route the flows is one of the main points of differentiation among the various models.

Once the precipitation has been translated into surface and subsurface flows, which in turn have been routed into existing waterways, and the overall model

18. Luna B. Leopold, *Hydrology for Urban Land Planning—A Guidebook on the Hydrologic Effects of Urban Land Use,* Geological Survey Circular 554 (Washington, D.C.: Geological Survey, 1968).

19. American Public Works Association, *Practices in Detention of Urban Stormwater Runoff,* Special Report No. 43 (Chicago, 1974) (NTIS No. PB-234-554). See also, Tourbier and Westmacott, op. cit.; and Meta Systems, Inc., *Land Use Environmental Quality Relationships* (Washington, D.C.: EPA, forthcoming).

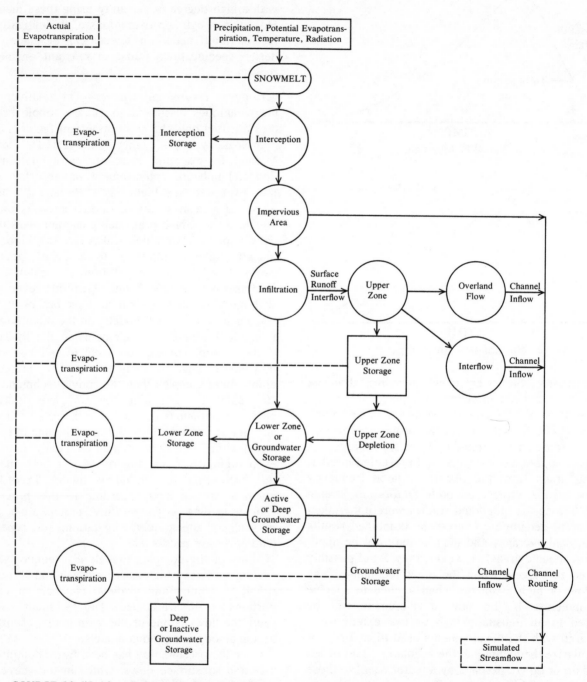

FIGURE 2-4
FLOW CHART OF COMPUTATIONS FOR A
COMPLEX HYDROLOGIC MODEL[a]

SOURCE: Modified from R. Linsley and N. Crawford, "Continuous Simulation Models in Urban Hydrology," *Geophysical Research Letters,* No. 1 (May, 1974): 59–62.

a. This diagram refers to the "lands" module of the Hydrocomp Simulation Program.

calibrated for a similar watershed with stream flow records, estimates of past and/or future flows are made for the watershed in question. The results are expressed in terms of continuous stream flow hydrographs for each of the stream reaches into which the stream has been divided. The past or future impact of changes in land cover (e.g., due to development, reforestation, conversion to agricultural uses), in channel configuration, or in flood control facilities can then be simulated.

This description is generally applicable to all continuous hydrologic models but especially those based on or modified from the Stanford Watershed Model.[20] An abbreviated evaluation of complex models, as well as simple hydrologic techniques, appears in the next section in tabular form to aid in comparative assessment.[21]

In summary, these models are much more satisfying from a theoretical perspective, although evidence for purposes of accuracy comparison is lacking. Most have the capacity to estimate short-term changes in flow and the effects of site design features, including changes to the drainage system.

One additional approach worth noting is the simulation of long-term stream flow by a mathematically produced stochastic process.[22] The concept is quite simple—hydrologic processes exhibit many features of a random series of events and could be simulated by an appropriately synthesized stochastic process. This requires the use of a digital computer. In addition, the results have not been as accurate as was hoped. For short-term stream flow prediction and for estimation of the impact of changing land use patterns, other approaches seem more desirable.

b. Comparison and Summary

A discussion of the comparative advantages and disadvantages of hydrologic techniques cannot proceed much beyond the obvious. The simple techniques are less expensive and produce less informa-tion with less accuracy than the complex ones. The almost total lack of reported information on costs and accuracy necessitates reliance on theoretical considerations as the basis for appraisal.

We have already mentioned the primary difference between complex hydrologic models and most simple techniques, but it is worth noting again. It is basically the difference between specifying relationships based on observed statistical associations and the simulation of underlying, empirically tested processes which are responsible for the observed associations. Both can be equally accurate for reproducing past events for the calibrated watershed, but the second approach is theoretically far superior for estimating future events, or events in a watershed to which the model has not been calibrated. Confirmatory empirical evidence is generally lacking, however. Table 2-4 represents an attempt to organize and present descriptive material on the various techniques in a standard format.

For the planner seeking to select from among the available techniques (especially in the absence of specific cost and accuracy figures), a very qualitative assessment may be valuable. All of the simple techniques described can be used in-house by planners who have some familiarity with them. In addition, flood frequency studies for individual watersheds may have already been undertaken by the local U.S. Geological Survey (USGS) field office. The more complex techniques will require the use of a computer and often a consultant. These will most likely give better results, but to an unknown degree.

All of the techniques require climatologic and hydrologic data as input. The National Weather Service (NWS) maintains daily precipitation records for various periods of time at 10,000 locations nationwide and hourly records at 2,500 of these. Hourly records of a variety of other meterological data for seventy years are available at approximately 600 first-order stations.[23] Local data, including that produced by the volunteer observer network, may greatly expand the official NWS system. The National Weather Records Archives are another rich source of meteorological data.[24]

The USGS operates most of the stream-gauging

20. See N. H. Crawford and R. K. Linsley, *Digital Simulation in Hydrology; Stanford Watershed Model IV,* Department of Civil Engineering Technical Report No. 39 (Palo Alto, Calif.: Stanford University, 1966).

21. Numerous events and continuous models are available. Recently, several comprehensive reviews of many of these have been published. See, for example, Marsalek, op. cit.; and A. Brandstetter, *Comparative Analysis of Urban Stormwater Models* (Richland, Wash.: Pacific Northwest Laboratories, Battelle Memorial Institute, 1974). See also the description of SWMM and STORM (two federally developed runoff models which can also be used to estimate stormwater runoff *quality*) in Table 2-4.

22. Leo R. Beard, *Simulation of Daily Streamflow,* Technical Paper No. 6 (Davis, Calif.: Army Corps of Engineers, Hydrologic Engineering Center, 1967); and Linsley, Kohler, and Paulhus, op. cit.

23. These data are available in the following Weather Bureau publications or data sets: regional Hydrological Bulletins, Climatological Data and Hourly Precipitation. These are available at Weather Bureau offices and at field offices of such agencies as the Corps of Engineers, Bureau of Reclamation, and Soil Conservation Service.

24. Environmental Data Services, National Weather Records Archives, Environmental Science Services Administration, Federal Building, Asheville, N.C. 28801.

Table 2-4. COMPARISON OF TECHNIQUES USED TO ESTIMATE CHANGE IN STREAM FLOW[a]

NAME	TYPES OF WATER BODIES	WATERSHED	COMPUTING REQUIREMENTS	INPUT	COST	OUTPUT	ACCURACY
Rational Method	Streams	Less than approximately 5 square mi.	Compilation of precipitation tables, manual computation	Precipitation depth-frequency-duration tables, percent impervious ground cover in the watershed	Relatively low	Peak stream flow for storms of various degrees of severity	Some reports of errors as great as 50% in reproducing past events[c]
Flood Frequency Analysis	Streams, lakes, estuaries	No limit	Access to a digital computer desirable to perform regression analyses and to fit flood data into the accepted distributional form	Stream flow records for gauged streams, watershed size and slope, average annual precipitation, and land use for numerous watersheds for several years	Low-medium (since additional time-consuming calculations are necessary)	Peak stream flow for storms of various degrees of severity	High for reproducing past events once it has been calibrated; unknown for future events
Hydrocomp Simulation Program (HSP)[b]	Streams, lakes, reservoirs	No limit	Designed for use on the IBM 360 or 370 computer	Hourly precipitation and evaporation; extent, location, type of sewerage, and ground cover in watershed; channel configuration (for snowfall—daily maximum and minimum temperatures, point, wind velocity, radiation and cloud cover desirable)	Approximately $10/acre for small watersheds, considerably less for large ones	Continuous stream flow hydrographs for as many points in the watershed and for as many years as desired	High for reproducing past events and "good" for future events as rated by the developers, although no documentation is available

a. Each of the techniques can estimate flows for almost any number of points within the watershed that is desired. The HSP is limited by the time needed to compute flow within river reaches. The smallest reach modeled has been about 1/2 mile in length.

b. Norman H. Crawford, *Studies in the Applications of Digital Simulations to Urban Hydrology* (Palo Alto, California: Hydrocomp International, Inc., September, 1971); and Hydrocomp International, Inc., *Hydrocomp Simulation Programming Operations Manual* (Palo Alto, California, February, 1972).

c. D. Earl Jones, op. cit., and J. C. Schaake, et al., op. cit.

stations in the United States. Records of stream flow are maintained at USGS regional offices and at numerous public libraries. Unfortunately, most gauged watersheds are located in rural areas.

4. Estimating Impacts on the Extent of Flooding

Once the change in runoff, and thus stream flow, from new land development has been ascertained, the next step is to translate this change into depth and extent of flooding. This involves construction of water surface profiles (i.e., the changing elevation of the water surface over the length of the stream) and the delineation of both flood plains and floodways (areas within the flood plain over which most of the flood water is discharged). Figure 2-5 contains an example of a map and a cross-sectional view of streams, floodways, and flood plains. The underlying computations (usually called backwater calculations) take into account river channel and valley configuration as well as the effect of manmade structures, such as dams, levees, and bridges. The latter may or may not be part of a new development, but even existing flood control devices or stream obstructions must be accounted for in estimating the height and extent of flood waters.

a. Analytical Techniques

Several highly developed computerized models are now available for making these calculations. However, the one developed by the Hydrologic Engineering Center (HEC) of the Corps of Engineers is by far the most widely used. Due to the popularity and representativeness of this model and to the existence of other, more detailed comparative reviews of hydraulic models, the following discussion is limited to the HEC model.[25]

HEC-2—The Hydrologic Engineering Center has been developing and refining models to compute surface water profiles for a number of years.[26] HEC-2 is the most efficient and comprehensive effort thus far but is only applicable to streams. To prepare inputs for the model, the river system in question is subdivided into a number of fairly homogeneous reaches. Measurements are made of stream bed slope, cross-

sectional areas at various points along the valley, "roughness" or indicators of flow impedance due to vegetation and other factors both in the stream channel and in overflow areas, and characteristics of manmade structures affecting flow. These data are then used as inputs for calculations of (1) total energy of the flowing water at each point where cross-sectional areas have been measured, and (2) energy losses due to frictional forces acting on the flowing water between cross-sections. These values are then combined with stream flow values for various patterns of precipitation for each reach, obtained by using one of the previously discussed techniques (or a similar one) and then translated into a water surface level above the stream bed in each reach.

The results can be presented in tabular as well as graphic or map form, similar to that found in Figure 2-5. Flood plain maps and diagrams must be prepared from the surface water profiles according to guidelines found in the guidebook prepared by the Federal Insurance Administration (FIA) of HUD as part of the Flood Disaster Protection Act.[27] The program has been written for use (with minor modification) with many high-speed computers.[28]

5. Estimating Impacts in Terms of Damages and Risks

Once the additional runoff caused by new development has been calculated and translated into flooding depth and extent, this information can be used to estimate the impact on the community in terms of potential dollar damage and people at risk (Measure 1).

FIA has developed a set of actuarial rate insurance premium tables based on correlations between flood severity and property damage in various geographical regions and over an extended period of time.[29] From these can be estimated the fraction of a structure likely to be damaged, given its location in the flood plain and the frequency of flooding. By estimating the expected damage to all flood-prone property within a watershed both with and without the new development, the impact attributable to the new development can be ascertained.

The insurance premium rates actually incorporate both the factors of location in the flood plain and of frequency of flooding, since they are based on the dif-

25. See Bill S. Eichert, "Survey of Programs for Water-Surface Profiles," *Journal of the Hydraulics Division, Proceedings of the American Society of Civil Engineers* 96 (HY2) (February, 1970): 547–63. This review article is purely descriptive, however. No attempt is made to assess relative costs and accuracies.

26. Hydrologic Engineering Center, *Water Profiles—Preliminary* (Davis, Calif.: Corps of Engineers, February, 1969) and Hydrologic Engineering Center, HEC-2: *Water Surface Profiles* (Davis, Calif.: Corps of Engineers, October, 1973).

27. Federal Insurance Administration, *Flood Insurance Study, Guidelines and Specifications* (Washington, D.C.: HUD, January, 1975).

28. Memory requirements are approximately 60,000 words and four or more magnetic tapes plus input-output units such as those available on the CDC 6600, IBM 360 or 7094, and GE 625.

29. For a discussion of the application of these tables in the construction of Flood Insurance Rate Maps under the Flood Disaster Protection Act, see Federal Insurance Administration, op. cit.

FIGURE 2-5
REPRESENTATIONS OF THE EXTENT AND
DEPTH OF FLOODING

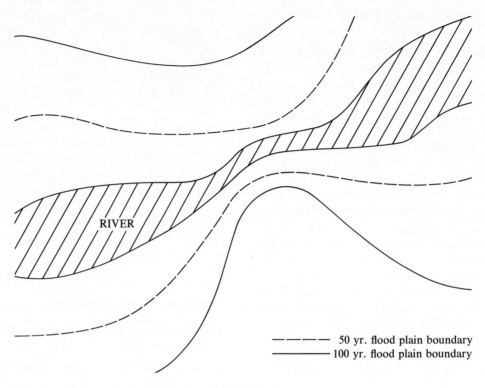

a. *Flood Plain Map*

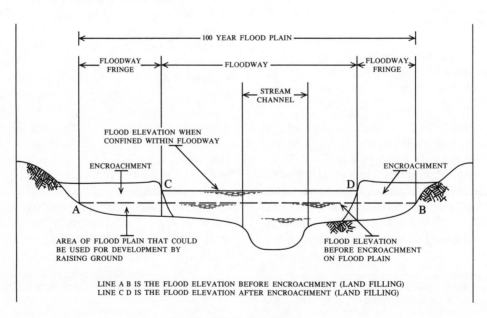

b. *Flood Plain Cross Section*

SOURCE: Federal Insurance Administration, op. cit.

ference in water depth between the ten-year and 100-year floods.[30] The difference in depth can be estimated for any location in the flood plain directly from the previous analyses. As an approximation of long-term expected damage, the appropriate actuarial rate (in dollars per one thousand dollars of value) can then be multiplied by the market value of each structure in the flood plain and summed up for all structures.[31]

A simpler but less detailed approach is to express expected damage as the number of structures and their total market value at risk for floods of various frequencies. Impact is again the difference (in market value) with and without the development.

We have also suggested that impact be expressed as numbers of persons at risk. This information should be obtainable from census tract data. Expected injury may be much more difficult to determine, although FIA or other federal agencies administering disaster relief may have attempted to correlate data on deaths and injuries due to flooding with flood severity, the size of the population exposed, and other related factors. This would allow the calculation of estimates for deaths and injuries.

B. IMPACTS ON WATER POLLUTION

The procedure to be described for assessing the impacts of land development on water pollution consists of four distinct steps: assessing current discharge levels, current ambient concentrations, future discharge levels, and future ambient concentrations. These steps are necessary in order to place the impact of development (either generalized development or specific projects) in proper perspective. In addition, the first three steps will generate the requisite data to be used as input for the analytical techniques to be used in the fourth step.

1. Measures, Standards, and Indices

Impacts on water pollution may be assessed by the following measures:[32]

1. Change in the permissible or tolerable usability of the water in question and the number of people affected.

OR

2. Change in the ambient concentration of each pollutant (relative to standards).

Measure 1 is the preferred measure, as it is more reflective of the end impact on man. "Change in the monetary value of the pollution-caused damage" is perhaps even more desirable as a quantitative measure of end impact, although the state of the art is not yet advanced to the point where its routine use could be recommended, as will be discussed subsequently. Measure 2 is less detailed and probably simpler to estimate. It thus can be used where limited resources for project evaluation preclude the use of Measure 1.

In order to make the values generated for Measures 1 and 2 more meaningful, reference must be made to the relationship of pollutant concentrations to safety and desired water use. At present, the standards proposed by EPA and other organizations reflect the current state of knowledge, although local communities may decide to use other standards as well.[33] Measures 1 and 2 may be stated in terms of average annual concentrations compared to the standard, the number of times the standard will be exceeded in a year, or some similar expression.

Once changes in values have been measured or estimated at specific points in a body of water, they can be viewed individually or combined to obtain a single or a few values for the entire body. An index can be used which combines values for each of the pollutants assessed and/or for each geographical point for which estimates were made. Several indices have been proposed and applied in numerous communities.[34] However, the use of indices tends to obscure the significance of changes in the concentration of any one pollutant or at any one point. We thus recommend that, if indices are used, values for individual pollutants and individual locations also be provided.

Measure 1 further assumes that the summations of changes in ambient concentrations for several pollutants and at several points in a body of water can be interpreted in terms of changes in permissible or tolerable uses. This interpretation must again rely on rules-of-thumb based on observed correlations between ambient concentrations and the behavior and/or preferences of water users.[35] In order to

30. Floods occurring more often than once every ten years or less than once every 100 years are thus ignored.

31. For a discussion of using assessment records as indicators of property value see, Thomas Muller, *Estimating the Impacts of Land Development on the Private Economy* (Washington, D.C.: The Urban Institute, forthcoming).

32. An alternative measure is "the quantity of effluent to be generated compared to the budgeted amount" where a budget has been prepared for the water body in question. See Part 2, III, Section A, for a more detailed discussion.

33. Suggested standards were discussed in Part 2, I.

34. See, for example, James W. Curlin, *National Environmental Policy Act of 1969, Environmental Indices-Status of Development Pursuant to Sections 102 (2) (B) and 204 of the Act* (Washington, D.C.: Congressional Research Service, Library of Congress, December, 1973); B. J. Berry, et al., *Land Use, Urban Form, and Environmental Quality* (Chicago: University of Chicago, 1974); and The Council on Environmental Quality, *Environmental Quality, CEQ's Third Annual Report* (Washington, D.C.: CEQ, 1972).

35. The most relevant data can be found in Bishop and Aukermann, op. cit.

express the evaluation results using Measure 1, a simple format such as that illustrated in Table 2-5 may prove effective.

In some situations it may be desirable to further subdivide the water uses listed in Table 2-5. Since the conditions necessary for trout fishing, for example, are considerably different from those for bass, sub-categorizations would be necessary if a trout stream were being degraded or improved.

2. Measuring/Estimating Current Discharge Levels

Discharges from point and nonpoint sources need to be considered in order to establish relationships between current discharges and current ambient concentrations. From these, relationships between future discharges and future ambient levels can be estimated.

The assessment of current emissions from point sources (i.e., specific identifiable outfalls, such as those found at sewage treatment facilities and certain industrial plants) is similar to that for air pollution. Direct measurement of effluent content is combined with analyses of industrial processes, product mixes, the amount of product used, and the types of pollution control devices employed. For water pollution, however, the number of sources to consider is much smaller than for air pollution. Still, wastewater emission inventories for most areas remain poorly developed. EPA is currently supporting research to refine wastewater emission factors for various industrial categories.

The assessment of emissions from nonpoint sources (e.g., runoff from agricultural fields and residential areas) is much more difficult. One approach is to construct a total materials balance or conservation of mass equation for each pollutant:

$$Q = P + N + I - (S + D)$$

where: Q = total quantity of pollutants leaving the water body

P = quantity of pollutant discharged by point sources

N = quantity of pollutant discharged by non-point sources

I = quantity of pollutant in the water entering the area

S = quantity of pollutant precipitated out of solution in the area

D = quantity of pollutant decayed or transformed in the area

If long-term (i.e., monthly or yearly) pollutant quantities are estimated from data on ambient concentrations and point source discharge, the relative proportion of emissions due to nonpoint sources can be quantified. However, since nonpoint source discharges are typically associated with rainfall which, in turn, can produce high ambient concentrations over short-time intervals, their impact far outweighs their relative quantity. These "shock loadings" can have disastrous effects on aquatic biology.

An alternative approach is to use a predictive model to estimate current nonpoint source discharges. The EPA and Department of Agriculture have both produced documents on simple techniques.[36] More complex techniques, some of which can estimate "shock loadings," will be discussed in the section on estimating future discharge levels.

Methods and procedures for conducting point and nonpoint source inventories appear in recently published EPA guidelines.[37]

---

36. C. H. Wadleigh, *Wastes in Relation to Agriculture and Forestry,* Miscellaneous Publication No. 1065 (Washington, D.C.: Department of Agriculture, March, 1968); and Office of Air and Water Programs, *Methods of Identifying and Evaluating the Nature and Extent of Nonpoint Sources of Pollutants* (Washington, D.C.: EPA, October, 1973).

37. Office of Water and Hazardous Materials, *Guidelines for Preparation of Water Quality Management Plans* (Washington, D.C.: EPA, September, 1974); and Office of Water and Hazardous Materials, *Draft Guidelines for Areawide Waste Treatment Management* (Washington, D.C.: EPA, May, 1974).

Table 2-5. AN ILLUSTRATIVE FORMAT FOR PRESENTING THE EFFECTS OF DEVELOPMENT ON WATER USE

LAKE CLEARWATER

WATER USE	CURRENT SUITABILITY	SUITABILITY AFTER DEVELOPMENT	APPROXIMATE NUMBER OF USERS	COMMENTS
Swimming	Suitable	Unsuitable	100,000/yr.	Rotting seaweed, floating materials and increased turbidity will also decrease the aesthetic quality.
Boating	Suitable	Suitable	20,000/yr.	
Fishing	Suitable	Suitable	5,000/yr.	

NOTES:

A much finer categorization of uses will probably be necessary.

Data on pollutant concentration levels relative to standards or rough thresholds and for various locations should also be presented.

Land Development and the Natural Environment

3. Measuring Current Ambient Concentrations

Analytical procedures for water sampling and measurement of pollutant concentrations are now standardized and widely accepted.[38] Although the accuracy of the methods is generally high, the paucity of historical water quality data in most communities from which patterns and trends could be established is a severe limitation. This is especially significant, since ambient concentrations are dependent on water flow and volume, which vary a great deal with changes in rainfall intensity, duration, and spatial distribution in the watershed. Thus, unless a clear picture of statistical fluctuations in ambient levels has been established, it may be difficult to estimate the importance of the typically small changes in pollutant concentration caused by individual land developments or urbanization in general.

Sampling points should be carefully located so as to measure, as far as possible, the effects of specific point sources. For example, water upstream as well as downstream of point sources should be sampled. In addition, the timing of sample collection should be such as to capture the effect of stormwater runoff and variations in flow. Continuous monitoring stations are desirable, since by definition they record continuous fluctuations in ambient levels. However, they are extremely expensive and cannot be recommended for routine use. The use of aquatic organisms as indicators of water quality has also been tested.[39] By carefully selecting indicator species and measuring population characteristics, such as diversity, estimates of ambient concentrations for various pollutants can be made. Local communities should consider using a biological monitoring network as a supplement to chemical analysis.

4. Estimating Future Discharge Levels

Although the primary interest here is in evaluating individual developments, it is important to place individual development in the context of community-wide growth. For large projects whose development will span several years it is essential in estimating the impact to add the generated emissions to those expected from growth in general over the intervening years.

Thus, we will discuss estimation procedures for both individual developments and generalized growth.

a. Point Sources

Future emissions from point sources depend on both the magnitude of future growth and the per unit generation of pollutants. The discussion of growth projections in Part 1 applies equally well here. Although estimates based on considerations of population growth, economic expansion, and in- and outmigration are far superior to assumptions of no growth or constant growth, understanding of growth processes is still primitive and the ability to accurately predict the future is still very limited. Low and high estimates should be used to describe the envelope of probable future states.

In determining the quantity of pollutants generated by a given level of future development, rates of generation must be applied to the various types of development. Although standard rule-of-thumb generation rates have been used in numerous communities, the suggested "standards" vary considerably for the same type of development and are generally reported with no documentation of empirical testing.[40] For this reason it is suggested that the possibility of determining generation rates locally be explored. For sewage, local wastewater, sanitation, and/or water supply, departmental files may contain information which can be used to determine volumes generated per capita or per unit area for various land use categories (residential, commercial, and industrial) and subcategories (e.g., high-rise apartments, townhouse, single family detached; strip commercial, shopping center).[41] The volumes calculated for single or collections of individual developments are often multiplied by the concentration of specific constituent pollutants in the effluent from the local sewage treatment facility, modified, of course, by any planned changes in treatment.[42] Information on pollutants generated by individual industries will have to be obtained from an analysis of the types of operations to be undertaken. Since this information must be provided in order to

38. National Training Program, Water Program Operations, *Water Quality Studies Training Manual* (Cincinnati: EPA, May, 1974) (NTIS No. PB237586).

39. See, for example, Patrick Ruth, "Use of Algae, Especially Diatoms, in the Assessment of Water Quality" and John Cains, Jr., K. L. Dickson, and Guy Lanza, "Rapid Biological Monitoring System for Determining Aquatic Community Structure in Receiving Systems" in *Biological Methods for the Assessment of Water Quality* (American Society for Testing and Materials, 1973); and J. L. Wilhm and T. C. Davis, "Biological Parameters for Water Quality Criteria," *Bioscience* 18(9) (June, 1968): 477–81.

40. For example, the suggested coefficients for sewage effluent from residential developments range from 65 to 300 gallons per day per person. For an example of standards for various types of developments see E. E. Seelye, *Data Book for Civil Engineers: Volume One—Design* (New York: John Wiley and Sons, Inc., 1968). A useful review can also be found in Meta Systems, Inc., op. cit.

41. If the sanitation department does not maintain data on household/industry size and/or structural size, a sample can be drawn and this information obtained for those properties in the sample from such sources as the local assessor's office.

42. Estimated efficiencies for various levels of sewage treatment can be found in Hydroscience, Inc. and Mitre Corp., *Simplified Mathematical Modeling of Water Quality*, (Washington, D.C.: EPA, March, 1971) (NTIS No. PB-227866).

obtain a discharge permit under the WPCA, the local or state pollution control agency should be consulted.

b. Nonpoint Sources

As an urban area expands in areal extent, vegetated and agricultural land is converted to urban uses. Thus, the nonpoint source pollution impact of urbanization (or the construction of a single development) is the difference between stormwater runoff quality before and after development.

The newest subset of water models, known as runoff quality or hydrologic transport models, deals with various aspects of pollution from nonpoint sources.[43] Although the algorithms (i.e., the set of computation-determining equations) differ among the individual models, they are all based on modeling mechanisms of pollutant transport by means of overland and/or subsurface water flow.

The transport models also simulate the manner in which the pollutants interact with water. Nitrate, for example, is transported primarily in a soluble form, while sediment is mechanically moved. In addition, mechanisms of pollutant decay or transformation while in transport must also be simulated.

Of primary interest here are urban runoff quality models, although runoff from the land before development has occurred should be estimated in order to make "before and after" comparisons. These models estimate the build-up of street contaminants and the extent of flush-out by surface flow. Typically, declining daily accumulation up to a limiting value and an exponential removal are assumed.

Table 2-6 is a compilation and description of some of the more well known or widely used transport models. Again, data on costs and accuracy are scarce. This is especially true if accuracy is to be determined by using observations other than those used to calibrate the model, that is, if accuracy is defined by the ability to reproduce pollutants generated in untested watersheds or at future points in time.

As indicated, each of the models requires computer support. However, since the Corps of Engineers and EPA are active in providing a user support service for STORM and SWMM, respectively, a local community may be able to utilize these models without employing a consultant (assuming the community's computer capability is adequate).[44] HSP, on the other hand, can only be obtained through a limited but growing number of consulting firms.

5. Estimating Future Ambient Concentrations

a. General Considerations[45]

Once current and future emissions and current ambient concentrations are known or estimated, the stage is set for estimating the impact of proposed development on ambient water quality.

The problem is basically one of estimating the assimilative capacity of the hydrologic environment in question, a quantity which is exceedingly variable from one surface water body to another and from one time to another within the same body. Generally, the greater the volume and flow, the greater the assimilative capacity. Thus, fast-flowing streams and very large lakes have high capacities, the former because the regeneration rate is high (i.e., high flow rates increase the rate of reaeration), the latter because the dilution volume is large. However, lakes generally do not make desirable dumping grounds. Some tend to become thermally stratified, thus inhibiting mixing and allowing pollutants to accumulate in the strata.

Estuaries represent unique problems. The cyclical reversal of flow due to the inflow of fresh water and the action of the tides may trap pollutants and impede dispersal. On the other hand, the turbulence created by the opposing forces of flow plus the additional mixing caused by salt gradients may increase the rate of regeneration.

The living and nonliving systems interact to determine the quality of hydrologic environments. Some pollutants are relatively inert and are assimilated by water bodies through dilution and deposition in bottom muds. Others, however, proceed through a complex and protracted series of chemical and biochemical reactions, often being recycled and modified innumerable times. Figure 2-2 depicts some of the major biotic pathways for pollutants which are nutrients (primarily phosphate and nitrate). Water quality models can likewise be classified according to the level of complexity of the processes they represent. But even for the simpler models which treat only the relationship of dissolved oxygen (DO) to biological

---

43. The Universal Soil Loss Equation is probably the only simple technique available for estimating water quality from nonpoint sources. However, it is only applicable to sediment and to agricultural land use. See EPA, *Methods of Identifying and Evaluating the Nature and Extent of Non-Point Sources of Pollutants* (Washington, D.C.: EPA, October, 1973); and Midwest Research Institute, *User's Handbook for Assessment of Water Pollution from Non-Point Sources* (EPA, forthcoming).

44. Research recently undertaken by Meta Systems, Inc., of Cambridge, Mass., involved an attempt to combine modules from both STORM and SWMM into a model for predicting stormwater runoff quality and impact on stream quality. Practical experience in applying the final product to a range of developments and watersheds will be reported. See Meta Systems, Inc., op. cit.

45. For more information, see Hydroscience, Inc. and Mitre Corporation, op. cit.

Table 2-6. URBAN RUNOFF QUALITY MODELS
(FOR ESTIMATING DISCHARGES FROM NONPOINT SOURCES)

NAME	POLLUTANTS MODELED	COMPUTING REQUIREMENTS	INPUT	COST	OUTPUT	ACCURACY
Hydrocomp Simulation Program (HSP), water quality (surface runoff component)[a]	BOD, COD,[b] organic N, phosphate, total solids	Same as for HSP, Table 2-4 (970,000 word core storage required to run all hydrologic and quality modules)	See HSP in Table 2-4, initial dust and dirt loadings on pervious and impervious areas and upper loading limits	No values available	Runoff pollutant concentration during all runoff events as simulated continuously by HSP	No reported data on accuracy of pollutant concentrations
Storage treatment overflow, runoff model (STORM)[c]	Suspended solids, settleable solids, soluble P, Total N, BOD	Program available for IBM 360/50, UNIVAC 1108, and CDC 6600 or 7600 machines, core storage of 35,000 words required plus 1–5 additional tape/disk units	Hourly rainfall for 10–30 years, land use type, percent imperviousness, runoff storage and treatment characteristics, initial dust and dirt loads and upper loading limits	No values available	Runoff pollutant concentration during storm events (pollutographs) simulated from rainfall records; also, quality of runoff after storage and possible treatment if applicable	No reported data on accuracy of pollutant concentrations
Storm water management model (SWMM)[d]	BOD, suspended solids, settleable solids, BOD, N, P and grease	Core storage of 350,000 bytes is required plus additional tape/disk units; has been used on IBM 360/70, UNIVAC 1108, and CDC 6400/6600	Hourly rainfall for many years, subbasin characteristics (area, width, slope, ground cover) storm sewerage (slope, length, roughness and storage capacity), initial dust and dirt loadings and upper loading limits	Effort for input data preparation has been described as "moderate" and, although computing time is 2–3 times longer than for similar models, computing cost is less than $10 per run[e]	Runoff pollutant concentrations during storm events (pollutographs) for the whole basin or at specific points therein	Very low accuracy for suspended solids reported in one test.[f] No other data available

a. Hydrocomp, Inc., Hydrocomp Simulation Programming, *Mathematical Model of Water Quality Indices in Rivers and Impoundments* (Palo Alto, California: Hydrocomp, Inc., n.d.).

b. Chemical Oxygen Demand. This is an alternative but not exactly equivalent measure for BOD.

c. Water Resources Engineers, Inc., Corps of Engineers (Hydrologic Engineering Center), and City of San Francisco (Department of Public Works), *A Model for Evaluating Runoff Quality in Metropolitan Master Planning* (New York: American Society of Civil Engineers, April, 1974); and Hydrologic Engineering Center, *Urban Storm Water Runoff "STORM,"* Generalized Computer Program, 723-58-12520 (Davis, California: Army Corps of Engineers, May, 1974).

d. W. C. Huber, et al., *Storm Water Management Model User's Manual*, vol. II (Cincinnati, Ohio: EPA, Office of Research and Development, March, 1975).

e. D. P. Heeps and R. G. Mein, "Independent Comparison of Three Urban Runoff Models," *Journal of the Hydraulics Division, Proceeding of the American Society of Civil Engineers* 100 (HY7) (1974): 995–1009; and J. Marsalek, et al., "Comparative Evaluation of Three Urban Runoff Models," *Water Resources Bulletin* 11 (2), (1975): 306–28.

f. N. V. Colston, Jr., *Characterization and Treatment of Urban Land Runoff* (Cincinnati, Ohio: EPA, Office of Research and Development, December, 1974).

Water Quality and Quantity: Methodological Approaches

demand (BOD), the number of physical and biological processes involved may number as many as fourteen.

Water quality models can also be classified by other characteristics. The simpler models represent a hydrologic environment as a steady state system, thus ignoring the dynamic elements such as changes in water flows, solar insolation, and changes in pollutant discharge with time. Others are time-varying. Some models represent each event in the water quality system as a probabilistic event, while others are deterministic and assume that an event will always occur if the precursor conditions are satisfied. Models are also characterized by the type of water body to which they apply and the extent to which they are spatially disaggregated.

As with several other types of water models, the fundamental equation upon which most water quality models are based is the conservation of mass or material balance relationship:[46]

$$Q_i = N_i + S_i + A_i$$

where Q_i = the change in the quantity of pollutant i in a small volume of water over time

N_i = the net movement of i into or out of the small volume

S_i = the summation of sources and sinks (sources of removal) for i in the volume

A_i = the amount of i added directly into the small volume from outside (i.e., pollutant discharge)

The manner and extent to which the various terms are represented mathematically will determine each model's complexity and fidelity to the real world.

b. Surface Water Models

Here we are again faced with the difficult task of selecting among a profusion of water quality models developed in recent years. As before, the criteria of representativeness and popularity have been utilized for discrimination purposes. In addition, our preference has been for the better documented models.

A number of recent reviews can be used to supple-

ment the information presented here.[47] The review by J. W. Brown et al. is especially useful in describing the characteristics of individual models. Even here, through information on cost and accuracy is sparse.

Streeter-Phelps—A number of water quality models have been based on the Streeter-Phelps equation first published in 1925.[48] This is a highly simplified version of the conservation of mass equation; it considers only the DO depletion due to the discharge of BOD containing effluent (and subsequent bacterial oxidation) and the replenishment of DO through surface reaeration. The model is also time-invariant (i.e., steady-state) and deterministic, and assumes complete, instantaneous mixing. DO concentrations are computed as a function of distance downstream from the outfall. It is basically an easy and inexpensive, but highly simplistic and inaccurate, approach to estimating water quality.

Simplified EPA Model—This model depends on relatively gross or averaged input data, rules-of-thumb, generalized relationships between watershed parameters and water quality, and a "worst condition" philosophy.[49] For example, the degree of stream reaeration is approximated by describing the depth of water relative to the size of bottom rocks, and analyses are typically made for points near outfalls and during low flows—the locations and times of lowest quality.

Due to the simplicity and manual nature of the model it is very attractive. Unfortunately, it is limited in applicability and may be misleading. Only average relationships between watershed parameters and water quality are used and are assumed constant in time and throughout the water body. The EPA has made an effort to limit distribution to those who are either knowledgeable in water quality analysis or who have attended special training courses.

Auto-Qual—The EPA's Middle Atlantic Region III has developed a water quality model which can be

---

46. More formally:

$$V_j \frac{dC_{ij}}{dt} = J_{ij}A_j + V_jS_{ij} + W_{ij}$$

where: C_{ij} = the concentration of pollutant i in segment j

V_j = the volume of segment j

J_{ij} = the net flux of i in segment j

A_j = the interfacial area of segment j

S_{ij} = the summation of sources and sinks of i in j

W_{ij} = the direct input of i to j,

Furthermore, J depends on the diffusion of pollutant i and the advective transport of i as determined by the flow velocity.

47. J. W. Brown, et al., op. cit.; Martin E. Harper, *Assessment of Mathematical Models Used in Analysis of Water Quality in Streams and Estuaries* (Pullman, Wash.: Washington State Water Research Center, June, 1971); and Pio S. Lombardo, *Critical Review of Currently Available Water Quality Models,* (Palo Alto, Calif.: Hydrocomp, Inc. July, 1973) (NTIS No. PB-222265); and Systems Control, Inc., *Use of Mathematical Models for Water Quality Planning* (Olympia: Washington Department of Ecology, June, 1974)

48. H. W. Streeter and E. B. Phelps, "A Study of the Pollution and Natural Purification of the Ohio River," *Public Health Bulletin 146* (Washington, D.C.: Public Health Service, 1925). (reprinted by HEW, 1958). For a description of other DO-BOD models, see Harper, op. cit.

49. For documentation, see Hydroscience, Inc. and Mitre Corporation, op. cit.

run in either a steady-state or a quasi-dynamic mode.[50] The model has a hydraulic component which is applicable to any body of water (except stratified lakes or impoundments) whose length is considerably greater than its width (i.e., rivers and many estuaries). The model estimates values for nonreactive pollutants and DO-BOD.

The computations are based on the conservation of mass equation as applied to a series of points or junctions evenly dispersed along the direction of flow. Quality variables are estimated at each junction, while the hydraulic (flow) variables are used to characterize the transport of substances between junctions.

Although the dynamic mode of operation allows for changes in pollutant and quality indicator values over time, the use of average or net daily flows "smooths out" the rapid response of these variables due to storm surges or tidal oscillations. However, the loss in fine tuning is compensated for by the model's compatibility with EPA's Water Quality Information System.[51]

HSP, Water Quality Component—This is the set of water quality routines used in conjunction with the HSP hydrologic model described previously.[52] Rivers are segmented into an unlimited number of reaches and lakes or impoundments into several layers. The water quality within each segment is estimated on a continuous basis, using the conservation of mass equation as an organizing framework and laboratory estimates of the various reaction rates to predict values for individual pollutant or quality indicators.

The model is extremely comprehensive. In addition to several nonreactive pollutants, various forms of N and P, temperature, coliform bacteria, and microscopic plant and animal organisms can be modeled. The DO-BOD system is also represented comprehensively.

Since the model is run with a surface runoff component (see Table 2-6), the contribution to water pollution from urban and agricultural nonpoint sources can be modeled.

On balance, the HSP system including the water quality submodel appears to be a comprehensive and well-integrated package. However, no quantitative in-

formation on accuracy for the quality component is in hand, although initial applications on the Green River in Washington are reported to have produced "reasonable" results.[53] The cost of operation is also unknown, although it probably is in the neighborhood of that reported for the hydrologic component of HSP (up to $10 per acre for small watersheds, less for larger ones).

Other Models—A number of advanced modeling efforts during the 1970s have been undertaken as part of the International Biological Program and as part of EPA's research and development. The ongoing EPA-sponsored projects are listed in Lombardo's review. Although most of these modeling studies are of a purely research nature, significant advances in the understanding of hydrologic and ecologic processes should ultimately result in improved operational models. Analysts involved in water-related planning and evaluation should contact the sponsoring agencies for descriptive and evaluative information as it becomes available.

c. Groundwater Models

Groundwater hydrologists have been involved with estimating the capacity of underground sources for several decades. The quantitative modeling of groundwater quality, on the other hand, has received only slightly more than passing attention.

The most dominant factor in explaining the non-aqueous components of underground water is the mineral composition of the aquifer (i.e., the water-bearing strata of rock or unconsolidated earth material). Since the movement of groundwater is often extremely slow (perhaps only a few hundred feet a year), the mineral content is usually high despite the slow dissolution rate of most minerals.

Human factors are increasingly important. Since surface water and groundwater are most realistically viewed as an interconnected system, degradation of rivers and lakes can also lead to groundwater deterioration. Pollutants from cropland, septic tank fields, and sanitary landfills are additional sources of degradation.

The degree to which a potential source will be polluting is largely dependent on the ground material overlying the aquifer and through which the pollutant-bearing water must pass. Properly managed, a liquid waste disposal site such as a septic tank leach field can be used to recycle nutrients with little or no net production of N or P. Soil particles are also effective in destroying bacteria and viruses. Improperly man-

50. Robert L. Crim and Norman L. Lovelace, *Auto-Qual Modelling System,* Technical Report No. 54 (Annapolis, Md.: EPA, March, 1973) (NTIS No. PB-227 032). EPA has developed alternative water quality models as well (e.g., HARO 3 and SNSM).

51. For more information contact the Monitoring and Data Support Division, Office of Air and Water Programs, EPA, Washington, D.C.

52. Hydrocomp, Inc., *Hydrocomp Simulation Programming Mathematical Model of Water Quality Indices in Rivers and Impoundments* (Palo Alto, Calif.: Hydrocomp, Inc., n.d.).

53. Lombardo, op. cit.

aged or operated in areas with inadequate soil characteristics (e.g., too fast or too slow percolation, too wet, too shallow), liquid or solid waste disposal sites can be severely polluting. Once polluted, aquifers may take years or decades to regenerate owing to their slow rates of flow. Techniques for estimating groundwater quality must consequently consider both the overlying unsaturated material and the water-filled aquifer, as well as direct communication between surface and groundwater.

Unfortunately, the movement of aqueous pollutants in media other than surface water is still not well enough understood to support the development of operational models. One of the most ambitious attempts to further the research in this area was recently undertaken by investigators from the University of Florida.[54] They coupled a surface water model, an unsaturated zone model, and a groundwater model in an attempt to simulate the entire hydrologic regime for a small Florida lake basin. Unfortunately, their set of models could not be validated due to data limitations.

In the absence of operational predictive techniques, estimates of causal relationships must rest on inferential evidence. Groundwater quality (as measured from well samples) should be correlated with land development activities and associated soil characteristics to the extent this is possible.[55] The relationships generated will obviously be general and approximate.

Most new developments should not present additional groundwater problems, since the majority will be serviced by sanitary sewers. In fact, they may cause an improvement in quality if older housing units with septic tanks are being replaced or if agricultural land is being developed.

A unique groundwater problem faced by communities in coastal areas is that of salt water intrusion. As this is a problem primarily related to water consumption it will be discussed in the next section, Water Supply.

d. Comparison and Summary

Various aspects of the previously described water quality models are summarized and compared in Table 2-7. These represent only a limited, albeit representative, sampling of extant models.

As with the other water models discussed in Part 2, those which are based on or simulate the fundamental

ecological interactions of living organisms and their environment should deliver more accurate results. Thus, the more complex models should provide more reliable predictions. Although the available data on accuracy tends to bear this out, much more extensive testing in a variety of lakes, streams, and estuaries is needed. The same can be said for operating costs. In some cases we have even experienced resistance on the part of the model developer to divulging whatever cost and accuracy documentation exists.

Even if reliable operating cost data were available, the question of costs for model start-up, validation, and calibration would remain. Lombardo reports that these costs for the HSP (quality component) model were in the neighborhood of $50,000 and $100,000 for Denver and Seattle, respectively.[56] Thus, any community which contemplates employing a water model should be prepared to expend the necessary and considerable funds for preparation. The justification for the utilization of any model should be made on its long-run benefits, in order to capture economies to be realized from long-term application.

6. Estimating the Number of People Affected

The number of people engaged in various water-related activities can be approximated using either direct observation survey techniques or written/telephone surveys of likely users. More detailed discussions of recreational survey techniques can be found in other references.[57]

7. Estimating Monetary Benefits

If the estimated water quality impacts of land development appear to be substantial in terms of the number of people affected and/or the types of other developments impacted, the local government may want to estimate the monetary value of the clean water benefits being reduced (or the "costs" of the additional deterioration). The principal approaches include the following:

(1) Willingness to pay—determining how much the affected individuals or firms are willing to pay for clean water.

(2) Expenditure method—determining the expenditures made by those using clean water.

(3) Cost method—determining the cost to ameliorate the pollution-caused damage.

54. Armando I. Perez, et al., *A Water Quality Model for a Conjunctive Surface-Groundwater System* (Washington, D.C.: EPA, May, 1974) (EPA-600/5-74-013).

55. In the case of confined aquifers with specific recharge areas, detailed knowledge of the location and nature of the recharge areas is a prerequisite for any correlation-type analysis.

56. Lombardo, op. cit.

57. See, for example, The Urban Institute, *How Effective Are Your Community Recreation Services?* (Washington, D.C.: Bureau of Outdoor Recreation, Department of the Interior, April, 1973).

Table 2-7. ASSESSMENT OF WATER QUALITY MODELS

NAME	TYPE OF WATER BODY	POLLUTANTS MODELED	COMPUTING REQUIREMENTS	INPUT	COST	OUTPUT	ACCURACY AND COMMENTS
Streeter-Phelps	Streams and reservoirs	DO-BOD	Hand calculations although a computer can greatly expand number of locations at which values are calculated	Effluent content of point sources, velocity of flow, and ambient DO concentrations	Very low if used manually	DO concentrations as a function of distance downstream from source	Low due to the simplifying assumption used in the calculations
EPA's Simplified Model	Streams and estuaries	Chloride, dissolved solids, total P, bacteria suspended solids, DO-BOD	Hand calculations	Effluent content of point sources, average and low flow velocity, general type of flow, channel geometry and slope, ambient water quality	Fairly low	Pollutant and indicator values as a function of location in stream/estuary	Less than for computerized models (EPA cautions against its use by those unfamiliar with water quality analysis)
Auto-Qual	Streams and elongated estuaries	DO-BOD based on both carbon and N compounds, suspended solids, temperature, chloride	Central core storage requirements are 105,000–115,000 bytes; has been run on IBM 370	Flow and velocity, channel configuration at each junction, effluent content of point sources, water temperature, rates of DO uptake by sediments, and production by photosynthesis	No figures available	Pollutant and indicator values as a function of location in stream/estuary and of time	Theoretically higher than the simple methods, although complex and rare events, such as storm surges, not represented well
HSP, water quality	Streams, lakes, impoundments	Dissolved solids, temperature, bacteria, DO-DOB based on both carbon and N compounds, phytoplankton, zooplankton, benthal organisms, various forms of N and P	See HSP Table 2-6	Effluent content of point sources. (See Table 2-4 for a description of the HSP nonpoint source component.) See HSP Tables 2-4 and -6 for other input requirements	Approximately $10/acre for small watersheds, less for large ones in addition to cost of the other HSP components	Pollutant and indicator values as a function of stream estuary location and of time	Subjectively estimated as "reasonable" and from theoretical point of view, relatively high; HSP is a comprehensive program so this submodel can be coupled with surface runoff and hydrologic submodels

(4) Local economy method—determining the effect in terms of reduced output.

(5) Property value method—determining the effect of clean water in terms of increased property values.

These methods are obviously not completely or perhaps even partially substitutable. Thus, results obtained by using one are not necessarily comparable to those obtained by using another. This fact, plus the difficulties involved with deriving reliable data regardless of the method employed, makes an economic analysis of water quality impacts a formidable task.

Discussions of the conceptual and technical problems, as well as examples of local studies, can be found in the references cited. The EPA is actively engaged in benefit research at the present time. Presumably, improvements in methodology as well as estimates of benefits (or damages) on a regional scale will be forthcoming.

C. IMPACTS ON WATER CONSUMPTION

Concern for the impact of new development on community water supplies, by and large, involves a consideration of quantities available and quantities consumed. In addition, problems of replenishment and salt water contamination are of concern for a small but growing number of communities.

1. Impact Measures

Following are suggested measures for both the quantity and quality aspects of the problem:[58]

Water Quantity

1. Change in the total duration and/or severity of expected shortages and the number of people affected.

OR

2. Change in the likelihood of a water shortage and the number of people affected.

Water Quality

1. Change in the concentration of those drinking water constituents that are important to health and the number of people affected.[59]

The first measure of water quantity best expresses the various aspects of the impact on man and is thus preferred. Measure 2 is the fallback measure. It is based on a largely qualitative rating of "likelihood" and is thus much less difficult to use.

The drinking water quality measure is quite similar to those suggested for water pollution. The concern here is for those health- or aesthetic- (color, odor, taste, clarity) related pollutants generated by the new development which may appear in the community or neighboring households' water supply, assuming the same level of purification. (Increased costs for purification necessitated by the development should be considered in its fiscal impact analysis.)[60] The discussion of standards and their use which appears in the water pollution chapter applies here as well.

2. Measuring/Estimating Impacts on Storage and Yield

Any analysis of impacts on water supply should consider existing and potential supplies. These are most conveniently divided into surface water and groundwater categories.

a. Surface Water

In many ways the estimation of water supply is analogous to flood prediction. In this case, though, the rare event to be predicted is low flow (or low volume) rather than peak flow. Thus, the general discussion and many of the specific techniques for estimating flood events apply here as well.

A river/reservoir system introduces a number of complicating factors, especially if the reservoir is used for purposes in addition to drinking water storage (e.g., flood control, irrigation, power generation, recreation) and if flows in the drainage system are influenced by water rights. Detailed discussions of both conceptual and technical aspects of the problem can be found in selected Corps of Engineers publications and many hydrologic texts.[61]

Where the probabilities of various low flows or storage volumes have been determined (i.e., the two, five, ten, fifty, 100, 500 year low flow/volume), the impacts can also be estimated probabilistically. The expected water use from the new development is added to the current use levels during the low flow

---

58. An alternative measure is "the amount of water to be consumed relative to the budgeted amount" where a budget has been prepared for the community. See Part 2, III, Section A for a more detailed discussion.

59. For a specification of drinking water standards, see HEW, *Public Health Drinking Water Standards, Revised,* (Washington, D.C.: Government Printing Office, 1962).

60. For a detailed discussion of the issues and methods involved in fiscal impact analysis, see Thomas Muller, *Fiscal Impact Analysis* (Washington, D.C.: The Urban Institute, 1975).

61. See, for example, Leo R. Beard, *Methods for Determination of Safe Yield and Compensation Water from Storage Reservoirs,* Technical Paper No. 3 (Davis, Calif.: Army Corps of Engineers, Hydrologic Engineering Center, 1965) and Linsley, Kohler, and Paulhus, op. cit.

period (obtained from the local water utility), and this new value is compared with the various low flows. The proposed development could then be said to cause a shortage during a five-year or greater low flow, for example (or a shortage with occurrence probability of 20 percent in any one year). Where adequate data on low flow frequency is not available or cannot be computed, qualitative descriptors such as "most likely" or "unlikely" will have to be used.

The duration and severity of shortages would appear to be more difficult to estimate. A rough estimate of duration could possibly be based on historical records of low flow duration for the various degrees of low flow. Severity could be expressed as the possible consequences of a shortage (e.g., no lawn-sprinkling, no swimming in pools, rationing of drinking water). Local water utility personnel may have useful data if past shortages have occurred. The experience of other communities in similar situations may also be useful.

b. Groundwater

The problem here is conceptually the same as that for surface water. Total inflows, outflows, and storage should be estimated with and without the land development in question. More realistically, "safe yield" from an aquifer is measured against demand with and without the new development.

"Safe yield" may be defined in several ways:[62]

1. *Maximum sustained yield*—the maximum *rate* at which water can be withdrawn perennially from a particular source.

2. *Permissive sustained yield*—the maximum *rate* at which water can economically and legally be withdrawn perennially from a particular source for beneficial purposes without bringing about some undesired result, such as salt water intrusion.

3. *Maximum mining yield*—the total *volume* of water in storage that can be extracted and utilized.

4. *Permissive mining yield*—the maximum *volume* of water in storage that can economically and legally be extracted and used for beneficial purposes, without bringing about some undesired result.

Most communities are interested in maintaining "permissive sustained yield," since this implies perpetual availability. Unfortunately, the calculation of permis-

sive sustained yield does not involve the simple comparison of inflows with outflows, even assuming that the characteristics of all recharge and discharge areas and the total amount of withdrawal were known. The mechanisms of underground water transmission are numerous and complex, and without complete and detailed information on the local hydrologic regime estimates of the effects of additional withdrawal remain of uncertain validity.[63]

This is not to say that approximations cannot be and are not made. By tracing the relative changes in precipitation, groundwater level, total withdrawal (usually from well logs), and natural discharge (usually by factoring out the surface and interflow[64] contributions to stream flow records), estimates of permissive sustained yield can be made.[65] Due to the delayed response of groundwater systems and the resulting difficulty in ascertaining when permissive sustained yield has been exceeded, the accuracy of this approach is difficult to specify.

Once the yield has been determined the impact of a proposed development is estimated by adding expected new demand to current demand and comparing the total to the estimated yield. However, since aquifer systems may be related to rainfall in a way that is difficult to understand, and since safe yield is difficult to determine, it is unlikely that the impact can be expressed in probabilistic terms, at least at this time.

In addition to the consumptive demand created by the new development, its location with respect to groundwater recharge areas should also be considered. These are areas where geologic structures allow precipitation to reach underground reservoirs. Most aquifers have rather extensive recharge areas, but for those confined by impermeable rock layers the areas of surface/underground communication may be limited and must be protected from coverage by impermeable materials. The local planner must depend on geologists from local, state, or federal agencies to conduct the requisite surveys of bedrock formations and overlying unconsolidated earth material from which the recharge areas can be mapped.

3. Measuring/Estimating Salt Water Intrusion

Salt water movement into fresh water aquifers is a phenomenon which may occur in coastal areas due to

---

62. American Society of Civil Engineers, *Groundwater Basin Management*, Manual of Engineering Service, No. 40 (Washington, D.C., 1961).

63. A brief description of an attempt to couple a surface water, an unsaturated zone, and a groundwater model appears in the section on water pollution, Part 2, I(B).

64. "Interflow" is water which flows under but close to the surface and is not considered part of the groundwater.

65. See Patrick A. Domenico, *Concepts and Models in Groundwater Hydrology* (New York: McGraw-Hill, 1972).

FIGURE 2-6
AN ILLUSTRATION OF SALTWATER INTRUSION

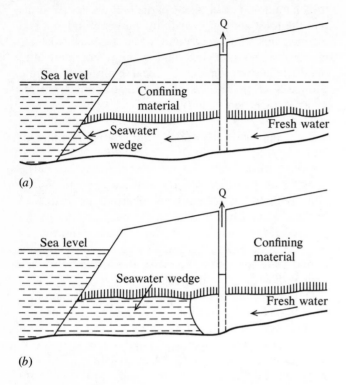

(a)

(b)

SOURCE: Adapted from Patrick A. Domenico, *Concepts and Models in Groundwater Hydrology* (New York: McGraw-Hill Inc., 1972). (Used with permission of McGraw-Hill Book Co.)

NOTE: The vertical shaft represents a well and Q, the withdrawal of fresh water. The height of freshwater in the well represents the pressure due to the freshwater in the aquifer.

excessive fresh water withdrawal. This is illustrated in Figure 2-6.

The Domenico text contains an excellent description of the phenomenon and a discussion of various fluid dynamic-based methods of quantifying it.[66] A few examples of applications are also included, although a discussion of results is lacking.

In the absence of information on the accuracy of specific analytical techniques, a qualitative approach is justified. Where the occurrence of intrusions has been observed it is safe to conclude that additional withdrawal will be exacerbating. However, the effects may possibly be ameliorated if additional corrective measures are taken, such as:[67]

1. A reduction or rearrangement of pumping patterns elsewhere.

2. Artificial fresh water recharge of the aquifer.

3. Establishment of a pumping trough along the coast, thus limiting the intrusion to the trough area.

4. Formation of a pressure ridge along the coast.

5. Construction of a subsurface barrier impermiable to salt water.

Details of these approaches can be found in the reference cited.

66. Ibid.

67. H. O. Banks and R. C. Richter, "Sea Water Intrusion Into Groundwater Basins Bordering the California Coast and Inland Bays," *Transactions of the American Geophysical Union* 34, (1953): 575–82.

III. CONCLUSIONS AND RECOMMENDATIONS

A. PLANNING VERSUS PROJECT REVIEW

The relationship between planning and project review has emerged as one of the key considerations in an impact evaluation program. Planning can greatly facilitate the evaluation of certain types of impacts resulting from individual developments. On the other hand, large-scale planning does not capture the idiosyncrasies of single projects, and the approximate relationships between impacts and development characteristics used to produce the plan may not be terribly accurate. These and other related points will now be elaborated on for each of the impact areas.

For those hydrologic considerations which are relatively insensitive to development design characteristics (e.g., sewage generation) the planning approach is decidedly superior. The review at the proposal stage then becomes almost perfunctory—for example, does adequate treatment capacity exist? For water-related project outputs which are more sensitive to design features the ability to minimize hydrologic impact through long-range planning is considerably reduced. Stormwater runoff, for example, is a function of landscaping and retention facilities (e.g., ponds) as well as the extent of impervious ground cover and the degree of sewerization. Thus, it is difficult to develop zoning classifications based on a single generalizable factor, such as impervious ground cover. A rather detailed site plan review is required in order to ascertain the actual volume and rate of runoff for various types of storms.

Impervious ground cover can be used, however, as an early warning indicator or target in comprehensive plans. That is, allowable degrees of "percent impervious ground cover" can be specified for different areas within a watershed based on acceptable or desirable degrees of flooding. (One of the simpler stream flow techniques could be used for this purpose.) These values can then be incorporated in comprehensive plans as targets. Once the target had been reached for an area the runoff-related problems in the vicinity would have to be investigated in greater detail, and development proposals would have to be carefully scrutinized on an individual basis before new development would be allowed.[1] A similar analysis for all hydrologic impact areas appears in Table 2-8.

It is clear that the planning activities outlined for water pollution of surface waters (sewage, industrial effluents, and, to some extent, stormwater runoff) are being or will be assumed by the special area-wide planning organizations as established by the WPCA. Existing city, metropolitan area, or county planning agencies are expected to cooperate with these special planning organizations and to implement the plans developed. Although individual local governments are responsible for flood plain planning and control, the process is controlled by HUD through the Flood Disaster Protection Act. Development outside the

1. A pervasive problem which typically attends the application of land use controls is the lack of public authority to require detailed site plans from developers at the point of variance or rezoning request. This argues strongly for the inclusion of quantifiable indicators in the general plan as the best way to control negative impacts. The higher the correlation between the indicator and the impact, the better. Thus, in the runoff example, "percent impervious ground cover" is superior to "housing density."

Table 2-8. LEVELS OF ANALYSIS APPLIED TO THE VARIOUS HYDROLOGIC IMPACT AREAS

	PLANNING	PROJECT REVIEW
Flooding	Specification of allowable development intensity based on watershed characteristics and expressed in terms of generalizable indicators such as "percent impervious ground cover" and "percent of the area served by storm sewers"	Assessment of (1) ground cover and sewerization variables, (2) mitigating design features such as retention ponds, and (3) potential for localized flooding problems
Water pollution: Sewage	(1) Specification of allowable effluent volumes based on hydrologic characteristics of receiving water body, uses to which it is subject, and degree of treatment to be used; (2) possible allocation of remaining volume to future land use categories	Assessment of available treatment capacity
Industrial	Same as for sewage plus specification of additional treatment levels of unusual pollutants	Same as for sewage plus assessment of special processing facilities if appropriate
Stormwater runoff	Specification of allowable development intensity based on watershed characteristics and general runoff loadings for development types, again expressed in terms of generalizable indicators such as "percent impervious ground cover"	Assessment of (1) ground cover variable, (2) mitigating design features such as retention ponds, and (3) planned management practices such as street cleaning
Water consumption	Specification of maximum flow available for consumption (and other uses) and possible allocation of remaining supply among future land use categories	Assessment of (1) available supply and (2) localized problems such as salt water intrusions or reduced availability of water for those in immediate vicinity

floodplain but within the watershed is not covered, however. Variance applications for locations within the flood plain must also be evaluated. In the area of water consumption, long-range planning is often conducted by the Corps of Engineers, especially if drinking water is provided by river regulation or impoundment.

It would thus appear that a complementary planning/project review system could be designed and implemented. Where planning is based on the specification of targets, reviews of individual projects could be significantly simplified.

Most plans, of course, do not use the target concept. Even worse, some comprehensive plans have been developed with very little regard for the consequences of development to water quality and quantity. In these cases the local government may wish to evaluate these or other alternative plans for hydrologic impacts. The impact measures we have suggested would seem to be applicable to this type of evaluation as well.

In selecting techniques and methods to be used in computing values for the measures, we have tried to offer some general guidance.[2] To obtain target figures for use in comprehensive plans or to evaluate existing plans the simpler and presumably less accurate large-scale techniques are probably adequate. On the other

hand, where a watershed or other community subarea is being developed quite rapidly and potential consequences may be quite severe, it may be preferable in the long run to utilize a complex model to specify more accurate targets. For evaluations of individual developments the selection of simple versus complex methods should be based on the size of the development (or more accurately, the potential severity of its impacts) and the ultimate cost of evaluation. Even for very large developments, the cost of using complex, computer-assisted models may not be justified. However, their application to watershed-wide evaluations—in a planning analysis—may be justified on the basis that the specification of accurate targets may greatly reduce the need for individual evaluations.

Although we have not been able to provide sufficient cost data for the various methods reviewed, we have tried to indicate which techniques could be used on an "in-house" basis, which ones require computer support, which ones would probably necessitate the use of a consultant, and which ones are supported to some extent by the federal government through user services.

B. SPECIFIC RECOMMENDATIONS AND CONCLUSIONS

1. Local governments should consider specifying runoff-, emission-, and water consumption-related "targets" in their land use or zoning

---

2. Additional assistance in writing requests for proposals and in negotiating with contractors for the use of water models can be found in Systems Control, Inc., op. cit.

plans, based on analyses of flooding hazards, desired levels of water quality, and available water supply. At a minimum, evaluations of individual developments would simply estimate future levels of such things as imperviousness, emissions, and consumption associated with each development. These values would then be added to the running sum kept for all developments and compared with the targets.

2. Where developments will cause targets to be exceeded or where special localized problems are likely, (or simply as a check on the assumptions used in preparing the plan), detailed evaluations of individual proposals should be undertaken.

3. The detailed evaluations should utilize the preferred measures suggested here (or similar ones) where possible, and the fallback measures at other times. In choosing between the measures, the potential magnitude of impact and the time and funding available for evaluation will probably be the most important considerations.

4. A variety of both simple and complex techniques exist for establishing the relationships between land development and flooding/water quality on a watershed-wide basis (e.g., for specifying targets). Calculations of surface water supply can be made with techniques similar to those used for flood hazard calculations. The more complex techniques are presumably more accurate than the simpler ones.

5. For conducting the detailed evaluations of individual developments the same watershed-wide techniques can be used. "Before and after" effects are calculated by using the technique to estimate flooding/water quality with and without the development.

6. Localized effects are estimated using detailed engineering procedures and/or experts in the appropriate disciplines.

7. Every technique reviewed needs additional verification. Assessment of accuracy for most of the models has been based on theoretical considerations or on extremely limited validation.

PART 3
WILDLIFE AND
VEGETATION

I. INTRODUCTION AND BACKGROUND

A. HUMAN WELFARE

Although concern for the environmental effects of urbanization has frequently focused on air and water pollutants, public interest in other environmental-related problems has been increasing. We now recognize that many plant and animal species are facing national and global extinction at an alarming rate. On a more local scale, natural areas rich in common plant species and frequently providing habitat for large numbers of interesting forms of wildlife are rapidly disappearing. The concern here extends beyond first-hand experiences with wildlife and vegetation. Some people feel a moral commitment to furthering the existence of all living things. In this sense the loss of any natural area or wildlife habitat is important, at least for those who hold these values. At the very least, the maintenance of natural life forms in developed areas permits people to become better acquainted with natural processes which then places them in a better position to make decisions related to environmental matters.

Although the primary subject of this part of the report is man's enjoyment of wildlife and vegetation and the way land development may affect the opportunity for such enjoyment, we should not lose sight of the fact that the presence of natural areas is intimately related to air quality, water quality, flooding, and noise. On a local, regional, and even global scale, the extent and distribution of vegetated areas may have pronounced climatic effects which in turn will affect temperature, humidity, precipitation, and wind

patterns. Vegetation may also help to cleanse air of certain pollutants and is known to have a significant effect on the quantity and quality of stormwater runoff. Certain types of plants may also serve as noise barriers. These and other roles which natural areas play in maintaining high levels of environmental quality are discussed further in other parts of this report.

Estimating impacts on man's opportunity to enjoy wildlife and vegetation will consist in large part of estimating how the abundance of various species will change. However, another important factor to consider is the value of this type of experience to the local population. In communities where residents value the nonmanmade environment highly this impact area should receive additional weight in decisions on land development. It must also be recognized, though, that some types of vegetation and wildlife in urban areas are undesirable or even a health hazard and that *some* people dislike many forms of natural life.[1] In these situations decision makers must face the unenviable task of balancing the desires of a subset of the current population with those of other subsets and with the interests of future populations.

---

1. See the results of an attitude survey conducted in Waterloo, Ontario, in Ann Dagg, "Reactions of People to Urban Wildlife," *Proceedings of a Symposium on Wildlife in an Urbanizing Environment* (Springfield, Mass.: Cooperative Extension Service, November 27–29, 1973) [hereafter cited as *Proceedings of Symposium on Wildlife*].

B. FUNDAMENTAL ECOLOGICAL PRINCIPLES[2]

Ecology is most generally the study of the *interrelationships* of organisms to one another and to the environment. All living organisms are seen as existing with their living and nonliving environments in a state of *dynamic equilibrium,* drawing from them sustenance (food and water), shelter, and the opportunity for reproduction and, in turn, being used by other components of the system. Within this dynamic equilibrium structure each organism has a position or *niche* determined by the function it performs. The most common and important types of organisms are the following: food producers (green plants); plant eaters (herbivores); first and second level meat eaters (carnivores); plant and meat eaters (omnivores); parasites; dead animal and plant eaters (scavengers); bacteria, yeasts, molds, and fungi which decompose dead organic material into basic chemicals (decomposers); and microorganisms which convert nutrients into compounds usable by green plants (transformers).

The complex set of interactions among the consumed and the consumers (sometimes known as the *food web*) can be characterized by the flow of nutrients and energy. *Nutrients* (water, minerals, and organic compounds) are continuously *recycled* by an ecosystem. *Energy* flow, on the other hand, is *pyramidal*. That is, the simple green plants which are the basic food producers are very efficient at converting the sun's energy into food. From this level on up the pyramid of prey and predator relationships there is a loss of useful energy at every step. By the time food reaches man at the top of the pyramid large quantities of energy have been used in its production.

As a result of the interdependence of ecosystem components, plants and animals tend to associate in a complementary fashion. Thus, ecologists speak of *associations* (groups of species) and *communities* (groups of associations). The type of biotic community found in any area at any given point in time is dependent on soil, moisture, and climatic characteristics as well as the biotic history of the area (what lived there in the past).

This leads to another fundamental ecological concept, that of *succession*. A biotic community changes over time, generally progressing toward an assemblage of climax species. In theory, the climax life forms which occur under a given set of environmental conditions will remain, unless disturbed by outside influences. However, it is often difficult to predict

which species will be present during the climax stage. In addition, climax associations are rarely observed, since succession is frequently interrupted by human intervention and such natural disturbances as floods, fires, droughts, and insect invasions.

Tolerance and *adaptation* are other key concepts. Individual plant and animal species are known to tolerate a range of environmental conditions. In some situations they have even been known to adapt to conditions far beyond the normal range.

Ecologists usually characterize an ecosystem by such features as its productivity (i.e., the amount and rate of living matter or biomass produced), by the types and magnitudes of energy and chemical flows, and by the abundance and variety of plants and animals. *Diversity* is the term used to describe the latter and is generally considered to be the best indicator of ecosystem stability. A diverse ecosystem is one which can withstand numerous perturbations because many of its species are at least partially substitutable. Thus, elimination of certain components will not destroy the entire system.

The implications of these principles for impact evaluation are several. First, the interconnectedness of the ecological system means that secondary and tertiary effects are the rule rather than the exception. What at first appears to be the rather innocuous primary impact of land development (e.g., the mowing of fields or the dredging of a pond) may result in an unexpected and dramatic reduction or increase in a particular species (e.g., loss of field birds or waterfowl).

A second but related point is that disturbances which affect organisms located near the bottom of the energy pyramid generally have far-reaching effects in terms of impact on other organisms. DDT is a case in point. Small organisms ingested and concentrated the chemical until levels toxic to susceptible bird species have been reached in insects and other prey.

Thirdly, impacts should also be viewed as changes in the direction or rate of natural succession. In this sense, "environmental preservation" may be a misleading term. Lakes, for example, often become overfertilized and fill in as part of natural processes, although the time scales are usually quite long. If the current lake condition is the desired state, then environmental manipulation may have to be undertaken. Developments which interfered with the natural processes of lake aging would then be considered to have favorable impacts.

Finally, the response to a given disturbance should be estimated with regard to the ability of many species to adapt to new environments. Ideal and tolerable environments may differ substantially. Squirrels and raccoons are good examples of wild-

---

2. For further information see any standard text on ecology, such as, Robert L. Smith, *Ecology and Field Biology* (New York: Harper & Row, 1974). A less technical discussion of general environmental principles is contained in Kenneth E. F. Watt, *Principles of Environmental Science* (New York: McGraw-Hill Book Company, 1973).

Land Development and the Natural Environment

life species which have adapted quite well to man's presence.

C. DEFINITIONS AND TERMS

The following terms will be used throughout the remainder of the discussion:

1. *Wildlife* is a collective term which refers to all nondomestic animals of a size to be seen and appreciated by the public. We have extended the usual definition to include fish.

2. *Open Spaces* are areas of the natural or nonbuilt-up environment, including forests, grasslands, deserts, agricultural land, parks, lawns, and bodies of surface water (with emphasis on their living constituents).

3. *Natural Areas* are open spaces which are relatively unmanaged.

4. *Wildlife Habitats* are areas which provide food, shelter, and general living space for wildlife.

The term "natural area" is used here in a slightly more general way than it appears in some of the literature. That is, "natural area" is used to designate any unmanaged "open space," regardless of quality, while elsewhere it frequently means a high-quality vegetated area of special scientific interest. On the other hand, "open space" usually includes manmade spaces as well as natural ones. Although "wildlife habitat" includes either open spaces or manmade environments which will support a wildlife population, the more desirable species are associated with open spaces.

II. METHODOLOGICAL APPROACHES

Although common and well-accepted techniques exist for characterizing existing natural areas and habitats, the estimation of impacts on wildlife and vegetation from proposed land development rests largely on inference. Simple techniques analogous to simple air or water pollution estimation models are not yet available. The explanation lies in man's limited knowledge of a very complex subject. In addition, standards (analogous to air and water quality standards) against which impact estimates could be gauged do not exist. Instead, the impacts are viewed in the context of how highly local residents (or in the case of rare and endangered species, state and national citizens) value wildlife and vegetation.

A. MEASURES AND INDICES

Measures of impact on wildlife and vegetation should reflect changes in the amount and kind of vegetation and wildlife added or lost. As indicated, quantitative estimates of change are difficult to make. Consequently, a simpler alternative measure is suggested together with the preferred one:

1. Change in the relative abundance and variety of vegetation and wildlife expressed as:
   (a) change in the number(s) of rare or endangered species.
   (b) change in the population size and diversity of common species (number of species, amount of cover, and possibly a diversity index score).

OR

2. Change in the extent and quality of vegetation (including the number of mature trees added or lost) and wildlife habitat (quality rating by animal type).

The first measure most directly reflects the number of species added or lost and is thus preferred. Diversity and abundance are the key variables.[1] The second measure is obviously simpler and should be used where detailed surveys of vegetation and wildlife are not feasible. The change in extent is expressed as the number of acres of open space. The impact on wildlife is inferred from changes in the quantity of habitat of a given quality.

The terms "quality" and "diversity" imply that rating scales and indices are to be considered. As with the pollution indices, these assessment schemes are designed to combine many factors into one or a few numerical scores. Unlike air and water pollution, however, there are no commonly accepted standards against which the scores can be compared. A more detailed discussion of rating scales and indices appears in the following section.

Communities should also consider measuring local residents' attitudes toward, and perceptions of, wildlife and vegetation. Questions on this subject could perhaps be included in a general survey of residents'

---

1. Other characteristics of vegetation can also be measured, such as cover (a product of abundance and massiveness), density, dominance (relative areal extent of various species), and productivity (the rate of production of living matter). Diversity is probably a better indicator of changes which will affect the experience of observing vegetation and wildlife.

perceptions and attitudes. For additional discussions of issues and methods of estimating citizen perceptions in the context of a social impact analysis, see a companion report in this series.[2]

A further consideration is the degree of public access to the areas affected. Total public access would imply that the "clientele group" is the community at large. However, accessibility is usually related to distance of residence from the area in question. It may thus be useful to identify those people within walking distance separately from those beyond for publicly accessible areas. For private areas the clientele group can be more accurately determined. Even for private areas, however, spillover affecting persons other than those with access to the area can occur. This is especially true for bird habitat areas or for private areas which are visible to a larger audience.

Consideration should also be given to the way evaluation results are presented to the decision makers. Analysis of impacts on open space readily lends itself to map presentation. "Before" and "after" development maps reflecting open space changes would appear to communicate the information well. The location of natural areas could be identified on these maps together with their quality ratings (if the preferred measure is used). If species lists have been compiled, a tabular presentation of impact is probably most suitable, as illustrated in Figure 3-1.

B. MEASURING/ESTIMATING CURRENT CONDITIONS

This section discusses ways to inventory predevelopment conditions in and around the proposed development site. This is necessary in order to determine the amount and the quality of the resource to be impacted.

Although the need to utilize experts in the various substantive areas throughout the impact evaluation process has been noted in other parts of this report, it is especially noteworthy in the areas of wildlife and vegetation. There is no substitute for expertise in identifying the various species of plants and animals. What follows, then, is a discussion of key factors which may suggest the type and degree of impact and, to a lesser extent, of techniques used by biologists to characterize natural environments. The latter is included so that the reader may develop an appreciation for the detailed types of ecological analyses which are frequently required to develop quantitative estimates of impact.

1. Vegetation

Natural vegetation is important both as habitat for wildlife and as a resource itself. The latter, in turn, can be considered from a social/psychological perspective (i.e., "open" space) and from an aesthetic/educational perspective (i.e., attractive or interesting combinations of vegetation).

a. Assessment of Areal Extent

Measuring the amount of open space is a straightforward operation. Change in cover areas currently in a natural state are readily estimated, if all or most of the site is to be altered (e.g., cleared or filled for home sites). Assessment of the current stock can be made from black and white or color aerial photos of the community and site in question. The segregation of open spaces into cover categories (forest, grassland, water, etc.) should be performed at this point if this information is to be used in the actual evaluation. An inventory of mature trees at the site might also be taken if there are relatively few and an areal description seems less appropriate. Sources of aerial photos include the National Aeronautics and Space Administration, the Soil Conservation Service and the Agricultural Stabilization and Conservation Service (U.S. Department of Agriculture), the U.S. Geological Survey (U.S. Department of the Interior), state departments of transportation, and private engineering/planning firms. Developers often obtain aerial photos for their own use, and these also may be available.

In measuring the extent of open space from aerial photos, a simple planimeter (i.e., an area measuring device) can be employed. Alternatively, a slightly more sophisticated and possibly more accurate point sampling approach can be used but is probably unnecessary unless open space is interspersed with developed areas.[3]

b. Assessment of Vegetation Quality and Quantity

A simple approach to the inventorying of natural areas is to use a quality rating scheme and data taken from aerial photos and/or obtained from brief field surveys. When available, color infrared photographs are especially useful, since the amount of infrared energy reflected from leaf surfaces during each season provides information on the type and general charac-

2. K. Christensen, *Estimating the Social Impacts of Land Development* (Washington, D.C.: The Urban Institute, forthcoming). See also, Dagg, op. cit.

3. Points are distributed over the photo according to a sampling design. The percentage of points falling on open spaces equals the percentage of land in open space in the community. See Brian J. L. Berry and Alan M. Baker, "Geographical Sampling," in Brian J. L. Berry and Duane F. Marble, *Spatial Analysis,* (Englewood Cliffs, N.J.: Prentice-Hall, Inc., 1968).

Land Development and the Natural Environment

FIGURE 3-1
EXAMPLE FORMATS FOR THE PRESENTATION OF ESTIMATED IMPACTS ON SPECIES ABUNDANCE AND DIVERSITY

NATURAL AREA "X"

Species	Present Abundance	Future Abundance	Diversity
Trees	(Typical entry for one line)	(Typical entry for one line)	(Typical entry for entire column)
_____	150 individuals	probably 25–50 individuals	Present Simpson diversity index score is approximately 20, future score is expected to be 10–15 (where 20 is "very diverse," 15 is "diverse," and 10 is "fairly diverse")[a]
_____			
_____			
	or	or	
Shrubs			
	very numerous	sparse	
_____			
_____	or	or	or
_____			
	covering 3 acres	covering 1/2 acre	Many species with evenly distributed populations now, fewer species with more uneven distributions expected
Grasses & sedges			
_____			
_____			
Aquatics			
_____			
_____			
Others (e.g., mosses, ferns, herbs, etc.)			
_____			
_____			
_____			

WILDLIFE HABITAT "Y"

Species	Present Abundance	Future Abundance	Diversity
Birds	(See above)	(See above)	(See above)
_____			
_____			
_____			
Mammals			
_____			
_____			
Amphibians			
_____			
_____			
Reptiles			
_____			
_____			
Fish			
_____			
_____			
_____			
_____			

NOTE: It may be desirable to present impacts on terrestrial (land based) and aquatic habitats separately or to discuss the latter as part of the water quality analysis.

a. Simpson's index is a mathematical expression of diversity. See footnote 8.

teristics of vegetation.[4] The identification of types of vegetation (both from photos and brief field assessment) is based primarily on identifying certain indicator species. Where the area under investigation is small (e.g., one hundred acres or less), interpretation of aerial photos may be almost as time-consuming as field studies. Judgments of resource quality are based on the current general understanding of resource value, health, and degree of disturbance. Several rating schemes have been proposed for assessing the quality of natural areas.[5] In general, these are based on the following considerations:

(a) The number of distinct plant communities.

(b) The uniqueness of each plant community (in the locality/region/state/nation).

(c) The presence of subareas which have been recently disturbed (e.g., by clear cutting, cultivating or grazing, burning, bulldozing).

(d) The accessibility of the area.

Values for these factors can be presented separately or, as suggested in references in Footnotes 4 and 5, be combined in order to assign a rank or score to individual areas. Although the mathematical manipulations differ among the various schemes, higher scores are generally assigned to areas which (a) have a greater number of or rarer plant communities, (b) are undisturbed, and (c) are accessible.

Relevant data sources on locally important[6] plant communities can be obtained from local universities and park departments and from state departments of natural resources or their analogs. The latter should also be consulted regarding the regional and statewide scarcity of community types.

A more detailed, more accurate analysis can be made using field surveys by trained observers. Through a sampling procedure the population of plants by species, species within plant communities, and communities within the area can be ascertained. This information can be used to either refine the simple quality assessment previously discussed or to provide baseline data for quantitatively estimating the impact of land development on species' abundance and diversity.

Field surveys can also provide data on the presence of rare or endangered species. Their presence would obviously increase the quality rating.

If the results of the field investigations are to be used for quantitative estimates of diversity, then a suitable diversity expression should be used.[7] The concept of diversity encompasses (a) the number of species in a community, and (b) the distribution of individuals among the species present. The greater the number of species and the more equal the distribution of individuals among the species, the higher the diversity. Although the number of individuals and species can be used alone, it may be useful to employ a mathematical expression which combines both elements.[8] For areas with more than one plant community the diversity scores for the individual communities can be summed.

Since the diversity index scores have little meaning by themselves (and indeed can be misleading if population sizes are not also specified), it would be useful to "calibrate" the index by applying it to a variety of natural areas in the local community. Subjective ratings of diversity by a trained observer could then be compared with the index score for each area so that a reference scale relating the two could be developed.

c. Methods of Field Measurement

Various standard methods of recording the presence of plants and measuring their various character-

4. For more information see Michael M. McCarthy, Richard A. Boots, and Bernard J. Niemann, Jr., "Remote Sensing of Infrared Energy: Critical Data for Land-use Decision Makers," *Landscape Architecture* (January, 1973): 133–47; D. M. Carneggie and D. T. Laver, "Uses of Multiband Remote Sensing on Forest and Range Inventory," *Photogrammeteria* 21 (1966): 115–41; and Lewis M. Cowardin and Victor I. Myers, "Remote Sensing for Identification and Classification of Wetland Vegetation," *Journal of Wildlife Management* 38 (April, 1974): 308–14.

5. See, for example, Peter A. Isaacson, "Aquatic and Terrestrial Consideration in Power Plant Siting" (Albany: Office of Environmental Planning, State Department of Public Service, 1974); Bernard J. Niemann, et al., *Recommendations for a Critical Resource Information Program (CRIP) for Wisconsin, Phase III Report,* (Madison: Institute for Environmental Studies, University of Wisconsin, February, 1974); and William Tans, "Priority Ranking of Biotic Natural Areas," *The Michigan Botanist* 13 (1974): 31–39.

6. Important plant communities are not necessarily rare. Importance refers as well to representativeness, quality, robustness, and aesthetic qualities.

7. A useful scheme for organizing the results of a field study is as follows: trees, shrubs, vines, grasses and sedges, aquatic vegetation, and others (e.g., herbs, mosses, ferns, lichens).

8. A number of diversity expressions have been developed. See, for example, Isaacson, op. cit.; C. E. Schannon and W. Weiner, *The Mathematical Theory of Communication* (Urbana: University of Illinois Press, 1963); and M. O. Hill, "Diversity and Evenness: A Unifying Notion and its Consequences," *Ecology* 54 (1973): 427–32. One of the simplest is Simpson's Index (E. H. Simpson, "Measurement of Diversity," *Nature* 163 [1949]: 688):

$$D = \frac{N(N-1)}{\sum_{i=1}^{M} n_i(n_i - 1)}$$

where D = the diversity index
N = the total number of individual plants in the community
n_i = the number of individuals of species i
M = number of different species

Note: This index was originally presented in an inverted form. It has been used in both forms and seems to be more intuitively satisfying when the numbers increase as diversity increases.

Land Development and the Natural Environment

istics can be found in the literature.[9] Commonalities and key differences in those methods appropriate for measuring abundance and diversity will be briefly highlighted here. Since the accuracy of field investigations is a product of statistical design, consistency in sample selection, and skill in plant identification (among other factors), any locality contemplating the use of biological field surveys is strongly encouraged to obtain the services of a person appropriately trained and qualified.

In order to ascertain the presence and abundance of plant species within a geographic area, the site is sampled and the sampled plants are identified and counted. Since both the presence and abundance of specific species are dependent on seasonal climatic factors, the sampling should preferably be done during each active season—spring, summer, and fall. For terrestrial (i.e., land-based) ecosystems the most salient considerations involve the manner of sample selection, the sampling intensity, and the techniques of plant identification and measurement. The alternative sampling units are "quadrats," "transects," and "points" (or "point-quadrats"). The first are circular or rectangular plots distributed throughout the natural area. The size, number, and location are determined by the density and distribution of vegetation.[10] Within each plot the vegetation is identified and individual plants counted. Transects are either linear arrangements of quadrats or lines which cross the area of interest at selected intervals. Plants are identified and counted if they lie under or over or touch the line. Points are individual positions from which plants are identified and counted.

For simply producing a list of the species present, the entire area is surveyed in a systematic fashion. No attempt is made to count the number present.

The most appropriate method in any situation will depend largely on the types and heterogeneity of vegetation characteristic of the area. Regardless of which method is used, the environment should be separated into from three to five vertical strata and each measured separately.

The time required can be significantly reduced if subjective measures of plant abundance are used. (In other words, if Measure 2 is used.) A limited number of abundance rating schemes have been tested, with

the Brown-Blanquet scale probably being the most popular.[11]

A thorough and quantitative analysis of a natural area is expensive. For a site of about fifty acres containing three or four plant communities, the cost could run to $10,000 or $15,000 for a professional biologist, depending on the number of times the site is sampled.[12] (Seasonal sampling is highly recommended.) A simple species list can probably be obtained for a few hundred dollars.[13]

Aquatic environments produce several distinct subenvironments, each of which should be sampled separately. Free-floating or submerged plants can be sampled directly. Plants attached to submerged objects can only be inventoried by collecting samples of these objects and then removing the plants. Bottom-dwelling plants are collected by special devices called bottom samplers.

2. Wildlife

Local wildlife can be inventoried directly by taking a population census, or indirectly by assessing the quality of local habitats.

a. Habitat Analysis

This is the simpler of the two approaches, as the analysis can be performed from secondary sources of information. Again, aerial photography is a prime data source.[14] The following factors for terrestrial ecosystems should be considered in such an analysis:

a. The number of and types of plant communities per unit area.

b. The number of forest openings (i.e., clearings in forested areas).

c. The presence of water.

d. The presence of movement corridors (e.g., trails, stream valleys).

e. The size of the area.

f. The rarity of the wildlife for which the habitat is appropriate.

The analysis should be performed separately for groups of animals requiring different types of habi-

---

9. See, for example, Robert L. Smith, op. cit., Appendix B; and Kenneth A. Kershaw, *Quantitative and Dynamic Plant Ecology*, (New York: American Elsevier Publishing Company, Inc., 1973).

10. The spatial distribution of vegetation and other natural resources and the implications for sampling design are discussed in D. Keyes, V. Basoglu, E. Kuhlmey, and M. Rhyner, "A Comparison of Several Sampling Designs for Geographical Data," *Geographical Analysis* (forthcoming).

11. For additional information on abundance rating schemes, see Kershaw, op. cit.

12. Personal communication with Forest Stearns, Professor of Botany, University of Wisconsin, Milwaukee.

13. Ibid.

14. See, for example, R. N. Colwell, "Remote Sensing as a Means of Determining Ecological Condition," *Bioscience* 17 (1967): 444–49; and H. K. Nelson, A. T. Klett, and W. G. Burge, "Monitoring Migratory Bird Habitat by Remote Sensing Methods," *Translations of the North American Wildlife Natural Resource Conference* 35 (1970): 73–83.

tats. But, in general, the greater the diversity of plant communities, the larger the area, and the greater the amount of edge or ecotones (i.e., areas of transition between communities), the better the habitat. The presence of water and movement corridors further improves the value of natural areas as wildlife habitats.

The quality of aquatic habitats is based primarily on the quality of the water. For this reason the reader is referred to Part 2 of this report for further information on tolerance limits for various species. Again, analysis should be performed separately for species requiring different habitat conditions.

Wetland areas (i.e., swamps, marshes, bogs) deserve special mention as habitats. Due to the juxtaposition of aquatic and terrestrial ecosystems, wetlands support a rich variety of animal and plant life. Freshwater wetlands are especially important as nesting areas for waterfowl, many of which have value as game species.[15] Saltwater wetlands are of critical importance as breeding grounds for a vast array of commercially valuable fin fish, shellfish, and crustaceans.[16]

Various schemes have been proposed for combining the various habitat quality variables into a single score.[17] Alternatively, subjective ratings can be assigned to a given area based generally on these variables. In either case it is desirable to catalog the habitat ratings by type of animal or animal groupings. Figure 3-2 is an *example* of a format that could be used to record this information. (Only a sampling of all possible habitat types is included.) The quality of the area being evaluated would be broken down by both type of wildlife and type of habitats found in the area. Descriptions based on the quality variables would appear in each cell.

b. Population Census

Since animals are mobile they are obviously harder to find and consequently much more difficult to survey than plants. In addition the observer may frighten the observed, thus reducing the accuracy of the survey. For these reasons, a population census is frequently used in combination with habitat assessment.

As in the discussion of vegetation surveys, only the highlights of field methods will be described. The as-

sistance of trained wildlife observers should be sought in undertaking a wildlife census.

Most methods employ either direct observation (sometimes preceded by trapping and tagging animals in the area) or the recording of indirect evidence. Direct observations of birds include both visual sighting and the identification of characteristic calls or songs (usually during mating season) at selected sample points. A modified procedure used to survey bird populations in Columbia, Maryland, relied on traverses rather than sample points, thus overcoming the problems of reduced visibility and audibility in urbanized areas.[18] Mammals and large reptiles are often "counted" by recording indirect evidence: pellets (i.e., fecal material), tracks, active dens and lodges, browse areas, and other signs). Due to the difficulties in relating this evidence to the number of animals present, indirect methods are less accurate.[19] Quantitative expressions of their accuracy are usually lacking, however.

Although the term "wildlife" is normally reserved for the more obvious or apparent species, the value of a study which will be used in an impact analysis may be increased if data on animals at all levels of the energy pyramid have been collected. Of course, the extent to which this data can be used, in combination with descriptions of the proposed developments, to estimate impact on wildlife will depend on current knowledge of such things as pollutant toxicity levels and interrelationships among organisms. Where information of this sort is at hand for certain "nonwildlife" animals, or where these animals represent a significant local resource themselves (e.g., clams in tidal areas), a population survey may be *justified*.

Measurement techniques for the smaller, less mobile organisms are similar to those for vegetation. Quadrats are often used to sample such animals as mollusks and earthworms, while zooplankton and other aquatic organisms are surveyed by taking water or bottom samples. Insects are collected with nets and populations determined by the intensity of netting effort and the number of individuals collected. In most cases the statistical accuracy of the results can be determined if care is exercised in the sampling and measurement activities.

---

15. See Niemann, op. cit.

16. See John Clark, *Coastal Ecosystems* (Washington, D.C.: The Conservation Foundation, March, 1974) and G. Lauff, ed., *Estuaries* (Washington, D.C.: American Association for the Advancement of Science, 1967).

17. See, for example, Isaacson, op. cit. and Niemann, et al., op. cit.

18. Traverses are divided into 100 yard long segments and birds within fifty yards on either side of the traverse line are counted continuously as the segment is walked. See Aelred D. Geis, "Effects of Urbanization and Type of Urban Development on Bird Populations," in *Proceedings of Symposium on Wildlife*.

19. For example, the relationship between number of pellets and number of animals is dependent on animal species, age, sex, diet, season, and type of vegetation present (which may cover the pellets, thus reducing visibility).

FIGURE 3-2
A CHART FOR CATALOGING BASELINE DATA ON HABITAT QUANTITY

HABITAT AREA "A"
HABITAT TYPES ON OR NEAR THE DEVELOPMENT SITE

	Deciduous[a] Forest	Coniferous[b] Forest	Old Field/ Grassland[c]	Wetland	Stream	Pond/Lake
Birds						
1.	Abundant					
2.	Absent					
3.	Common					
.						
.						
Mammals						
1.						
2.						
3.						
.						
.						
Reptiles						
1.						
2.						
3.						
.						
.						
Amphibians						
1.						
2.						
3.						
.						
.						
Fish						
1.						
2.						
3.						
.						
.						

NOTES:

For those habitat types which are generally appropriate for the species listed, the quality is described (e.g., excellent-poor) and possibly given a rating based on the factors listed in the text.

a. Deciduous trees are those which lose their leaves seasonally.

b. Coniferous trees are those which do not lose their leaves.

c. Old fields are abandoned pastures, while grasslands are areas characterized by native species (i.e., they have not been farmed).

Regardless of the method used to survey wildlife populations, it is important to employ them at several points in time. Climatic and other factors often produce yearly as well as seasonal fluctuations. Ideally, the baseline values used in impact evaluations would be long-term averages. Unfortunately, the data needed to construct such averages are rarely available. Quantitative expressions of species diversity similar to those cited for plants can be used.[20]

Quantitative animal surveys tend to be expensive. Bird populations are the easiest to measure and

20. Again, the Simpson formula (Simpson, op. cit.) is appropriate.

would probably cost several hundred dollars, using a professional biologist for a site of about fifty acres and containing three or four plant communities.[21] Surveys of mammals would probably cost several thousand dollars under similar circumstances.[22]

C. ESTIMATING FUTURE CONDITIONS[23]

Most estimations of future impacts rely on logical deduction and analogy to similar, well-documented situations. We have yet to find specific predictive techniques for estimating the impacts of land development.[24] The discussions to follow will highlight key considerations, relevant research, and impact evaluation findings where appropriate.

1. Vegetation

The most direct and usually most significant development impacts on open spaces and natural areas are also the most obvious—removal or addition of trees and underbrush, filling of wetlands, grading and replanting of grasslands or fields. The vegetation left standing may benefit or suffer from an increased exposure to wind and sun and from changes in soil moisture content. Less obvious impacts may be manifest in terms of interruptions in plant reproduction mechanisms. Land developments which reduce those types of wildlife upon which some plants depend for seed propagation may reduce the ability of these plants to compete for space. For example, berry-producing plants depend on birds for propagation, while animals with hair or fur often assist in the distribution of thorny seeds. Land development can also cause the introduction of nuisance species (e.g., dandelions), which compete well with more "natural" species.

The effect on vegetation of additional air pollutants emitted by, or as a result of, new development should also be considered. Even low levels of certain pollutants may have dramatic effects. However, it may be extremely difficult to separate the effects of a single development from the cumulative effects of urbanization in general. This is especially true of the most serious transportation-related pollutants—photo-oxidants. Even where the new source will be a single point and the emissions are well-specified, accurately predicting the effects on plant growth is difficult.[25]

Some of these effects will be quite obvious from the developer's plans (e.g., tree-cutting and wetland filling). Others are more subtle and will probably require the judgment of local biologists familiar with the environmental requirements and characteristics of plant species found in the local area.

The effect of a specific development is also dependent on the management practices employed once the development is completed. Mowing of common areas and the elimination of tree seedlings on the periphery of privately owned parcels will effectively eliminate wildflowers and reduce the effectiveness of buffer zones around natural areas, respectively. On the other hand, new types of trees and shrubs may be introduced by new residents or the developer. Comparison with similar types of developments elsewhere in the community may be helpful here.

The actual procedures employed in the analysis primarily involve the comparison of the project site plan with the baseline assessment of the existing open spaces and natural areas in the immediate vicinity. A statement of landscaping plans and future management intentions would be desirable.

2. Wildlife

a. Key Considerations

Land developments can affect wildlife populations in the following ways:

(a) Direct removal of habitats.

(b) Indirect destruction of habitats through the introduction of air and water pollutants.

(c) Interference with movement, especially by the construction of highways through habitat areas. (On the other hand, the clearing of trees in forested areas may actually facilitate movement.)

(d) The introduction of predators, such as cats and dogs.

(e) The elimination of natural predators.

21. Personal communication with Forest Stearns, Professor of Botany, University of Wisconsin, Milwaukee.

22. Ibid.

23. For a general discussion of urbanization and its effects on the natural environment, see D. Gill and P. Bonnett, *Nature in the Urban Landscape: A Study of City Ecosystems* (Baltimore: York Press, Inc., 1973).

24. Models developed to simulate the interractions of specific ecosystems have been used primarily as management tools for largely undeveloped areas (e.g., rangeland management). However, some water quality models incorporating biological parameters and applicable to urbanizing areas are available. See "Water Quality and Quantity," Part 2 of this report.

25. Retrospective studies on the impacts from power plants have underscored the difficulty in controlling for all nondevelopment factors and thereby being able to assign the observed changes to the power plant. See, for example, D. E. Willard, *Preliminary Documentation of Environmental Change Related to the Columbus Electric Power Generating Site* (Madison: Institute for Environmental Studies, University of Wisconsin, May, 1973). However, the EPA secondary ambient air quality standards are designed to protect vegetation and materials, and can be used as an indicator of potential impact. (For more information, see "Air Quality," Part 1 of this report.)

(f) The introduction of urban-adapted species which are superior competitors.

(g) The infringement on feeding and nesting activities due to increased noise and disturbance levels.

(h) The addition of new habitats which will cause increased populations of certain species.

b. Research Findings

Since predictive wildlife impact techniques analogous to air dispersion and water quality models are not at hand, the importance of case studies of similar developments in similar environments is greatly increased. The results of retrospective analyses must be applied with caution. For studies which have measured population over time, checks should be made to see if proper controls were used. Since wildlife populations can fluctuate dramatically from year to year, the measured changes in urbanizing areas should be compared with those in rural areas for the same time period. In addition, if the results of a study in one geographical area are to be applied to another, the validity of such a transfer will depend on the similarity of the developments and environments in question. Care must also be exercised in interpreting the results of urban wildlife studies which summarize the cumulative results of urbanization (e.g., increased air temperatures, increased average noise levels, decreased sunlight, increased street lighting, increased community-wide pollution levels). The findings are often difficult to apply to single developments, which may contribute only infinitesimally to the cumulative impact.

Although the listing of research findings to follow is undoubtedly less than exhaustive, it does provide a set of representative findings:

Birds—Aelred Geis has monitored the changes in bird populations over a period of several years in Howard County, Maryland. During this time the new town of Columbia was undergoing development.[26] He found:

(a) The cropland species (e.g., bobwhite), field species (e.g., redwinged blackbird), and woodland species (e.g., wood thrush) all declined due to habitat removal and possibly predation by cats.

(b) One adaptable species, the cardinal, showed no change. Ornamental shrubs and bushes appear to provide a ready supply of food and nesting areas.

(c) Urban species (e.g., house sparrows, starlings) increased as eaves and vents provided attractive nesting sites. These populations were also associated with poorly designed or constructed homes. More desirable urban species (e.g., song sparrow, mockingbird) also increased due to the landscaping around homes.

(d) Detached homes in areas where some original trees were retained provided the greatest diversity of species.

Geis has also reported that populations of individual species and overall diversity can be increased by not mowing open spaces, by leaving water areas in natural vegetation, and by planting grasses and shrubs of high nutritional value to birds.[27]

A comparison of bird populations across an environmental gradient in Washington, D.C., by Robert Williamson provides additional information on bird populations in urbanizing environments.[28] The following results were obtained from a population census in each of three city environments—a large, forested park; a moderately dense, landscaped townhouse neighborhood; a denser neighborhood lacking in landscaping and open spaces:

(a) Mockingbirds and cardinals were associated with the number of deciduous trees and the diversity of yard vegetation.

(b) Robins and blue jays were associated with the percentage of unpaved ground cover and with dense housing.

(c) Wood thrushes were associated with the number of coniferous trees which provided food and protection.

(d) Catbirds were associated with dense thickets and water.

(e) Starlings, house sparrows, and pigeons were associated with dense housing.

A third study provides more detailed information on necessary habitats for various species:[29]

(a) Cardinals need tree cover at least five feet in height and are found in urban areas only when trees are above this height.

(b) Bluejays nest only in mature deciduous trees.

(c) Both bluejays and cardinals are attracted to feeders in developed areas, even if not to nest.

Mammals—Most pertinent studies of mammals

26. Geis, op. cit.

27. Personal communication.

28. Robert D. Williamson, "Birds in Washington, D.C.," in *Proceedings of Symposium on Wildlife.*

29. Darrell L. Cauley, "Urban Habitat Requirements of Four Wildlife Species," in *Proceedings of Symposium on Wildlife.*

have concentrated on squirrels and raccoons. The findings are as follows:

(a) Squirrels adapt well to urban environments provided that "mature, uncrowded trees with large canopies" are present.[30] Chimneys and attics will provide shelter but are hardly an acceptable alternative.[31]

(b) Raccoons will co-exist with man in urban environments provided that fallen trees or other natural enclosures are available as nesting sites. (When forced to seek alternative shelter, garages, attics, and sewers are the preferred choices.) A supply of water is also required. Garden vegetables can be substituted for naturally occurring food sources.[32]

Amphibians and Reptiles—Because many amphibian and reptile species have water-associated habitats, they are susceptible to alterations in water quality as well as to physical changes in their habitat. Craig Campbell has reviewed a number of relevant studies regarding impacts on amphibians and reptiles.[33] A sampling of these follows:

(a) Modification of natural storm drainage systems (e.g., channelization of streams, installation of sewers, dredging) reduces habitat for various frog, snake, and salamander species.

(b) Frogs are extremely vulnerable to roads, which create barriers to their movement. Snakes and turtles, which use roadways for warm resting areas, also exhibit high death rates from cars.

(c) Increasing levels of pollution from septic tanks, municipal sewage facilities, and industrial sources have been associated with decreasing populations of aquatic amphibians and reptiles in many geographic areas.

(d) Species which inhabit transitional areas between plant communities seem to be more tolerant to disturbance; land-based species tend to survive longer in the face of urbanization than do aquatic ones.

(e) Some amphibians and reptiles may find "artificial" habitats suitable (e.g., sewers, reservoirs, ponds).

c. Estimation Procedures

Although quantitative techniques are not available for estimating impacts, meaningful conclusions about the effects of future development can be reached. These conclusions should be based on baseline studies of local wildlife populations and/or habitat conditions, information on development characteristics, and the results of other impact studies similar to the ones just described.

The analysis can be organized around the primary mechanisms of impact: (a) removal of habitat, (b) deterioration of water and air quality, (c) interference with wildlife movement, (d) introduction or removal of predators, (e) introduction of more competitive species, and (f) increase in noise levels. The proposed development can then be assessed for each of these changes. Special attention should be given to the proposed design features and management practices. Consideration should be given to the extent to which original vegetation can be retained, the extent to which grass mowing can be confined to small areas, the extent to which development in general and roads in particular can be directed away from key habitat areas (especially wetlands), the types of vegetation which will be planted, the types of new water areas created (and the intended management practices thereof), the design of the proposed buildings, and, of course, future levels of air, water, and noise pollution. Attempts to circumvent probable negative impacts (e.g., culverts beneath roadways to facilitate wildlife movement) should also be noted.

Once the development-induced changes have been enumerated, they can be related to the wildlife found in the area. In many cases the probable direction of impact (e.g., the red winged blackbird population will be reduced, a high-quality habitat will be disturbed) and, in some cases, the relative magnitude of impact (e.g., mallard ducks will be eliminated from the area, the wetland will be totally drained and filled) can be ascertained. In order to translate these into quantitative estimates of impact and areal extent of habitat removal can be estimated. If present wildlife populations are known, a range of estimated changes in species populations (high, low, most likely) can be used to estimate changes in diversity.

30. Vagn Flyger, "Tree Squirrels in Urbanizing Environments," in *Proceedings of Symposium on Wildlife.*

31. Cauley, op. cit.

32. Ibid.; and James R. Schinner and Darrell L. Cauley, "The Ecology of Urban Raccoons in Cincinnati, Ohio," in *Proceedings of Symposium on Wildlife.*

33. Craig A. Campbell, "Survival of Reptiles and Amphibians in Urban Environments," in *Proceedings of Symposium on Wildlife.*

III. CONCLUSIONS AND RECOMMENDATIONS

A. PLANNING VERSUS PROJECT REVIEW

Although most of the prior discussion focused on the evaluation of individual developments, planning for the protection of a community's wildlife and vegetation resources should be coordinated with and supportive of the project review process. First, the identification and assessment of open spaces, natural areas, and wildlife habitats can be used as the basis for the application of land use controls and inducements designed to protect these areas (and thus possibly eliminate the need for evaluations of individual developments). Secondly, community-wide baseline studies may facilitate individual evaluations when they are necessary. Thirdly, knowledge of alternative habitat areas into which wildlife may relocate (carrying capacity permitting) and of the total remaining community resource base will allow more accurate estimates of impacts from single projects to be made, on the one hand, and more meaningful interpretations of the estimates, on the other.

Although a few local governments have undertaken field studies of selected types of natural areas or habitats on a community-wide basis,[1] most planning-type studies are of a reconnaissance nature. Aerial photographs are typically employed to inventory all open spaces and to make initial assessments of natural areas and habitats. More detailed studies can thus be made of selected areas as time and funding permit.

Aside from the obvious fact that eliminating development in and around high quality areas will minimize impact, little in the way of generalizations can be made about types of development and the probable severity of their impact. Certainly the largest (in area) and the most polluting developments will have the greatest impact, but translating these variables into general types of development is difficult. Even a correlation of impact severity with population density is tenuous. A well-designed, high-density cluster development can be much more consonant with neighboring habitats than a large-lot subdivision with its manicured and often fenced-in yards. Perhaps the one general statement which is justified is that zoning which provides for design flexibility should be used in buffer areas. The more important point to be made, however, is that planning can never totally substitute for project reviews. Design features and future management practices (e.g., for planned unit developments) are very important considerations which only the evaluation of individual developments can capture.

B. ALTERNATIVE DATA COLLECTION APPROACHES

Although ecological field studies may be time-consuming and costly, alternative data collection options are available. Any community located near a college or university should investigate the possibility

---

1. Dane County, Wis., for example, has initiated a detailed field analyses of all wetlands in the county.

of employing biology students supervised by appropriate faculty members. Information already collected as part of class research projects may be highly relevant for the purpose of evaluating impacts. Departments of natural resources or analagous agencies at the state level should also be queried for locally relevant data. Private environmental interest groups and other organizations with knowledge of local resources (e.g., bird-watching groups) are other sources of data. The possibility of employing the latter on a volunteer or limited pay basis should also be explored. In many northeastern states active participation by local interest groups and resource experts has been formalized through the establishment of local environmental conservation commissions. Some of these commissions act purely as an official forum for environmental advocacy groups (and thus the subjects for discussion extend far beyond maintaining vegetation and wildlife resources), while others are more technically oriented and attempt to undertake original data collection and analysis on their own.[2]

Although the utilization of data sources compiled by volunteers is attractive, a word of caution is necessary. In those cases where the data collector may also be a strong adversary (or advocate) regarding related land use issues, the accuracy of the data may be questioned. Without supervision of the data collection by an independent and reputable expert, it may be impossible to resolve this issue.

---

2. For more information on conservation commissions, see Charles C. Morrison, Jr., "Local Environmental Conservation Commissions—The Beginning of a National Movement," *Outdoor Recreation Action,* No. 29 (Fall, 1973): 7–13.

C. SPECIFIC RECOMMENDATIONS AND CONCLUSIONS

Following is a list of recommendations and conclusions based on our investigation of issues and methods of analysis relevant to the assessment of wildlife and vegetation impacts from proposed land development:

1. Evaluations of individual developments should include consideration of the expected change in the amount of vegetation and numbers of wild species; communities should consider using impact measures such as are suggested here. In choosing between the preferred and fallback measures, the potential magnitude of impact and the time and funding available for evaluation will probably be the most important considerations.

2. The estimation of impacts on wildlife and vegetation must be based on analogies to similar and well-documented case studies and/or inferences made by experts knowledgeable about the local environmental conditions. Predictive models analogous to air and water pollution models are not available.

3. Communities should consider supplementing individual project evaluations conducted by trained observers with data collected by local universities and private naturalist associations.

4. The identification and characterization of high-quality natural areas and wildlife habitats during the process of developing community-wide plans would probably facilitate the preparation of individual project evaluations.

PART 4
NOISE

I. INTRODUCTION AND BACKGROUND

Noise has been commonly defined as unwanted sound. A proposed land development, by the nature of its design and function, can be a potential source of noise for residents in the surrounding neighborhoods. This section provides a brief background discussion of the physical properties and measurement of noise, as well as information on a few approaches to estimating noise impacts from proposed developments.

In evaluating a proposed land development for noise the concern is primarily on how the sounds emitted directly (e.g., from people or machinery at the site) or indirectly (e.g., from increased traffic flows) will affect people living or working in the surrounding areas.[1] The impact is related to the magnitude and pitch of the sounds (together, the perceived loudness), the frequency of occurrence of the various noise levels, and the compatibility of new sounds with existing noise levels.[2]

A. HEALTH AND WELFARE CONSIDERATIONS[3]

Biomedical research has shown that there are a variety of adverse effects on human health and wel-

fare that may be caused by variations in the magnitude, pitch, and timing of noise. These may be classified into three broad groups of adverse effects which are known to be caused by noise. These are:

1. The physiological effects on human hearing.
2. The nuisance effects on personal comfort, resulting in annoyance.
3. The nuisance effects on specific activities (e.g., interference with oral communication and sleeping).

These findings have been based on extensive epidemiological studies, that is, studies conducted on man in real-life situations.

There has also been extensive laboratory testing on animals and humans to ascertain nonauditory physiological responses from noise. These relationships, however, have not been shown to be causal. That is, the effects may be caused by other factors found in noisy environments. It is also not presently possible to generalize these findings to humans exposed to normal day-to-day noises. There are a number of variables that may affect response (e.g., context, timing of occurrence), although the extent of influence is not known. A review of the literature on

---

1. Although most new developments will increase noise levels, it is conceivable that some could provide barriers and noise absorbing surfaces to decrease levels.

2. Additional background material can be found in EPA, *Information on Levels of Environmental Noise Requisite to Protect Public Health and Welfare with an Adequate Margin of Safety* (Washington, D.C.: EPA, March, 1974) (NTIS No. PB 239–429) [hereafter cited as *Information on Levels of Environmental Noise* . . .]; and Karl D. Kryter, *The Effects of Noise on Man* (New York: Academic Press, 1970).

3. For further discussion of this topic, see Kryter, op. cit.; EPA, *Information on Levels of Environmental Noise* . . . ; and Louis Sutherland, Marial Braden, and Richard Colman, *A Program for the Measurement of Environmental Noise in the Community and Its Associated Human Response,* vol. 1: *A Feasibility Test of Measurement Techniques* (Washington, D.C.: DOT, Office of Noise Abatement, December, 1973) (DOT-TST-74-5).

human effects suggests that noise exposure, under controlled situations, can lead to decreased respiratory rates and cardiovascular changes, constriction of the blood vessels, changes in blood pressure and heart rate when sound reaches seventy decibels (dB) and above. Studies on animals indicate that ". . . continued exposure leads to imbalance of blood electrolytes, blood glucose levels, size of adrenal cortex and ultimately changes in kidneys, liver and gastro-intestinal tissues."[4] Even though researchers do not know the full extent of the nonauditory physiological responses to noise, many assume that if noise control is sufficient to protect persons from ear damage and hearing loss it is probable that humans will also be protected from other nonauditory physiological impacts.[5]

Table 4-1 summarizes some of the findings on nuisance and physiological effects of environmental noise stimulus.

B. FUNDAMENTAL PRINCIPLES[6]

Sound is a vibration or wave conveyed by molecules of air. As such, it has an amplitude (volume) and a frequency (pitch). The amplitude is the magnitude of air pressure fluctuations caused by changes in the concentration of air molecules as the wave passes, while frequency reflects how rapidly the pressure fluctuates. Both amplitude and pitch contribute to the loudness or "sound level" as perceived by man.

Most noise is a combination of many individual sounds. That is, it consists of a wide range of pitches and amplitudes and is known as "broad band noise." "Pure tone" or single pitch noise, when it does exist, can be extremely annoying, as in chalk screeching on a blackboard.

The pitch of a sound is expressed in cycles per second, or Hertz (Hz), while amplitude is measured in decibels (dB). Decibels are calibrated on a logarithmic scale directly related to air pressure levels.[7] Man's audible spectrum ranges between twenty and 20,000 Hz and between zero and slightly more than 140 dB.

In order to better reflect the subjective loudness of different sounds as perceived by man, the A-weighted decibel scale (dBA) has been developed. Values on this scale reflect amplitude weighted by the pitch at which the amplitude is measured in a manner which reflects man's responsiveness. The scale is again logarithmic and an increase of 10 dBA corresponds roughly to a doubling in perceived loudness. Figure 4-1 shows the amplitude of some common sounds.

The loudness of noise at any point in space depends on features of the source, the distance between

4. Sutherland, op. cit.

5. EPA, *Information on Levels of Environmental Noise. . . .*

6. For additional information, see Kryter, op. cit.; and Theodore Schultz, *Noise Assessment Guidelines: Technical Background*, HUD Report No. TE/NA 172 (Washington, D.C.: HUD Office of Research and Technology, 1971).

7. More precisely: $\quad dB = 20 \log_{10} \dfrac{P}{P_0}$

where P = the pressure of the sound in question
$\quad\quad P_0$ = a reference pressure (usually 20 micronewtons/cm²)

Table 4-1. A SUMMARY OF HUMAN HEALTH AND NUISANCE RELATIONSHIPS TO ENVIRONMENTAL NOISE[a]

APPROXIMATE NOISE LEVELS[b]	SETTINGS WHERE NOISE LEVELS ARE LIKELY	PROBABLE EFFECTS
>45dB	Urban residential (indoors)	Speech interruption indoors (interruptions of normal conversations at distances up to 2 meters)
>55B	Urban residential (outdoors)	Speech interruption outdoors (interruption of normal conversations at distances up to 2 meters)
>60dB	Urban residential and residential near airport (outdoors)	Average community reaction: Complaints and threats of legal action
>70dB	Industrial settings (indoors) and very noisy urban residential (outdoors)	Hearing loss

a. These thresholds are based on the summary findings of the Environmental Protection Agency in *Information on Levels of Environmental Noise . . .* (Washington, D.C.: EPA, March, 1974).

b. These noise levels are approximations and may be subject to change given variations in such factors as the frequency of noise and the intermittency of occurrence. These are outdoor day-night noise level averages, or average levels for twenty-four hour periods with night noise given increased weighting due to its sleep interruption characteristics. See p. 111 for a further discussion.

Land Development and the Natural Environment

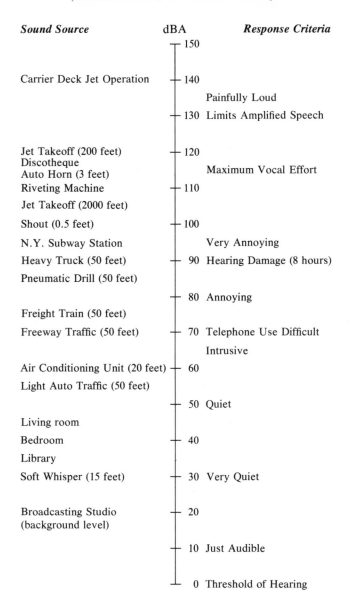

FIGURE 4-1
LOUDNESS RANGE OF COMMON SOUNDS
(Measured at Source or Indicated Distance)

Sound Source	dBA	Response Criteria
	150	
Carrier Deck Jet Operation	140	
		Painfully Loud
	130	Limits Amplified Speech
Jet Takeoff (200 feet)	120	
Discotheque		
Auto Horn (3 feet)		Maximum Vocal Effort
Riveting Machine	110	
Jet Takeoff (2000 feet)		
Shout (0.5 feet)	100	
N.Y. Subway Station		Very Annoying
Heavy Truck (50 feet)	90	Hearing Damage (8 hours)
Pneumatic Drill (50 feet)		
	80	Annoying
Freight Train (50 feet)		
Freeway Traffic (50 feet)	70	Telephone Use Difficult
		Intrusive
Air Conditioning Unit (20 feet)	60	
Light Auto Traffic (50 feet)		
	50	Quiet
Living room		
Bedroom	40	
Library		
Soft Whisper (15 feet)	30	Very Quiet
Broadcasting Studio	20	
(background level)		
	10	Just Audible
	0	Threshold of Hearing

SOURCE: Council on Environmental Quality, *Environmental Quality, The First Annual Report* (Washington, D.C.: CEQ, August, 1970).

the source and the point in question, and characteristics of both the intervening land and atmosphere. Noise attenuates in amplitude exponentially with distance. A doubling in distance will reduce the amplitude by a factor of four, everything else held constant. Additional attenuation can be accomplished by wind and temperature fluctuations and by the presence of vegetation "screens" and physical barriers.[8] The latter two are by far the most important factors. The degree of attenuation will depend on the size, type, and location of the screen or barrier with respect to the source and receiver. For example, tall trees with many branches and thick foliage are quite effective in reducing sound levels.

Reverberation from reflecting surfaces, such as highrise buildings found in many central cities, represents a complicating factor. Any method used to estimate noise levels in these locations should be carefully calibrated in order to account for these effects.

---

8. For further information on atmospheric effects, see B. A. Kugler and A. C. Piersol, *Highway Noise—A Field Evaluation of Traffic Noise Reduction Measures,* NCHRP Report No. 144 (Washington, D.C.: Federal Highway Administration, Highway Research Board, 1973). For further information on vegetation and barrier effects, see B. K. Huang, *An Ecological Systems Approach to Community Noise Abatement—Phase I* (Raleigh: North Carolina State University, June, 1974) (NTIS No. PB 234-311).

II. METHODOLOGICAL APPROACHES

A. MEASURES, STANDARDS, AND INDICES

The suggested measure of noise impact is as follows:

1. Change in the level of noise, the frequency with which it occurs, and the number of people affected in the area surrounding the development.

Estimates of noise levels and frequencies of occurrence produced by proposed developments could be based on analogies to other similar developments (and in similar settings) or on detailed calculations of noise sources and the subsequent propagations of sound into surrounding areas. Since the suggested measure requires an estimation of the number of people affected, noise levels should be estimated for a variety of locations around the development.

Noise is a multifaceted problem which resists reduction to a few simple rules of thumb. Nevertheless, the EPA has attempted to relate hearing damage and activity interference to levels of exterior and interior noise.[1] Although the recommended standards do not represent inviolable breakpoints, they can and should be used as points of reference.[2] The Swedish National Board of Urban Planning has also specified interior and exterior standards for various types of structures, while the Federal Highway Administration (FHWA) has developed design guidelines which contain stan-

dards for different types of land uses.[3] HUD has issued standards applicable to outdoor noise for HUD-sponsored residential developments.[4] Table 4-2 lists standards suggested by still others.

One of the basic problems in developing standards is to capture the most significant aspects of noise variability: pitch, magnitude, frequency of occurrence, compatibility. Reference has already been made to the dBA scale, which reflects both pitch and magnitude. Some sets of standards (e.g., the FHWA guidelines) are specified directly in terms of the dBA scale. In order to capture frequency of occurrence, standards are typically specified in terms of L_{10}—the level which is exceeded 10 percent of the time.[5] This is true for the FHWA guideline. The HUD Standards are in terms of L_{33} and L_4. The EPA standards, on the other hand, refer to L_{eq} values. This is a scale which expresses patterns of intermittent noise as equivalent constant-level noise. L_{eq} is thus dependent on the distribution of noise levels over time and can be easily converted to L_{10} values.[6] The compatibility factor has

---

1. EPA, *Information on Levels of Environmental Noise.* . . .

2. EPA refers to these standards as "guidelines" since they are not legally binding.

3. Sten Ljunggun, *A Design Guide for Road Traffic Noise* (Stockholm: National Swedish Building Research, 1973) (NTIS No. PB-227-258); and Federal Highway Administration, *Interim Noise Standards and Procedures for Implementing Section 109(i) of Title 23, U.S.C.,* FHWA PPM 90-2 (Washington, D.C., n.d.).

4. HUD, (1390.2 chp. 1).

5. Similarly, L_{50} and L_{90} are levels which are exceeded 50 and 90 percent of the time, respectively.

6. In order to translate L_{eq} to L_{10} values, the distribution of noise levels over time and the standard deviation of this distribution must be known. See EPA, *Information on Levels of Environmental Noise.* . . .

Table 4-2. RECOMMENDATIONS OF SOUND LEVELS IN VARIOUS SPACES

	KNUDSEN-HARRIS 1950 dbA	BERANEK 1953 dbA	BERANEK 1957 dbA	LAWRENCE 1962 dbA	KOSTEN-VAN OS 1962 dbA	ASHRAE 1962 dbA	DENISOV 1967 dbA	KRYTER 1970 dbA	TOKYO 1971 dbA	USSR 1971 dbA	BERANEK 1971 dbA	DOELLE 1972 dbA	WOOD 1972 dbA	RETTINGER 1973 dbA	SWEDEN dbA	SWITZER-LAND 1970 dbA	CZECHO-SLOVAKIA 1967 dbA
RESIDENT																	
Home																	
Bedroom	35–45	35	35–45	25	30	25–35		40		35	34–47	35–45	35	34–42	25	35–45	40
Living Room	35–45	35		40	35	30–40		40		35	38–47		40		25	35–45	40
Apartment	35–45		35–40	30		35–45		18			34–47			38–42		35–50	40
Hotel	35–45		35–40	35–40		35–45		38		35	34–47	35–54	30–40	42		35–50	40
COMMERCIAL																	
Restaurant	50–55	55	55	40–60	50	40–55		55		55	42–52	45–60	45–50	50		40–50	55
Private Office	40–45	50	30–45	35–45	30–45	25–45	40–45	35			38–47	30–45	40–45	46			
General Office	45–55		40–55	40–60	60	35–65	50–60			50	42–52	45–55	45–55	50	40		
Transportation						35–55		35–40		60							
INDUSTRIAL																	
Workshop																	
Light		50		40–60	70						52–61		55–65			45–55	
Heavy		75		60–90			85				66–80		60–75	70		50–60	
EDUCATION																	
Classroom	35–40	35	35	30–40	30	35–45	40–50	35		40	38–47	35	35–45	38	35	35–45	
Laboratory				40–50		40–50					47–46		45–50	42			
Library	40–45	40	42–45	35–45	35	35–45		40			38–47	40–45	40–45	42			40
HEALTH																	
Hospital	35–40	40	42	20–35	35	30–45		40		25	34–47	40	40–45	38	25–35	25–35	35–40
RECREATION																	
Swimpool						45–60								50			
Sports		60	30			35–45						60	50–60	46			
Gymnasium					55	40–50				60		55–60	45–55	46		60	60
AUDITORIUM																	
Assembly Hall	35–40	35	35–40	40–45		30–40		38			30–42	35–45	35–45	38–42			
Church	35–40	40	40	35–40	35	25–35		40		35	30–42	35–40	35–40	34			
Concert Hall	30–35	30–35	25–35	25–35	30	25–35		28–35			21–30	25–35	30–35				35
Court Room	40–45	40	40–45	40–45	35			40			42	35–40	35–40				
Record Studio	25–30	30	25–30	20–30	20	25–35		28			21–34	25–30	30	30			
TV Studio	25–30	30	30	25–35	30	25–35		28			21–34	30–35	35	34–38			
Mot. Pict. Studio	25–30	30	25–30		25–35			28				35	25				
Mot. Pict. Theater	35–40	40	40	35–40	35	35–45		40			21–34	40		38			
Leg. Theater	30–35	35	30–35	25–35	25	30–40		33		40	30–34	30–35	35–40	34			35
OUTSIDE																	
Rural									35–45	35							
Suburb									40–50	45							
Urban									50–60								
Industrial									50–60								
Res. Areas															55		

SOURCE: EPA, *Information on Levels of Environmental Noise* . . . (1974).

been used in designing still another scale of noise levels—L_{dn}. This is basically a day-night or 24-hour L_{eq} scale with nighttime noises weighted more heavily to reflect their intrusive nature.

Additional indices which attempt to integrate the various noise considerations in other ways include

Table 4-3. TABULAR PRESENTATION OF NOISE IMPACTS FOR A HYPOTHETICAL DEVELOPMENT[a]

| | **NUMBER OF RESIDENTS EXPOSED**[b] | | |
NOISE LEVEL	ELDERLY	OTHER	TOTAL
(L_{10} in dBA)			
>65	50		50
55–65			
45–55			
<45			

Local standards:
>65—clearly unacceptable
55–65—potentially unacceptable
45–55—normally acceptable
<45—clearly acceptable

a. Another table should be prepared showing the levels to which the population groups are currently exposed. Changes in the number of people exposed to the various levels could then be calculated.

b. Socioeconomic and demographic data can be obtained from the census. Supplemental information on individual units such as nursing homes can be used to further refine the population distribution data.

the Community Noise Equivalent Level (CNEL), the Composite Noise Rating Method (CNR), the Noise Exposure Forecast (NEF), and the Noise Pollution Level (NPL)[7]. Although any one of these indices may be best suited for a given situation, they tend to correlate well with one another. They can also be readily translated into L_{eq} values.[8]

A local government may well desire to use different standards in different parts of the community. Citizens presumably desire quieter residential than working or shopping environments. Determining the appropriate standards, however, is not a trivial task. Eliciting preferences, assigning levels of acceptability, and translating these into statistical values for noise levels require a considerable survey effort.

Regardless of which standards or categories of acceptability are used, a map format becomes extremely useful for an intermediate, if not a final, display of information. If estimates are made for enough geographical points (perhaps fifty, 100, 200, and 300 feet back from the roadway and every 100 feet along the roadway), then

7. For further information, see ibid.; and Bolt, Beranek, and Newman, Inc., *Noise Assessment Guidelines, Technical Background,* No. TE/NA 172 (Washington, D.C.: HUD, n.d.).

8. See EPA, *Information on Levels of Environmental Noise . . . ,* for specific instructions.

Table 4-4. APPROXIMATE NOISE LEVELS FOR CONSTRUCTION EQUIPMENT

TYPE OF EQUIPMENT	TYPICAL SOUND LEVEL dBA AT 50 FT.
Dump truck	88
Portable air compressors	81
Concrete mixer (truck)	85
Jackhammer	88
Scraper	88
Dozer	87
Paver	89
Generator	70
Piledriver	101
Rock drill	98
Pump	76
Pneumatic tools	85
Backhoe	85

SOURCE: *Federal Register* 39 (121) (June 21, 1974): 22298.

noise contour lines can be interpolated. By overlaying these on maps showing population by block or some other spatial unit, approximate values for the number of people exposed to various levels of noise can be obtained. Figure 4-2 illustrates a population and noise distribution map.

Once these values for both the "with" and "without development" situations have been obtained from such a map overlay process, they could be displayed in a tabular format, as illustrated in Table 4-3. It may also be desirable to indicate the impact on especially susceptible population groups (e.g., older persons, persons living in poorly insulated homes, or, from an equity perspective, disadvantaged groups), as shown. At a minimum, the location of noise sensitive activities or facilities, such as schools and hospitals, should be noted in the map presentation.

B. ANALYTICAL TECHNIQUES

A new development will generate noise in several different ways. Depending on the type and number of buildings constructed and the degree of terrain modification required, significantly high construction-related noise levels may be attained. After occupancy, commercial and residential developments will produce transportation-related noise. Industrial developments will also produce various on-site noises specific to each type of industry.

1. Construction-Related

The degree to which objectionable levels of noise will be produced during the construction stage is largely dependent on the type of equipment and machinery to be used. Table 4-4 presents average

Noise: Methodological Approaches

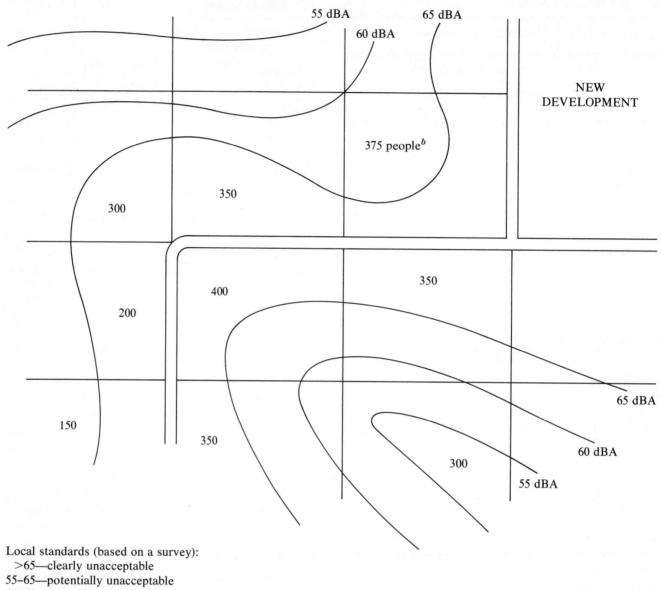

FIGURE 4-2
MAP PRESENTATION OF NOISE IMPACTS
FOR A HYPOTHETICAL DEVELOPMENT[a]

Local standards (based on a survey):
  >65—clearly unacceptable
55–65—potentially unacceptable
45–55—normally acceptable
  <45—clearly acceptable

a. This displays the estimates for noise levels with the proposed development. A similar map should be prepared for the existing conditions so that the change in noise levels can be calculated. For this example, the loudness (dBA) estimates are given at the L_{10} levels.

b. The residents are assumed to be evenly distributed throughout each spatial unit (e.g., the block or block group).

noise levels for various types of construction equipment at a distance of fifty feet. Rough estimates of total noise generated by the construction of a proposed development could be made simply by estimating the number and different types of machinery required and adding the noise generated by those that

will be used at the same time.[9] The estimates should reflect changes in noise by time of day and by phase

9. The noise produced by several sources is calculated by adding the sound pressure levels rather than the decibels. Thus, two cranes each producing 80 dBA of noise would produce 83, not 160 dBA, together.

Land Development and the Natural Environment

of construction. (The duration of each construction phase should also be noted.) Estimates for distances other than fifty feet can be made, based on the fact that sound *pressure* changes exponentially with a change in distance from the source.[10] The effects of terrain, barriers, and possibly meteorology can be simulated according to techniques found in references cited in the next section.

2. Transportation-Related

The discussion here will be limited to vehicular traffic. Noise from aircraft and trains is covered in numerous other sources.[11] Residential, commercial, and industrial developments will all cause an increase in traffic at least on the surrounding streets, if not on a significant portion of the entire road network. The degree of impact will be determined by the type and number of vehicles added (by time of day), the average speed and "stop-and-go" nature of the trips, the physical characteristics of the streets (e.g., elevation, grade, natural or manmade barriers), and the distance from source to receptor. The noise levels once the development has been constructed are then the sum of existing levels and the increment added by the development.[12]

Besides data on traffic generation, information on population distribution is needed to select the points where estimates should be made and to specify the number of people affected. For residential populations the census provides population data on a census tract, block group, and individual block basis. (In most cases the smaller units will allow more accurate estimates.) Population dot maps would also prove useful if they are available on a large-map scale. For daytime nonresidential populations local transportation studies of trip origins and destinations are a potential source of information. Rarely, however, is the data available for small areas. (Traffic zones are usually a square mile or more.) Planning departments or assessment offices may have data on office and re-

tail space for smaller areas which could be used to supplement the transportation data.

a. Specific Examples

The available techniques for making transportation-related noise estimations range from simple approximation based on the use of tables and graphs to rather complex computer models. Three of the more promising and/or popular of these techniques will be discussed.

HUD Noise Assessment Guidelines—Bolt, Beranek, and Newman, Inc. have developed a set of simple procedures to estimate the suitability of potential settings for proposed HUD-sponsored developments.[13] That is, proposed sites are rated for their current acceptability, based on noise emanating from the surrounding environment. For estimating noise impacts *from* a development on the community, the same procedures can be used, but at several geographic points. Although the guidelines deal with aircraft and railroad as well as with automobile and truck noise, our concern is largely with the latter two.

In order to use the guidelines the following must be specified:

1. The mix of cars and trucks.
2. The average flow (number per hour) and speed of the vehicles.
3. Whether the flow is continuous or "stop and go."
4. The road grade (i.e., percent slope).
5. The existence and position of large reflective barriers (e.g., billboards, buildings).
6. The distance from each of the street lanes to the geographic points where estimates are desired.

The noise levels are then estimated by using a series of nomographs and charts. The impact due to the new development would thus be based on the additional number and type of vehicles generated, their effect on traffic speeds and volumes, and changes to noise barriers.[14] In order to estimate the total impact on the community estimates should be made for a number of points at various distances along each side of every street affected, with the points chosen to reflect the distribution of population and the location of especially sensitive facilities, such as hospitals.

The results are expressed as one of four levels of acceptability (from clearly acceptable to clearly unac-

---

10. Mathematically, the relationship is:

$$\frac{P_1}{P_2} = \left(\frac{d_2}{d_1}\right)^2$$

where: P_1 = pressure level at distance "1"
P_2 = pressure level at distance "2"
d_1 = distance "1"
d_2 = distance "2"

This translates into an approximate decrease of 6 decibels with a doubling of distance.

11. See, for example, Bolt, Beranek, and Newman, Inc., op. cit.

12. For a discussion of methods for estimating traffic levels associated with proposed developments, see the chapter on transportation in P. Schaenman, D. Keyes, K. Christensen, *Estimating the Impacts from Land Developments on Public Services* (Washington, D.C.: The Urban Institute, forthcoming).

13. Bolt, Beranek, and Newman, Inc., op. cit.

14. The development may also reduce noise levels by adding barriers or other sound dampening devices.

Noise: Methodological Approaches

ceptable), rather than in terms of decibels. Thus, the HUD standards are built-in. If desired, the levels of acceptability can be adjusted to reflect local standards. A modification of this type is presumably a straightforward operation. However, we know of no one who has attempted it.[15]

Unfortunately, no data on accuracy are provided in the user manual or supporting document. The only related notation that does appear concerns the fact that the technique does not estimate noise levels from more than one source very well. This lack of information on accuracy levels detracts considerably from what otherwise appears to be an extremely simple approach to noise estimation.

TSC Methods—Two versions of a technique for estimating highway-associated noise have been developed by the FHWA's Transportation Systems Center (TSC).[16] Similar to the HUD guidelines, the simple version of the technique specifies parameters which characterize the traffic and the environment, with estimates being derived from nomographs. However, fewer parameters are used and thus the results are less sensitive to variations in traffic and other variables. The effects of "stop-and-go" flow and street grade are ignored.

As with the HUD guidelines, the impact from a development would be described by estimating the noise levels at numerous locations on either side of each street where significant additions to traffic volumes are expected. The actual number of estimates required depends on initial results (i.e., low estimates near the street eliminate the need to estimate levels at greater distances) and the uniformity of the environmental and street characteristics.

The results of the simple version are L_{10} values and are reported to be within 3 dBA of measured values.[17] However, validation experiments for the presumably more accurate complex version (discussed below and in the Summary and Comparison section) would indicate that this is an overstatement of accuracy.

The more complex version allows a greater number of input variables to be used (and thus allows for a more detailed description of the area), produces estimates in terms of various statistical measures (e.g., L_{50}, L_{10}) and indices (e.g., Noise Pollution Level), and increases very little in cost as the number of points at which estimates are to be made increases.

The model is sensitive to such factors as the noise spectrum[18] of different types of vehicles, the heights of the source and the receptor, and various types of ground cover (trees, shrubs, high grass), as well as to the variables used as input to the simple version. Thus, the results should be more accurate than those produced by the simple version. Validation experiments, however, indicate that the accuracy even of the more complex version is disappointing. (See the Summary and Comparison section.)

NCHRP Report 117 Method—Bolt, Beranek, and Newman, Inc., as part of the National Cooperative Highway Research Program (NCHRP), have developed a guide to be used by highway engineers in designing highways for noise minimization.[19] Much of the input data and many of the relationships underlying the calculations are the same as those for the HUD noise guidelines. In this case, however, the technique was designed to estimate impacts of increased traffic levels due to a proposed development at selected sights in the surrounding neighborhoods rather than existing noise from the neighborhood at a proposed site for development.

The analysis involves the use of charts and tables to relate the input values to levels of noise at each point specified, a new analysis being required for each point. One relevant application of this technique was the analysis of noise impacts from increased traffic levels due to new high-rise office buildings in San Francisco.[20] A discussion of the advantages and disadvantages from this and other applications appears in the Summary and Comparison section.

Other Techniques—Since the degree of roadway, traffic, and environmental characterizations necessary to make accurate noise-level estimates tends to be necessarily large and to involve numerous calculations, several efforts are now underway to develop computer models of noise generation and propagation. One such model, albeit a relatively crude one—the TSC model—has already been discussed. Another promising but as yet unverified example is the Noise-Environment-Ecology System Model under development at North Carolina State University.[21] Approximately the same level of detail is required for

15. The acceptability categories can be related to statistical expressions of noise levels (dBA) in a general way from Figure 29 in Bolt, Beranck, and Newman, Inc., op. cit. This graph plus those found in Part 4 of this report provide the basis for recalibration to locally determined levels of acceptability.

16. J. E. Wesler, *Manual for Highway Noise Prediction* (Cambridge, Mass.: DOT, TSC, March, 1972) (NTIS No. PB 226088).

17. Ibid.

18. The noise spectrum is the relative magnitude of noise produced at various pitches or frequencies. The spectrum of new vehicles can presumably be altered in such a fashion that those noises which are irritating to man are reduced.

19. C. G. Gordon et al., *Highway Noise—A Design Guide for Highway Engineers,* NCHRP Report 117 (Washington, D.C.: Highway Research Board, 1971).

20. David M. Dornbusch & Co., Inc., *Intensive Commercial and Residential Development Impact Study,* San Francisco. Phase I Report (San Francisco: Dornbusch & Company, Inc., n.d.).

21. Huang, op. cit.

descriptive data on roadway and traffic characteristics, but the required descriptions of factors affecting propagation are much more refined. The latter include the type and density of grass, shrub, and tree zones, atmospheric temperature and pressure, and wind patterns. The computations are based on relationships derived from extensive field studies on the effect of these factors on propagation of sound. Noise levels can be expressed as L_{10}, L_{50}, L_{90} and Noise Pollution Level values, each of which in turn can be plotted as isopleths on maps of the area under investigation.[22] Although the cost of operation is unreported and the accuracy of the results remains to be determined, the model seems promising.

b. Summary and Comparison

Three operational techniques for estimating the noise impact of increased traffic have been described. The key considerations from an application perspective are the relative cost and accuracy of these techniques.

Perhaps the simplest measure of accuracy is the difference between estimates from observed values under a variety of field conditions. Table 4-5 shows the results of several such experiments by an independent organization. As shown, the NCHRP 117 Method proved to be considerably more accurate than the computerized version of the TSC Method (average deviation of 1.8 versus 7.2 dBA),[23] although the investigators report that the TSC model was

---

22. Isopleths are lines connecting points of equal values.

23. The reader should recall that noise is perceived to double with a 10 dBA increase. An error factor of ± 7.2 could *easily* make a difference between acceptable and unacceptable levels if the estimate is close to a threshold.

Table 4-5. COMPARISON OF PREDICTED AND ACTUAL NOISE LEVELS AT SELECTED SITES

SITE[a]	DISTANCE	MEASURED dBA	TSC dBA	TSC DIFF.	NCHRP 117 dBA	NCHRP 117 DIFF.
1	50'	77.1	80.3	+3.2	79.0	+1.9
	100'	74.7	78.7	+4.0	74.9	+0.2
	200'	71.3	76.5	+5.2	69.6	−1.7
2	50'	71.4	76.7	+5.3	74.4	+3.0
	100'	65.4	75.0	+9.6	71.1	+5.7
	200'	58.4	67.9	+9.5	60.0	+1.6
	400'	55.4	67.6	+12.2	57.1	+1.7
3	50'	74.6	79.4	+4.8	76.7	+2.1
	100'	68.5	75.8	+7.3	70.7	+2.2
	200'	64.8	73.7	+8.9	66.4	+1.6
	400'	60.6	70.9	+10.3	60.6	0
4	50'	75.5	80.1	+4.6	78.5	+3.0
	100'	72.0	77.8	+5.8	73.5	+1.5
	200'	68.4	75.0	+6.6	68.4	0
	400'	59.5	70.8	+11.3	61.5	+2.0

SOURCE: E. W. Babin, *Highway Noise Study* (Baton Rouge, Louisiana: Louisiana Department of Highways, Research and Development Section, May, 1974).

a. Sites are various highways.

better adapted to making large numbers of estimates and to situations where roadway geometrics became more complicated (e.g., interchanges). Additional validation studies of NCHRP 117 produced deviations ±3 dBA or less for observed versus estimated reductions in noise levels due to barriers.[24] However, the best-drawn line through plots of observed versus esti-

---

24. The reductions were due to physical shields and to roadway configurations. Kugler and Piersol, op. cit.

Table 4-6. SUMMARY OF THREE NOISE ESTIMATION TECHNIQUES

TECHNIQUE	OUTPUT	COST	ACCURACY	COMMENTS
HUD noise assessment guidelines	Noise level as one of four acceptability categories	Inexpensive, although repeated applications are tedious (a new calculation is required for each point for which an estimate is desired)	Unreported	This is an extremely simple technique whose utility is limited by the unknown accuracy and the already interpreted nature of the estimates.
TSC method	L_{10} for the manual version; L_{10}, L_{50}, L_{90}, "noise pollution level" for the more computerized version	Same as for the HUD guidelines (for the manual version); more expensive for the computerized version but to an undetermined degree	Suspect for the simple version,[a] fair for the computerized version	The manual version should be used only for very rough approximations; the computerized version is probably better than the NCHRP 117 method only for complex roadway configurations. Neither version of TSC is applicable to stop-and-go traffic.
NCHRP 117	L_{10}, L_{50}, L_{90}, "noise pollution level"	Inexpensive, although the computations are not as quickly performed as with the HUD guidelines	Good	This appears to be the most widely applicable of the three methods reviewed here.

a. The accuracy should be less than that for the computerized version but was reported to be fairly good by one investigator.

Noise: Methodological Approaches

mated values often deviated significantly from the ideal 45° line.[25] The authors of the study report that, in general, the NCHRP 117 method tends to overpredict reduction in noise levels due to barriers at points distant from the roadway and to underpredict reductions for trucks. No validation efforts have been reported for the HUD guidelines.

Information from these and other sources is used to summarize the three methods in Table 4-6. NCHRP 117 would appear to be the most accurate but TSC (computerized version) the most practical for impact evaluation where large numbers of estimates are needed. If the TSC method is used, the analyst should anticipate a consistent pattern of overpredictions for continuous traffic and unknown accuracies for stop-and-go traffic.[26] Regardless of which technique is employed accuracies should be determined locally, since the reported accuracies are only for a limited range of conditions.

25. If *on the average* the observed and estimated values were equal, then a line drawn through plotted points would be at a 45° angle to each axis.

26. Stop and go traffic tends to produce louder but more intermittent noise levels than continuous traffic of the same speed.

III. CONCLUSIONS AND RECOMMENDATIONS

Much has already been said, either implicitly or explicitly, about the utilization of measures and techniques for estimating noise impacts. This chapter will attempt to tie together some loose ends and offer further guidance to those in local governments responsible for impact evaluation.

A. PLANNING VERSUS PROJECT REVIEW

Unlike the situation for many of the other types of impact, advanced planning does not appear to offer great potential for impact mitigation in the case of noise. Of course, some areas will be more or less predisposed to noise problems owing to topographical features or vegetative cover, and planners can encourage the segregation of noise-producing activities. In general, downtown areas will be noisier than mixed central city residential/commercial areas, which will be noisier than suburban residential areas, which will be noisier than rural areas. Noise mitigation thus lies primarily in source controls and project design.

Impact evaluations of individual developments can be used to (1) assess the seriousness of the additional increment added by the development (perhaps by reference to some set of standards), and (2) determine the effect of special design features used to reduce noise levels (e.g., physical barriers or trees). Baseline noise studies (not necessarily part of a *planning* activity) can be used to identify those areas where noise is either currently a severe problem or where noise is an increasing but not yet severe problem (and thus where the impact of new development should be care-

fully evaluated). Quiet areas can also be identified for the purpose of preservation, if this is desired. It is worth reemphasizing that in the process of determining problem areas communities may wish to use different standards, or "targets," in different areas.

B. SPECIFIC RECOMMENDATIONS AND CONCLUSIONS

Following are recommendations and conclusions regarding the estimation of noise impacts from land development:

1. Local governments should consider using impact measures similar to the ones suggested here. Where practical, they should be quantitative and reflect the number of people affected.

2. Standards should be used to interpret the estimated noise levels. Standards suggested by various experts (such as the EPA standards) can be employed for the purpose, although communities may wish to establish their own levels of acceptability, based on surveys of the local residents. Different areas of the community may thus have different standards.

3. Success in reducing noise or in maintaining low levels will probably depend on the incorporation of barriers, buffer zones, and other noise-abating features in the project design.

4. Analytical techniques appear to be available for use in quantitatively estimating noise impacts.

5. Much remains to be done in the area of technique development and validation.

PART 5
OTHER TYPES OF IMPACT: NATURAL DISASTERS AND SCARCE RESOURCE PREEMPTION

PART 5

I. INTRODUCTION

Although the discussions in the preceding parts of this report have been wide-ranging, a few topics have not been covered fully or have been left untouched. Among the many types of natural disasters, for instance, only floods have been mentioned thus far. (See Part 2.) As for topics not yet broached, problems associated with the substitution of development uses for other types of land use is an obvious candidate for discussion.

Hence, this part of the report deals with *natural disasters* and *scarce resource preemption*. The manner in which new developments may (a) create disaster hazards for the occupants or other community residents, or (b) preclude other valuable uses of the land will be highlighted. Key considerations for impact evaluation will be noted. Since many of the salient issues have been discussed elsewhere, the treatment here will be of a summary and reference nature.

The relatively superficial treatment given these topics compared to other impact areas in this report should not be misinterpreted. Natural disasters and scarce resource preemption are extremely serious problems for specific communities. But the quantitative methods for evaluating the impacts occurring to or caused by land development is generally less advanced for these types of impacts. In addition, what we do know about impact estimation is reasonably well documented elsewhere, although this information is contained in many diverse documents. We have elected to highlight key considerations and reference primary sources of information.

II. NATURAL DISASTERS OTHER THAN FLOODS

In spite of improvements in our understanding of natural processes and in our technical ability to circumvent undesirable events, man still is seriously affected by natural disasters, such as earthquakes and landslides. Many developments are built in or near hazardous areas in the absence of clear identification of the risks involved. Whether to allow development of land when the risks are known is another matter left to local or higher governmental judgment. The reader should also keep in mind that the subject of this report—estimating the impacts associated with land development—is but one small aspect of a comprehensive disaster prevention program.[1]

The factors which lead to natural disasters are often localized geographically. Earthquakes occur near fault lines; landslides in areas of steep, unstable slopes; forest fires on forested land. In order to estimate damage to future inhabitants (and thus to reduce the potential monetary impact on the population as a whole), the hazard potential in the locality of the proposed development should be evaluated.

Impact measures for any type of disaster can be patterned after that suggested for flooding:

Change in the likelihood of the disaster and the number of people and the value of the property endangered.

It is difficult to specify quantitatively the probability of occurrence for most disasters other than floods and, in some cases, earthquakes. The discussion of data needs and procedures for estimating people and property at risk which appears in Part 2 applies equally to other types of natural disasters.

A. LANDSLIDES AND SUBSIDENCE

Landslides are the result of forces exerted on earth material located on sloping bedrock and can be due to the characteristics of the soil or to weaknesses in the bedrock. *Subsidence* is the vertical collapse of the ground due to underground mining, overpumping of groundwater, cavern formation, and other causes. The scale and location of a development and, to some extent, the degree of landscape alteration, will largely determine the potential for landslides or subsidence.

The basic procedure involves determining the hazard potential at the development site from geologic and hydrologic evidence and from records of past landslides or subsidence episodes in the area or in other areas of similar topographic, geologic, hydrologic, and soil characteristics.[2] In order to reduce the

---

1. For a discussion of key issues involved in the design of disaster prevention and relief programs, see Gilbert F. White and J. Eugene Haas, *Assessment of Research on Natural Hazards* (Cambridge, Mass.: The MIT Press, 1975) and Office of Emergency Preparedness, *Disaster Preparedness—A Report to the Congress,* (Washington, D.C., Executive Office of the President, January, 1972).

2. For information on specific data requirements and methods of landslide hazard assessment, see E. B. Eckel, ed., *Landslides and Engineering Practice* (Washington, D.C.: Highway Research Board, 1958); Building Research Advisory Board, *Methodology for Delineating Mudslide Hazard Areas* (Washington, D.C. National Academies of Sciences and Engineering, 1974); and John H. Sorensen, et al., *Landslide Hazard in the United States: A Research Assessment* (Boulder, Col.: Institute of Behavioral Science, University of Colorado, 1975).

need to evaluate each proposed development on a site-by-site basis, regional hazard maps can be prepared using similar data and assessment methods but at a smaller geographic scale. For example, a landslide hazard map has been prepared for the San Clemente area of California based on a geologic model which relates landscape stability to (1) background factors (e.g., critical angle of natural slope and type of vegetation), (2) energy factors (e.g., amount of precipitation and fire potential), and (3) special factors (e.g., presence of swelling clays and adverse geologic structures).[3]

B. EARTHQUAKES

Numerous areas within the United States are subject to earthquakes. The West Coast in particular has been the site of significant episodes of seismic activity, although some of the largest earthquakes in history occurred in the Midwest and on the East Coast.

In conducting an earthquake impact analysis the key questions are these: Will the new development be in a high risk zone? What is the frequency of expected earthquakes of various magnitudes? And what is the expected loss of life and property damage? In order to predict the frequency and severity of future earthquakes, past records of seismic activity are combined with geological information in the vicinity of the site in question. Future damage is also a function of the size, nature, and method of construction of the proposed development.

Earthquake risk maps should be a starting point for the analysis. Although the National Seismic Risk Map does not contain information on the probability of future earthquakes, it does indicate what the severity may be and can be used where other risk maps are unavailable.[4] The U.S. Geological Survey (USGS) is completing a national risk map which incorporates both the frequency and severity factors. This is expected to be available sometime in 1976. Techniques have also been developed by USGS and HUD which provide a basis for more detailed mapping.[5]

Where a proposed site is located in a high risk zone, a site-level evaluation should be conducted. This is based on detailed information concerning the location of fault lines, soil type and depth, bedrock type, and water table conditions. Detailed guidelines regarding the site-level assessment of risk are found in various federal agency publications.[6]

The estimation of expected damage should be based on detailed information regarding the location, design, and construction of the proposed development. Several reports by various federal government agencies provide relevant information for damage assessments and hazard reduction through improved construction practices.[7]

This highly abbreviated discussion may create the impression that earthquake hazard assessment is a simple, straightforward operation. Quite the contrary is true. These calculations require the collection of considerable quantities of data and are fraught with uncertainty. The error in estimating the expected damage for a single building may be 100 percent and for several hundred structures, 50 to 75 percent.[8]

Before undertaking an assessment of earthquake impacts for proposed developments, it is recommended that the USGS be contacted regarding the extensive body of research on the subject.

Many communities in seismically active areas now have special building codes designed to mitigate earthquake damage. New development in these communities must meet these codes, thus reducing somewhat the need for special attention to impact evaluation. However, improved earthquake resistance is only a partial solution.[9]

C. OTHER TYPES OF DISASTERS

Hurricanes, tornadoes, avalanches, and forest fires all extract a toll in human life and property damage. In some cases the high risk areas are so widespread and the forces of destruction so great that few pre-

3. California Division of Mines and Geology, "Mudslide and Landslide Prediction," *California Geology* 25 (June 1975): 136.

4. *National Seismic Risk Map*, Department of Commerce, Environmental Science Services Administration, Coast and Geodetic Survey, circa 1969 (also contained in HUD's Minimum Property Standards).

5. USGS, *Studies for Seismic Zonation of the San Francisco Bay Region, Professional Paper 941-A* (Washington, D.C.: U.S. Department of the Interior, 1975).

6. See, for example, Walter W. Hays, et al., *Guidelines for Developing Design Earthquake Response Spectra* (Champaign, Ill.: Army Construction Engineering Lab, June 1975) (NTIS No. AD-A012 728/2GA).

7. See, for example, The National Bureau of Standards, *Building Practices for Disaster Mitigation,* NBS Building Science Series #46 (Washington, D.C.: U.S. Government Printing Office, 1973) and National Oceanic and Atmospheric Administration, *A Study of Earthquake Losses in the San Francisco Bay Area* (Washington, D.C.: Government Printing Office, 1972). Additional information can be obtained from Charles Culver at the National Bureau of Standards.

8. Personal communication with Charles Thiel of the National Science Foundation.

9. Improvements in our ability to predict earthquakes may reduce the safety hazard if not the property damage. See, Frank Press, "Earthquake Prediction," *Scientific American* 232 (May, 1975): 14–23; and Christopher N. Scholtz, "Toward Infallible Earthquake Prediction," *Natural History* 83 (May 1974): 54–59.

Land Development and the Natural Environment

ventative measures can be taken. Tornadoes are a case in point.[10] Forest fires and avalanches, on the other hand, are more localized. Damage from the latter can thus be minimized by preventing development in the high-risk areas and, in the case of forest fires, undertaking certain preventative maintenance activities, such as removal of dead plant material in forest fire-prone areas and clear-cutting of trees in corridors to be used as barriers to the propagation of fire.[11]

For hurricanes the key considerations involve building strength and potential evacuation problems for those likely to be affected. For example, one argument for limiting development in the Florida Keys is based on potential evacuation problems caused by too few bridges linking the Keys with the mainland. In order to provide local governments in hurricane hazard areas with more information on the extent and severity of the problem, the National Oceanic and Atmospheric Administration is planning to publish about 185 storm evacuation maps showing the potential flood zone areas.[12]

10. Even for tornadoes, attempts at identifying high risk zones have met with some success. See Illinois Emergency Services Agency, *Hazard Analysis for the State of Illinois* (Springfield, Ill.: October, 1975).

11. For a discussion of factors which can be used to estimate the potential for or risk from forest fires, see R. D. Nelm, B. Neal, and L.

Tayler, *A Fire Hazard Severity Classification System for California Wildlands* (Sacramento: California State Division of Forestry, April 1, 1973) (NTIS No. PB-237 951/9WV).

12. Raymond Wilcove, "The Mapping of Hurricane Alley," *Water Spectrum* (Summer 1975): 18–25.

III. SCARCE RESOURCE PREEMPTION

For every parcel of land used for urban development, alternative uses must be foregone. In some cases the preemption of alternative uses may carry with it significant social costs which are borne by the population as a whole or large portions thereof. This may be the case when certain scarce resources, such as agricultural land, land overlying mineral deposits, and land with unique natural features are used for residential, commercial, or industrial development.

The suggested impact measure is as follows:

> The type and value of the scarce resource and the degree of the preemption.

Although the calculation of the costs of preemption in monetary terms is far from a straightforward process and is not practical for routine evaluations at the present time, an articulation of the land uses being preempted by development will allow decision makers to consciously formulate value judgments about these costs. Descriptions in terms of land area, and perhaps qualitative assessments of "value," are more practical.

A. AGRICULTURAL LAND

Recent food shortages in various parts of the world have heightened the concern of many for the conversion of agricultural land to other uses in metropolitan areas. Although much of the land converted to urban uses tends to be well-suited for crop production, the impact of these conversions on total food production is far from clear. Improvements in technology and the reclamation of farmland elsewhere in the country may render urban preemption relatively insignificant.[13] Still, metropolitan farmland may affect the local price of certain agricultural products.

In assessing the value of farmland to be converted, the following factors should be considered.[14]

1. Productivity—this can be expressed directly as yield (by crop type) or indirectly as soil fertility, topography, and available moisture.

2. Specialty crops—certain land may be uniquely suited for the production of certain specialty products, such as cranberries or seed potatoes.

3. Viability—even productive land is of limited value if its size is too small or if support industries have left the community or region.

These factors could be used to specify a qualitative measure of resource "value." The impact of development could then be expressed as amount of land of the specified value converted to other uses.

---

13. For a discussion of these issues, see George E. Peterson and Harvey Yampolsky, *Urban Development and the Protection of Metropolitan Farmland* (Washington, D.C.: The Urban Institute, 1975); and Richard L. Barrows, et al., *Wisconsin Natural Resource Policy Issues: An Economic Perspective,* Working Paper No. 6 (Madison: Center for Resource Policy Studies and Programs, School of Natural Resources, University of Wisconsin, July 1973).

14. For additional elaboration see, Bernard J. Niemann, Jr., et al., *Recommendations for a Critical Resource Information Program (CRIP) for Wisconsin, Phase III Report,* (Madison: Institute for Environmental Studies, University of Wisconsin, February, 1974).

B. MINERAL DEPOSITS

Less well-publicized but certainly as important is the preemption of mineral extraction by urban development. The loss of gravel pits on Long Island, for example, has reportedly cost New York State $30,000,000 per year in increased building costs.[15] This is not to say that the value to society of developing land overlying mineral deposits is not equal to or even greater than the value of the deposits themselves. But investigation of this issue prior to development is certainly in order.

Mineral resources encompass nationally scarce fossil and nuclear fuels and metallic minerals, as well as less scarce but locally significant construction minerals, such as sand and gravel. Key considerations in any planning study or impact evaluation include scarcity, quality and size of the deposit, ease of extraction, and (usually) the availability of water.[16] Unfortunately, an adequate assessment of these variables frequently requires costly test borings. Even though potential deposits can be inferred from general geologic data, only about 1 percent of potentially valuable deposits are economically exploitable. Where the potential mineral is extremely valuable and the proposed development represents a sizable investment, test borings might be conducted.

The impact of the development should be measured not only by direct physical interference with mining activity. Development in close proximity may effectively preclude future mining activity, since mine operators may well decide to close their operations rather than spend the money necessary to reduce the level of noise and pollutant output in a manner appropriate for residential or commercial areas. Unless the proposed development will be compatible with surface or deep mining operations (e.g., heavy industry), a buffer area should be secured sufficient to screen the mine and to mitigate accompanying noise and dust.

C. UNIQUE NATURAL FEATURES

Unique natural features are those geologic or physiographic features which are of scientific, educational, or aesthetic interest.[17] They include such items as waterfalls, canyons, natural bridges, mountain ranges, escarpments, or simply combinations of more common features which provide a scenic view.

Many states have undertaken an inventory of these resources as part of critical area or other programs. The relevant state agencies should be consulted for this information. If planning or inventory studies have not been conducted at the state or local level an assessment of the impacted environment should be made as part of the impact evaluation of individual developments. Criteria to use as basis for these assessments can be found in the literature.[18] A further discussion of aesthetic evaluation appears in another volume of The Urban Institute's land use series of reports.[19]

---

15. E. Dale Trower, "Land Use and Mineral Industry" (Paper presented at the Annual Meeting of the American Association for the Advancement of Science, January 30, 1975).

16. For a further description of these variables and their application to various types of minerals, see Niemann et al., op. cit.

17. Biological features (i.e., natural areas and wildlife habitats) have already been discussed. See Part 3 of this report.

18. See, for example, Niemann, et al., op. cit.

19. K. Christensen, *Estimating the Social Impacts of Land Developments* (Washington D.C.: The Urban Institute, forthcoming).